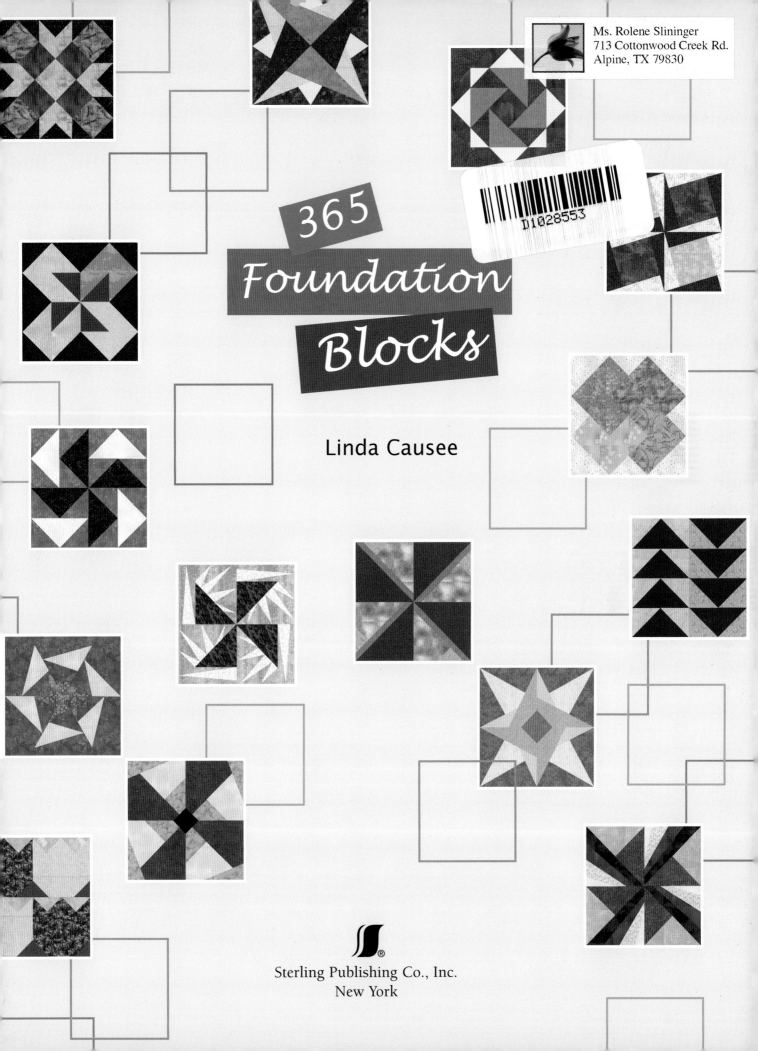

365

Foundation
Blocks

Linda Causee

Sterling Publishing Co., Inc.
New York

Contents

Photography: Carol Wilson Mansfield
Graphic Artist: April McArthur
Quilters: Kathryn Causee, Jackie Green, Ann Harnden, Wanda MacLachlan, John Schiller
Book design: Joyce Lerner
Produced by: The Creative Partners™, LLC.

Library of Congress Cataloging-in-Publication Data Available

10 9 8 7 6 5 4 3

Published in paperback in 2006 by Sterling Publishing Co., Inc.
387 Park Avenue South, New York, NY 10016
© 2005 by Linda Causee
Distributed in Canada by Sterling Publishing
c/o Canadian Manda Group, 165 Dufferin Street
Toronto, Ontario, Canada M6K 3H6
Distributed in the United Kingdom by GMC Distribution Services,
Castle Place, 166 High Street, Lewes, East Sussex, England BN7 1XU
Distributed in Australia by Capricorn Link (Australia) Pty. Ltd.
P.O. Box 704, Windsor, NSW 2756, Australia

Printed in China
All rights reserved

Sterling ISBN-13: 978-1-4027-2315-5 Hardcover
        ISBN-10: 1-4027-2315-6
        ISBN-13: 978-1-4027-4041-1 Paperback
        ISBN-10: 1-4027-4041-7

For information about custom editions, special sales, premium
and corporate purchases, please contact Sterling Special Sales
Department at 800-805-5489 or specialsales@sterlingpub.com.

Before You Begin

If you are an aficionado of foundation piecing, then you already know the joys of this simple quilting technique. If you have never considered foundation piecing, then welcome to the world of absolutely perfect patchwork, without tedious cutting of templates, where every piece meets every other piece perfectly and where even the smallest of blocks can be created with a minimum of work.

In this wonderful method, the patchwork pieces are sewn on a foundation of either paper or cloth following a specific numeric sequence. If you have a printed pattern for a block, the rest is easy.

In this book you will find patterns for 365 foundation-pieced quilt blocks. Yes, there is one for every day of the year, and some of the blocks actually commemorate that special day. You'll find a block to observe holidays like St. Patrick's Day and Christmas, but you'll also find a block to celebrate the day the Beatles landed in America. In addition, there are blocks that just honor that time of the year. The January blocks depict ice and snow; the May section is filled with flower blocks. Each month has a gemstone, a flower, a bird, a house, a basket, a star, and a pinwheel. You'll find some old favorite quilt blocks like Log Cabin, but you'll also find some new and very creative blocks like the Golden Gate Bridge and the Chicago Skyline.

The majority of the blocks in this book are 7" x 7". This means that they can be combined to make interesting quilts, some samples of which introduce each month. You can also combine the basket blocks to create a basket quilt, or the house blocks to make a beautiful gift for someone's new home. Because miniature quilts are so easy to create using the foundation method, we've also included a number of 3½" x 3½" blocks. These smaller blocks can also make creative additions to your quilt.

Included with each pattern is a photo of the completed block. Be sure to note that the completed block will be a mirror image of the pattern. **(Figure 1)**

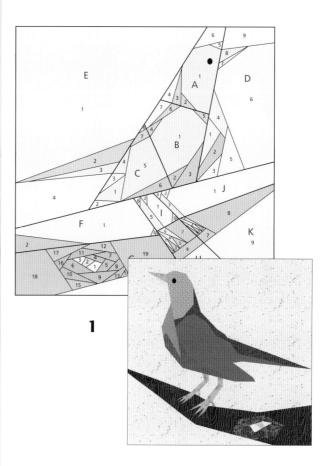

1

If you've never made a quilt using the foundation method, or if you need a brief refresher course, here are the basic instructions on how to create blocks using this wonderful method.

If, however, making foundation-pieced quilts is your passion, choose your favorite blocks and get started!

3

The Material Used for a Foundation

Before you begin, decide the kind of foundation on which you are planning to piece the blocks. The most popular choice is paper. It's readily available and fairly inexpensive. You can use copy paper, newsprint, tracing paper – even computer paper. The paper does not remain a permanent part of your quilt as it is removed once the blocks are completely sewn.

You can also use fabric as your foundation, especially if you choose to hand piece your block. Just remember that fabric is not removed after you make your block so you will have another layer to quilt through. This may be a problem if you are planning to hand quilt. Using fabric might be an advantage, however, if you want to use some non-traditional quilting fabrics, such as satin, since the fabric foundation will add stability to the block. If you do decide to use fabric, choose a lightweight and light-colored fabric, such as muslin, that will allow you to see through for ease in tracing.

Another option for foundation materials is Tear Away® or Fun-dation™, translucent non-woven material combining the advantages of both paper and fabric. They are easy to see through but like paper they can be removed with ease.

Currently a new kind of foundation material has appeared in the market place: a foundation paper which dissolves in water after use. Two companies, W.H. Collins and EZ Quilting by Wrights are producing this product.

Preparing the Foundation

Place your foundation material over your chosen block in this book and trace the block pattern. Use a ruler and a fine-line pencil or permanent marker, and make sure that all lines are straight. Sometimes short dashed lines or even dotted lines are easier to make. Be sure to copy all numbers. You will need to make a foundation for each block you are planning to use.

If you have a home copier, you can copy your block from the book right onto the paper that can then be used for the foundation. Since the copy machine might slightly alter the measurements of the block, make certain that you copy each block from the original pattern.

You can also scan the block if you have a home scanner and then print out the required number of blocks.

The Fabric Used in Foundation Piecing

One hundred per cent cotton fabric has always been recommended for quiltmaking, and fabric for foundation piecing is no exception. Pieces cut from 100% cotton, as opposed to a cotton/polyester blend, will not slip and will respond to finger pressing.

While it is not necessary to pre-wash fabric for foundation piecing, you should test your fabric to make certain that it is colorfast. Do this by placing a 2"-wide crosswise strip of fabric into a bowl of very hot water. If the fabric is not colorfast, the color will bleed into the water. You often can salvage the fabric by washing it until the excess dye has been washed out, but if a fabric continues to bleed after it has been washed again and again, it should be eliminated.

If you are concerned that your fabric might shrink, you may want to test it for shrinkage. Take one of the strips used in the colorfast test and iron it dry. Then measure it, comparing it to the original 2" measurement.

Cutting the Fabric

In foundation piecing, you do not have to cut perfect shapes!

You can, therefore, use odd pieces of fabric: squares, strips, rectangles. The one thing you must remember, however, is that every piece must be at least 1/4" larger on all sides than the space it is going to cover. Strips and squares are easy: just measure the length and width of the needed space and add 1/2" all around. Cut your strip to that measurement. Triangles, however, can be a bit tricky. In that case, measure the widest point of the triangle and cut your fabric about 1/2" to 1" wider.

Other Supplies for Foundation Piecing

Piecing by hand:

You will need a reasonably thin needle such as a Sharp Size 10; a good quality neutral-colored thread such as a size 50 cotton; some pins, a glue stick; fabric scissors; muslin or fabric for the bases.

Piecing by machine:

You will need a cleaned and oiled sewing machine; glue stick; pins, paper scissors, fabric scissors, foundation material.

Hint: *Before beginning to sew your actual block by machine, determine the proper stitch length. Use a piece of the paper you are planning to use for the foundation and draw a straight line on it. Set your machine so that it sews with a fairly short stitch (about 20 stitches per inch). Sew along the line. If you can tear the paper apart with ease, you are sewing with the right length. You don't want to sew with such a short stitch that the paper falls apart by itself. If you are going to use a fabric foundation with the sewing machine, use the stitch length you normally use.*

Using the Patterns

The numbers on the blocks show the order in which the pieces are to be placed and sewn on the base. It is extremely important that you follow the numbers; otherwise the entire process won't work.

If you have never made a foundation-pieced block, you may want to start with an easy block, such as "Boxes" on page 19, or "Log Cabin" on page 68. One of the miniature blocks, such as the two on page 237 would also provide a good introduction to foundation piecing.

Making the Block

The important thing to remember about making a foundation block is that the fabric pieces go on the unmarked side of the foundation while you sew on the printed side. The finished blocks are a mirror image of the original pattern.

Step One:
Hold the foundation up to a light source – even a window pane – with the unmarked side facing you. Find the space marked 1 on the unmarked side and put a dab of glue there. Place the fabric right side up on the unmarked side on Space 1, making certain that the fabric overlaps at least 1/4" on all sides of space 1. **(Figure 2)**

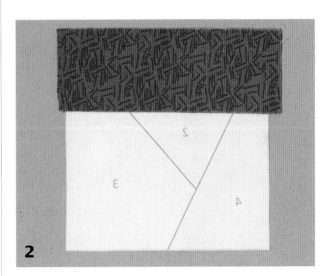

Step Two:
Fold the foundation along the line between Space 1 and Space 2. Cut the fabric so that it is 1/4" from the fold. **(Figure 3)**

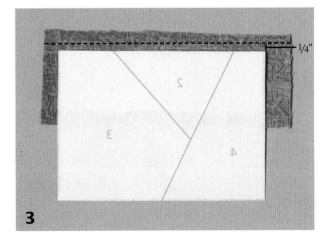

Step Three:

With right sides together, place Fabric Piece 2 on Fabric Piece 1, making sure that the edge of Piece 2 is even with the just-trimmed edge of Piece 1. **(Figure 4)**

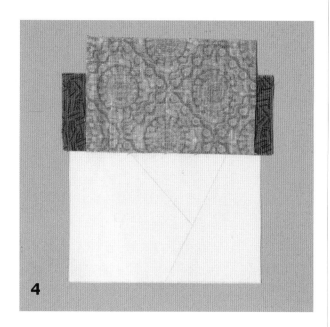

Step Four:

To make certain that Piece 2 will cover Space 2, fold the fabric piece back along the line between Space 1 and Space 2. **(Figure 5)**

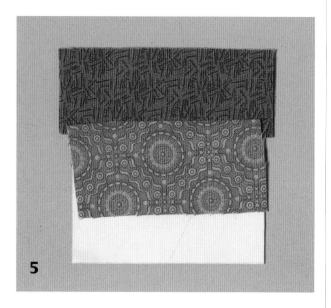

Step Five:

With the marked side of the foundation facing up, place the piece on the sewing machine (or sew by hand), holding both Piece 1 and Piece 2 in place. Sew along the line between Space 1 and Space 2. **(Figure 6)**

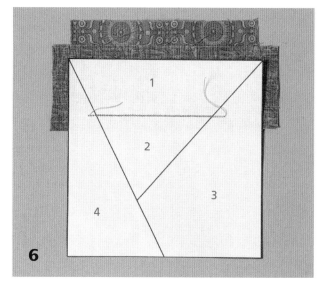

Hint: *If you use a small stitch, it will be easier to remove the paper later. Start stitching about two to three stitches before the beginning of the line and end your sewing two to three stitches beyond the line, allowing the stitches to be held in place by the next round of stitching rather than by backstitching.*

Step Six:

Turn the work over and open Piece 2. Finger press the seam open. **(Figure 7)**

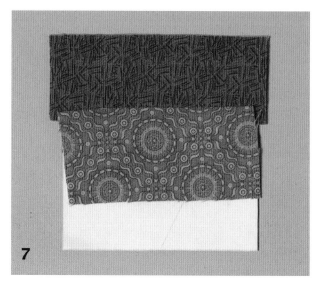

Step Seven:
Turning the work so that the marked side is on top, fold the foundation forward along the line between Space 1+2 and Space 3. Trim about 1/8" to 1/4" from the fold. **(Figure 8)**

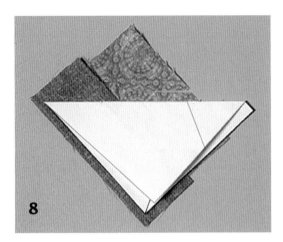

Hint: *It is easier to trim the paper if you pull the paper away from the stitching. If you use fabric as your foundation, fold the fabric forward as far as it will go and then start to trim.*

Step Eight:
Place Fabric #3 right side down even with the just-trimmed edge. **(Figure 9)**

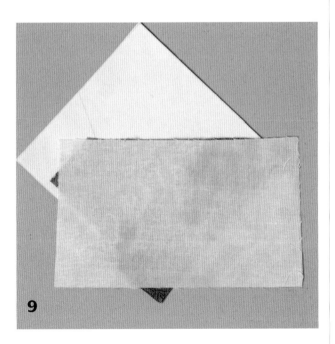

Step Nine:
Turn the block over to the marked side and sew along the line between Space 1+2 and Space 3. **(Figure 10)**

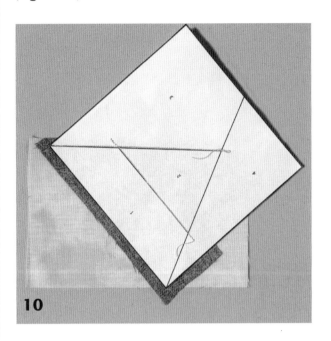

Step Ten:
Turn the work over, open Piece 3 and finger press the seam. **(Figure 11)**

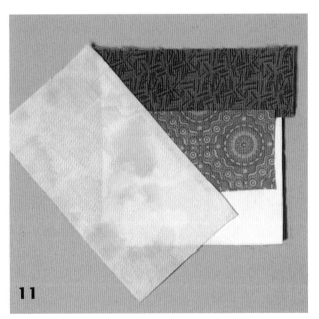

Step Eleven:

In the same way you have added the other pieces, add Piece #4 to complete this block. Trim the fabric 1/4" from the edge of the foundation. The foundation-pieced block is completed. **(Figure 12)**

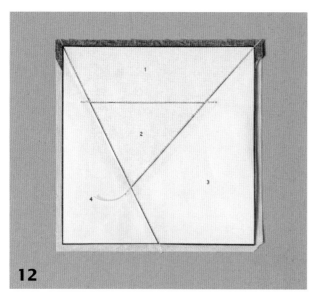

12

After you have finished sewing a block, don't immediately remove the paper. Since you are often piecing with tiny bits of fabric, grainline is never a factor. Therefore, some of the pieces may have been cut on the bias and may have a tendency to stretch. You can eliminate any problem with distortion by keeping the paper in place until all of the blocks have been sewn together. If, however, you want to remove the paper, stay stitch along the outer edge of the block to help keep the block in shape.

Sewing Multiple Sections

Many of the blocks in this collection have been created with two or more sections. These sections, which are indicated by letters, are individually pieced and then sewn together in alphabetical order. The cutting line for these sections is indicated by a bold line. Before you start to make any of these multi-section blocks, begin by cutting the foundation piece apart so that each section is worked independently. Leave a 1/4" seam allowance around each section as you sew.

Step One:

Following the instructions above for Making the Block, complete each section. Then place the first two sections right side together. Pin the corners of the top to section to the corners of the bottom section. **(Figure 13)**

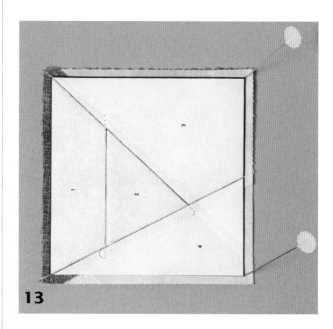

13

Step Two:

If you are certain that the pieces are aligned correctly, sew the two sections together using the regular stitch length on the sewing machine. **(Figure 14)**

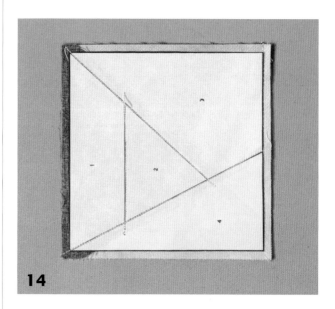

14

Step Three:

Press the sections open and continue sewing the sections in pairs. **(Figure 15)**

15

Step Four:
Sew necessary sections together to complete the block. **(Figure 16)**

16

The blocks are now ready to sew into your quilts.

The Quilts in This Book

You'll find examples of quilts made with these foundation blocks on the following pages: 10 (January), 38 (February), 64 (March), 94 (April), 122 (May), 152 (June), 180 (July), 210 (August), 238 (September), 266 (October), 296 (November), 324 (December).

What You Don't Want to Forget

1. If you plan to sew by hand, begin by taking some backstitches which will anchor the thread at the beginning of the line. Then use a backstitch every four or five stitches. End the stitching with a few backstitches.

2. If you plan to sew by machine, start stitching two or three stitches before the start of the stitching line and finish your stitching two or three stitches beyond the end.

3. Use a short stitch (about 20 stitches per inch) for paper foundations to make it easier to remove the paper. If the paper falls apart as you sew, your stitches are too short.

4. Finger press (or use an iron) each seam as you finish it.

5. Stitching which goes from a space into another space will not interfere with adding additional fabric pieces.

6. Remember to trim all seam allowances at least 1/4".

7. When sewing points, start from the wide end and sew towards the point.

8. Unless you plan to use it only once in the block, it is a good idea to stay away from directional prints in foundation piecing.

9. When cutting pieces for foundation piecing, don't worry about the grainline.

10. Always remember to sew on the marked side, placing the fabric on the unmarked side.

11. Follow the numerical order when piecing and alphabetical order when sewing sections together.

12. Once you have finished making a block, do not remove the paper until the entire quilt has been finished unless you stay stitch around the outside of the block.

13. Be sure that the ink you use to make your foundation is permanent and will not wash out into your fabric.

January

Is there anything more pleasant on a cold January day than to sit curled up next to the fire staring out of the window at a lovely winter scene? The window won't be necessary when you create this intriguing quilt from some of the blocks in the January section. Start with a group of snowflakes at the top, add those scenes you might see from the window: a snowman, a snow covered cottage, a snowy pine tree, a red cardinal, and finish with a quartet of winter blocks. Now sit back and let those winter winds blow while you're as warm as toast.

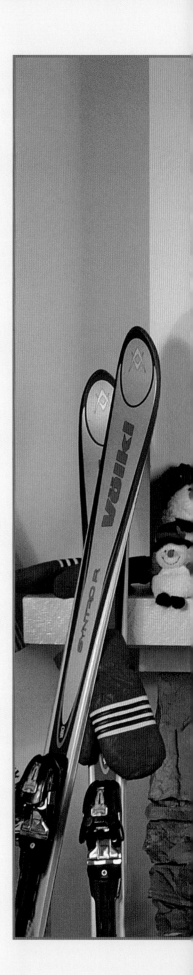

Happy New Year

A
1
2
4
3
5
7

B
3
1
2
6
4
5

6

7

7

6

C
5
4
2
1
3

D
5
3
2
4
1

6

7

Snowflake

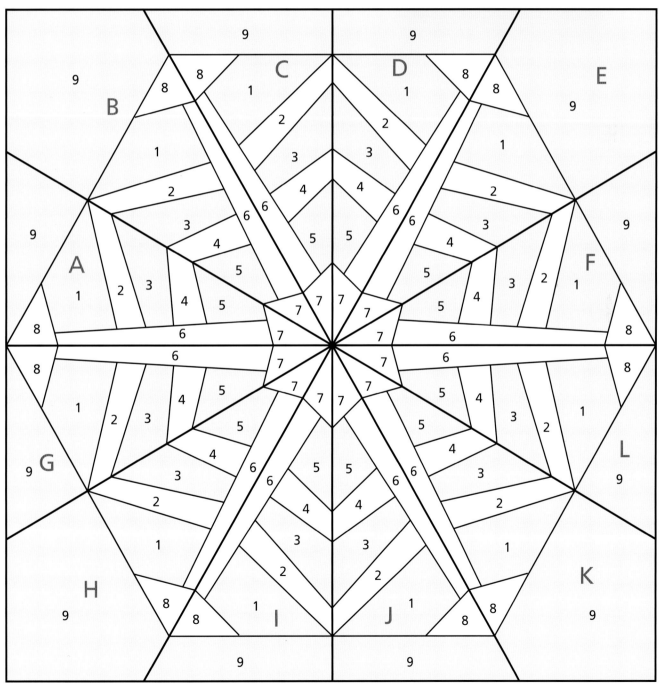

3

Snowflake

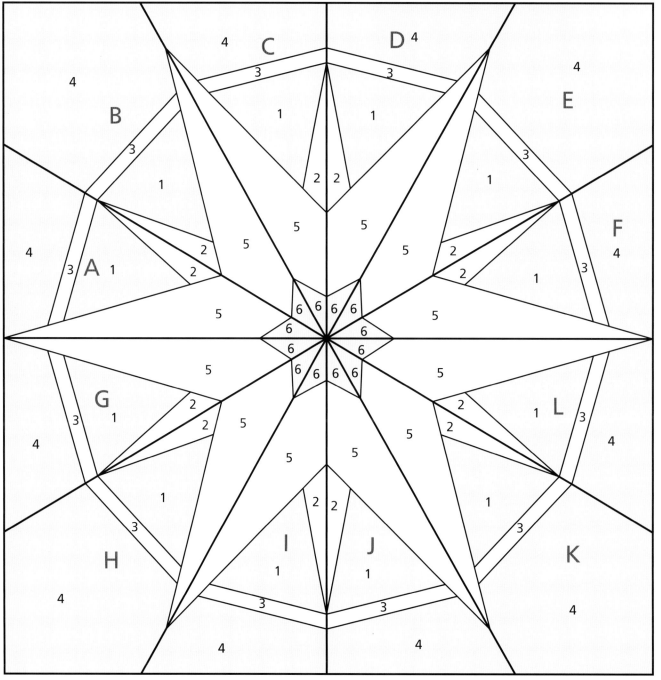

Snowflake

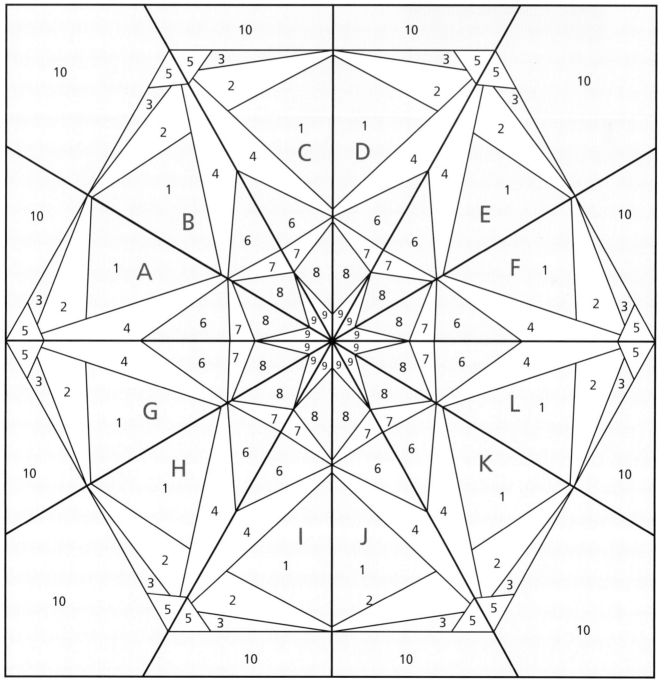

Snowman

EMBELLISHMENT NOTE:
Use orange felt for the nose and permanent fabric markers:
black for eyes, green and red for the buttons. You may use small
buttons in place of the permanent markers if desired.

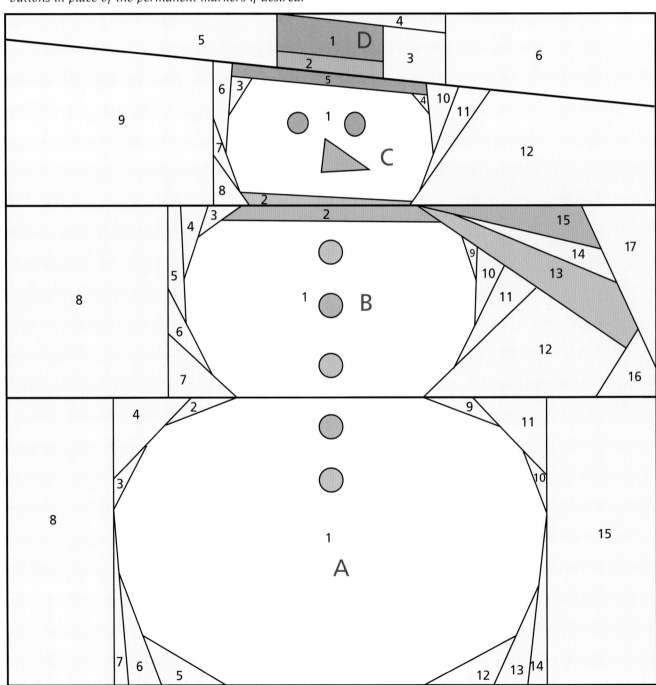

Snowy Pine

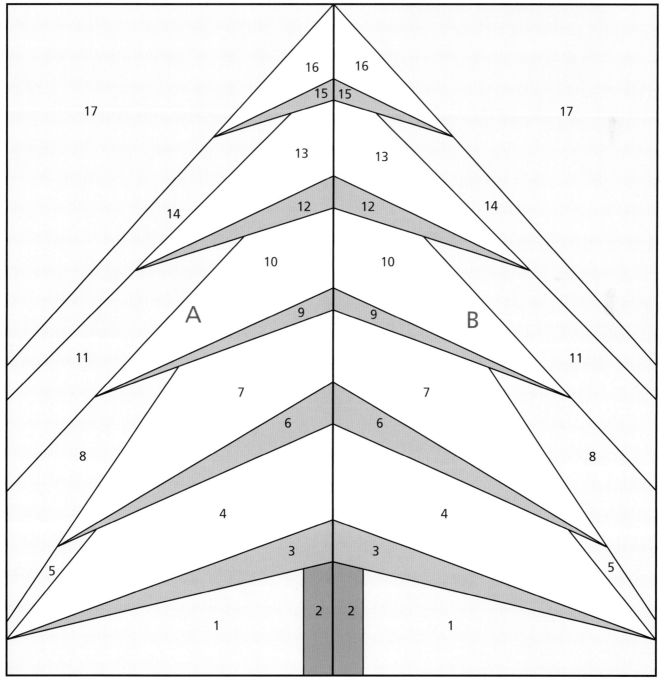

Snowy Cottage

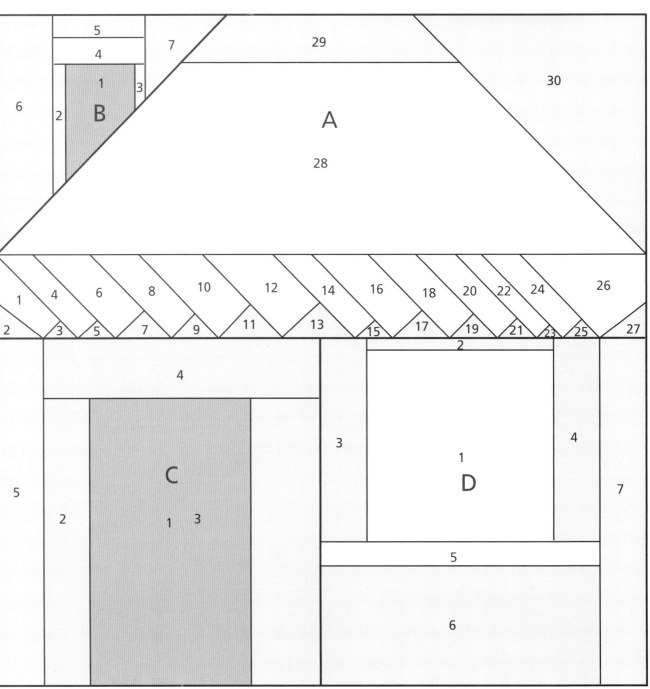

Boxes

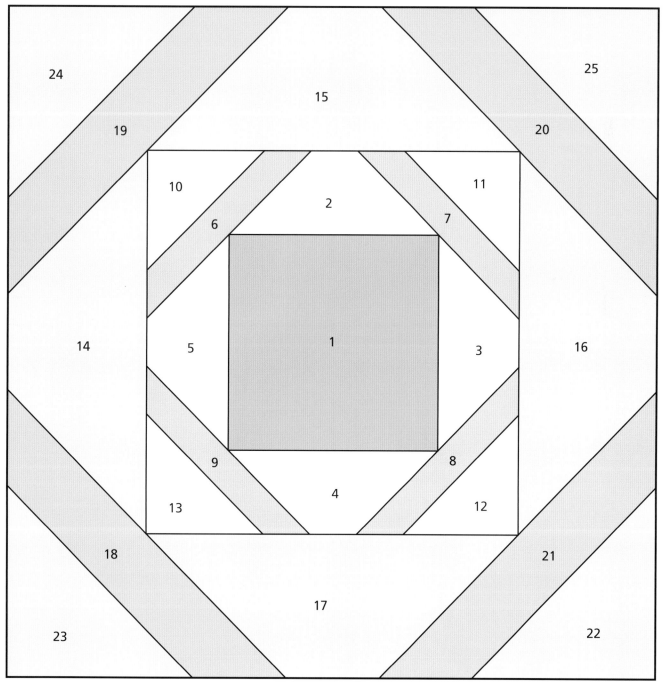

9

Winter Geese

A
5
6
4

2
1
3

B
2
5
1
4
3
6

C
5
2
4
1
3
6

D
1
2
3
5
4
6

10

Snowflake

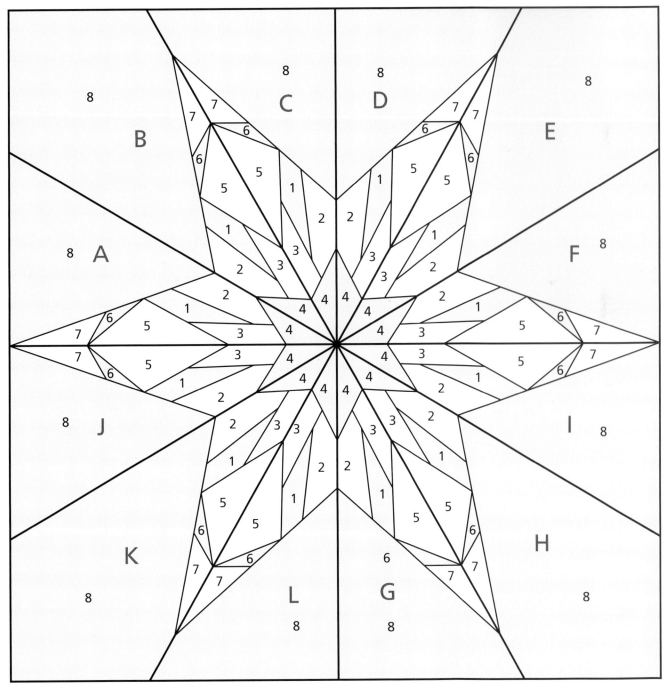

Cardinal

EMBELLISHMENT NOTE:
Use permanent black fabric marker for eye. A small black button or bead may be used for the eye if desired.

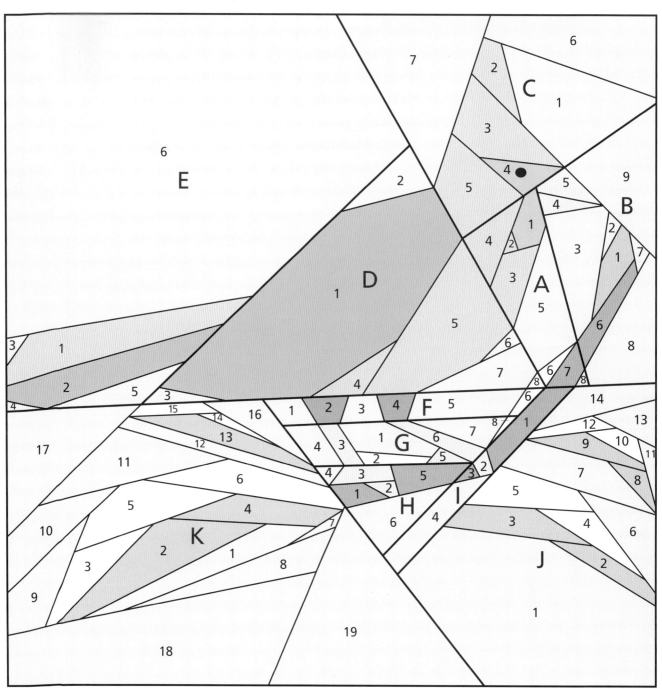

12

Winter Star

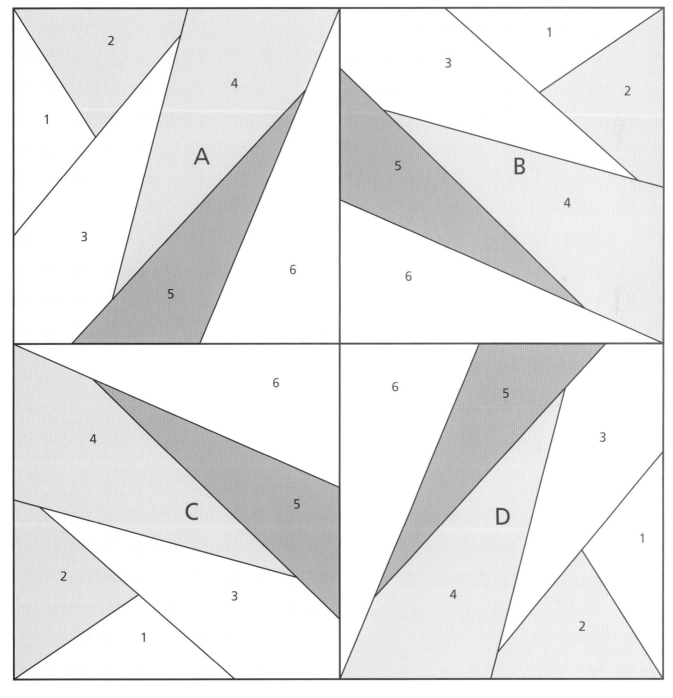

Snowdrop —
January Flower

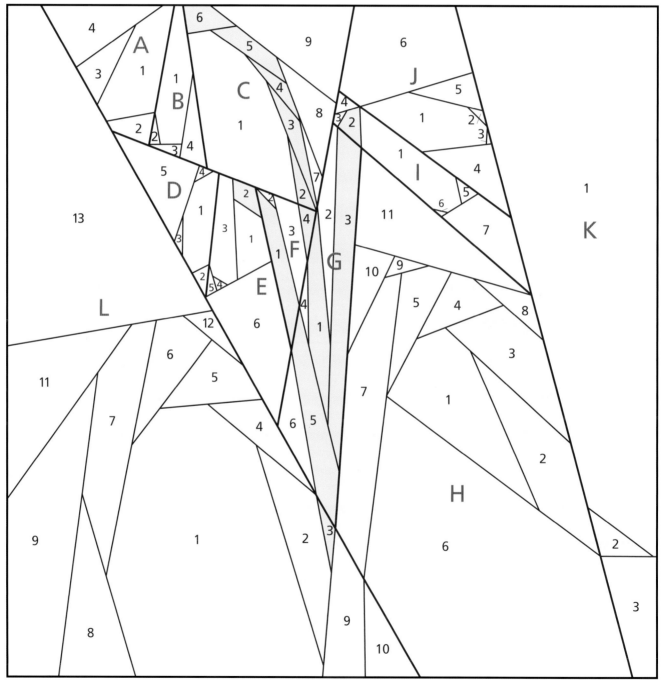

Garnet—
January Birthstone

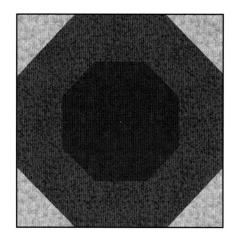

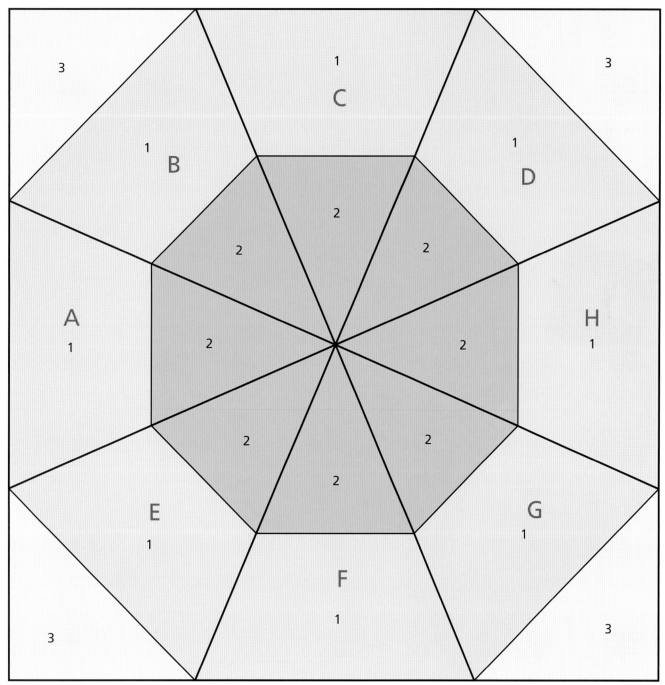

3

1
C

1
B

1
D

2

2

2

A
1

2

2

H
1

2

2

3

2

2

E
1

F
1

G
1

3

3

15

Pinwheel

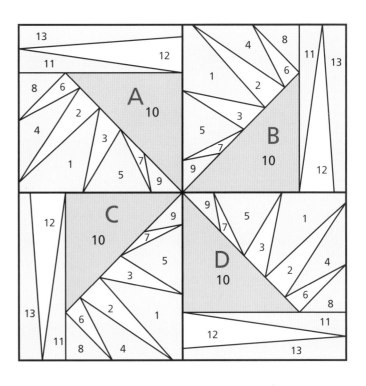

16

Log Cabin

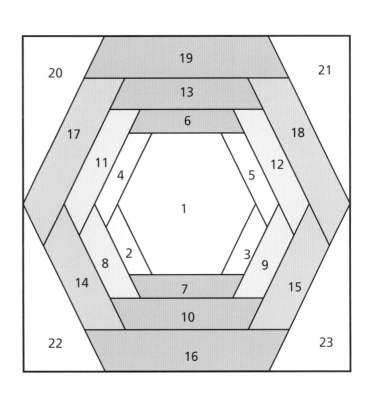

17

Angel

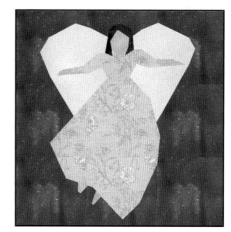

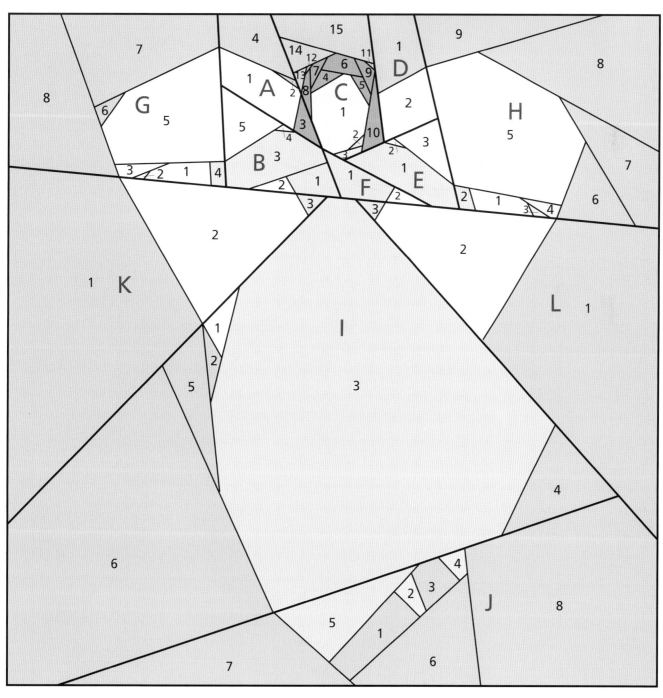

Celebrate

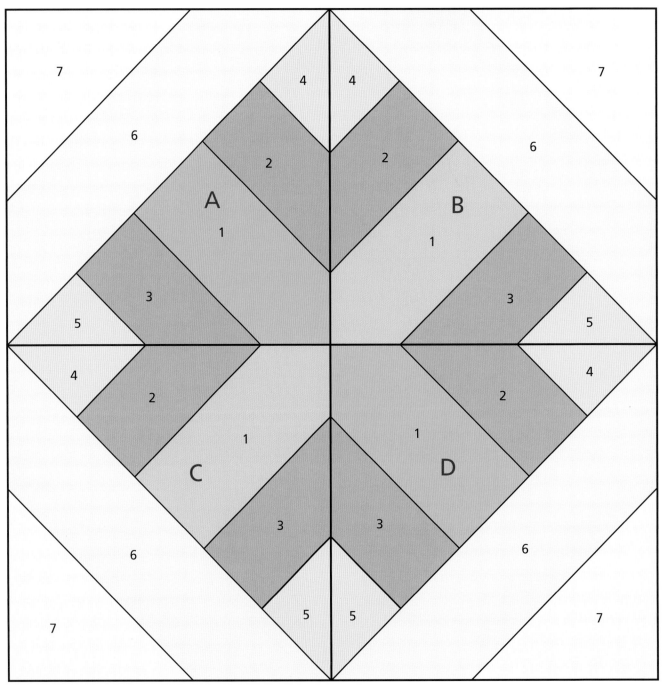

19

*Pentagon Opened
in Wahsington
D.C.*

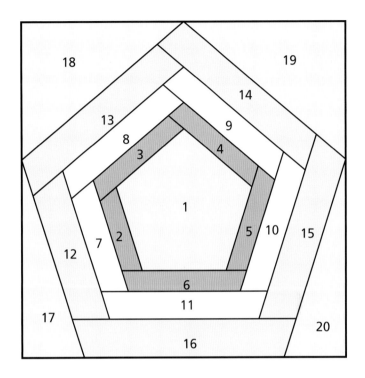

20

*Martin Luther
King's Birthday*

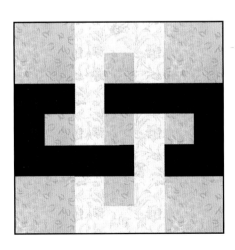

Snow Crystal

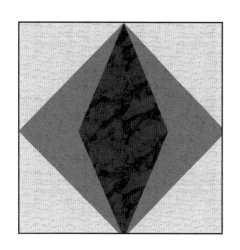

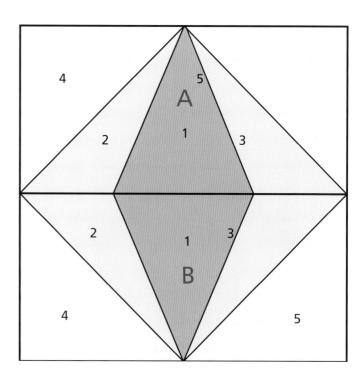

Square in a Square

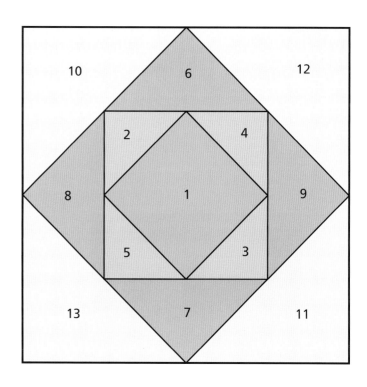

23
Star Search

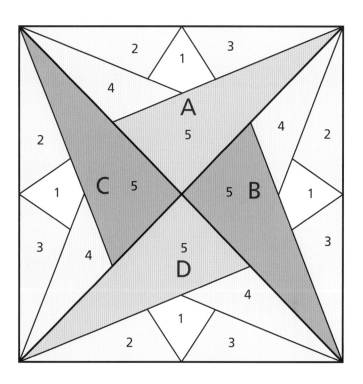

24
Winter Bud

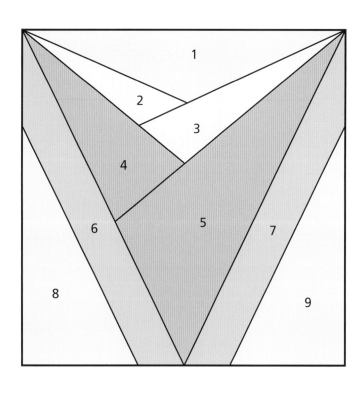

Winter Olympics

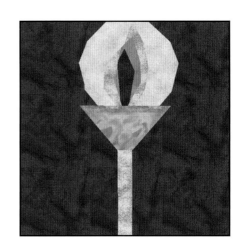

A

B

C

D

20
19
3
2
15
4
1
5
8
2
3
18
22
9
6
12
1
5
4
6
10
7
13
17
21
16
11
14
2
3
1
4
1
2
3

26

Winter in the Mountains

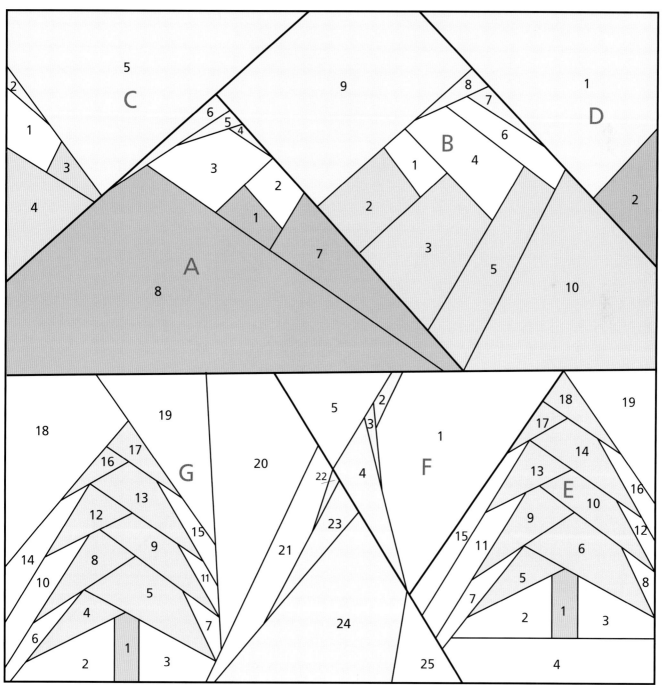

27

Puzzle

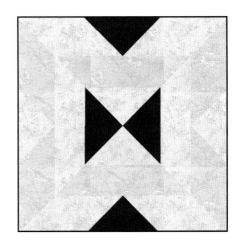

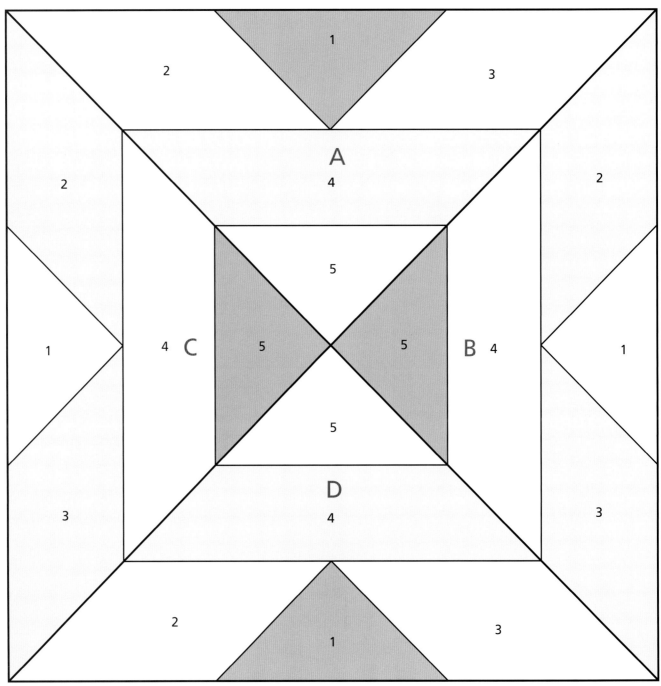

28

Space Shuttle

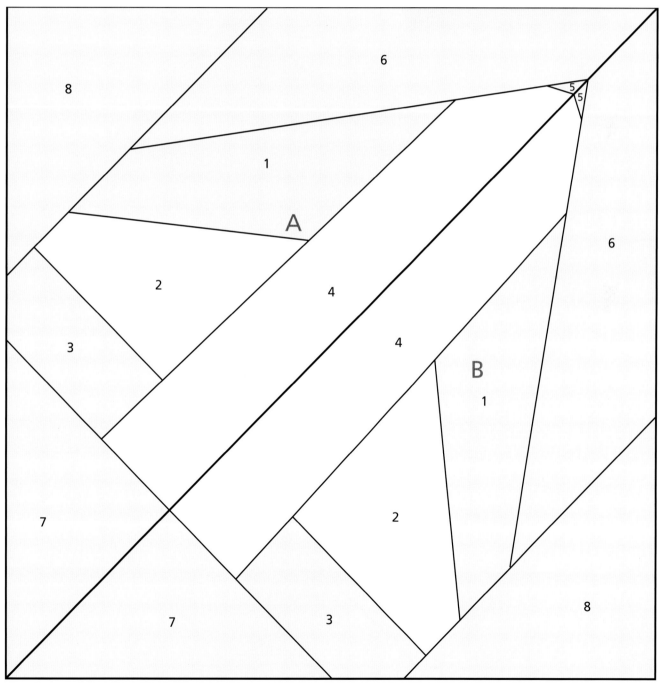

8

6

5
5

1

8

6

A

2

4

3

4

B

1

7

2

3

7

8

29

Snow Tulips

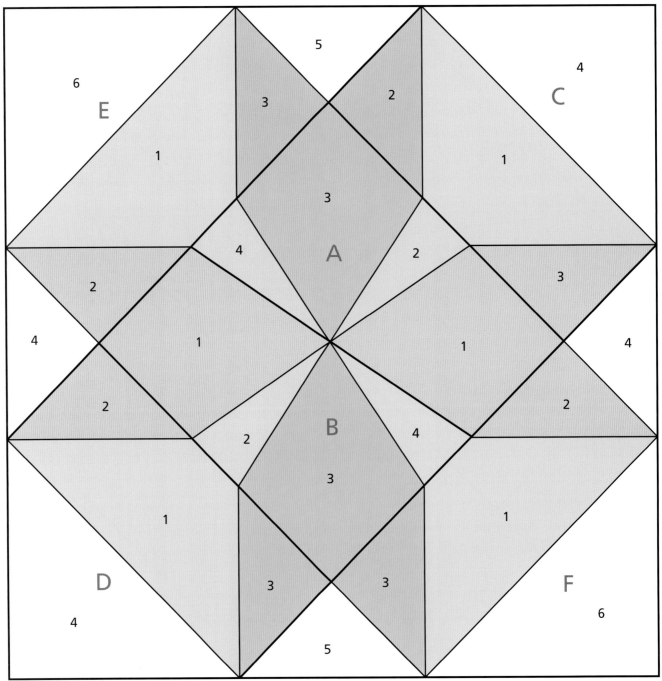

5

6

E

4

C

3

2

1

3

1

3

4

A

2

2

1

3

1

4

4

2

2

1

B

4

2

3

1

1

D

F

3

3

4

6

5

30

Mosaic

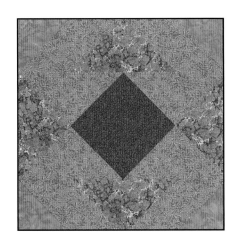

31

Woven Ribbons

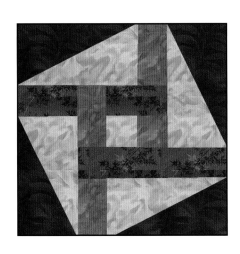

It's time to celebrate Valentine's Day with a flurry of hearts. And this charming quilt can be made in no time at all. It's actually created with only two blocks, and because those blocks are foundation pieced, it will be completed in record time. The center medallion is made with four Windblown Flower blocks, each one turned to create an entirely new design. The heart borders are made with sixteen Framed Heart blocks, a great example of how these smaller blocks can be used to make wonderful borders.

Log Cabin Heart

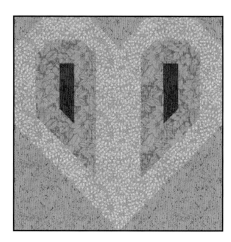

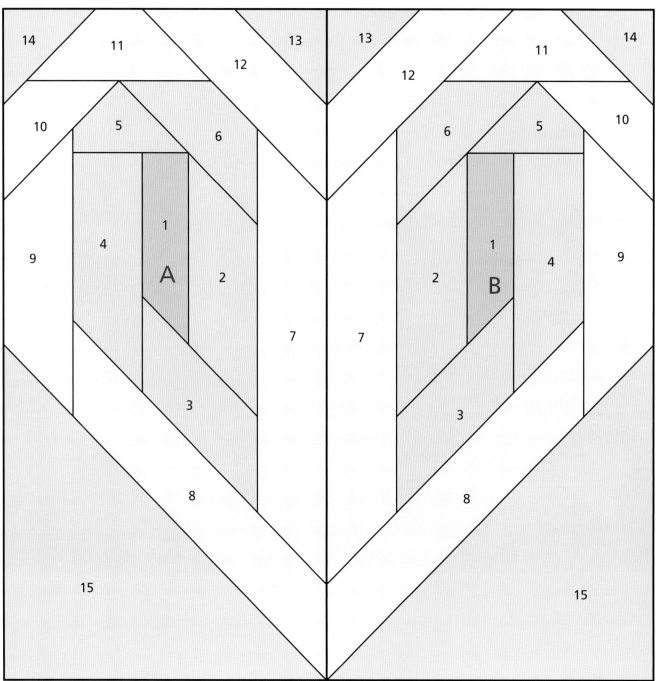

Groundhog Day

EMBELLISHMENT NOTE:
Use white and dark blue felt for eyes, black felt for nose and white felt for tooth. Draw mouth with black permanent fabric marker.

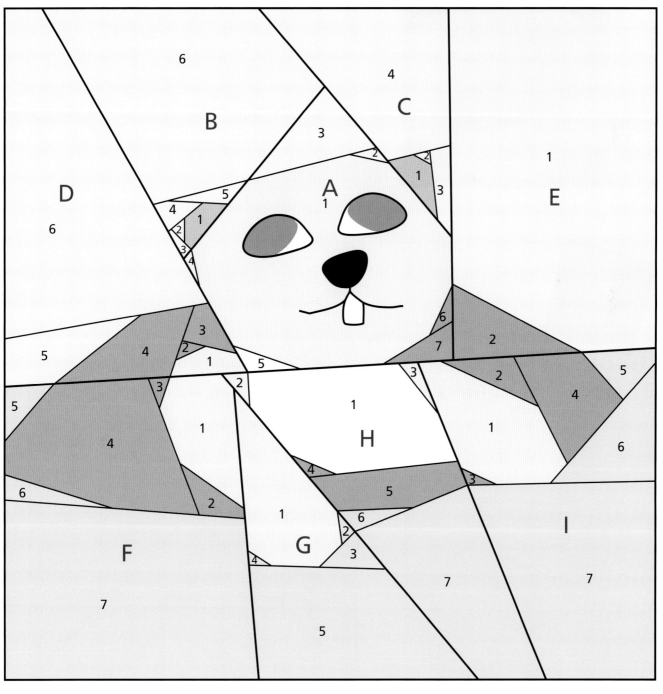

3

Topsy-Turvy

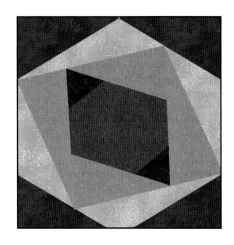

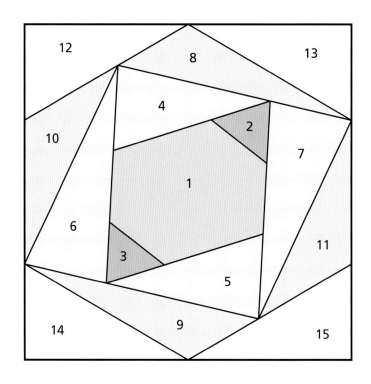

4

Fractured Geese

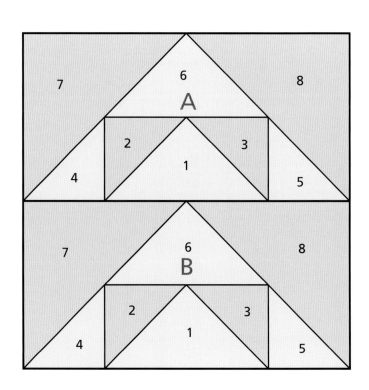

5

Framed Heart

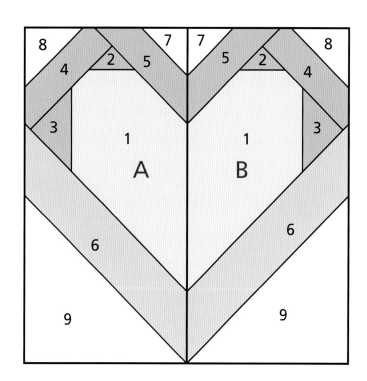

6

Fading Heart

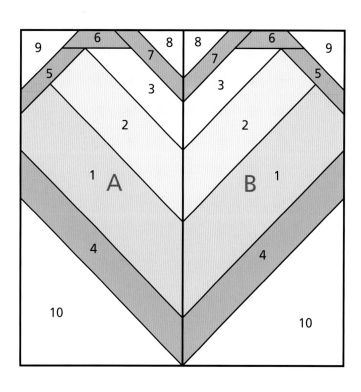

Yellow Submarine –
Beatles come to America

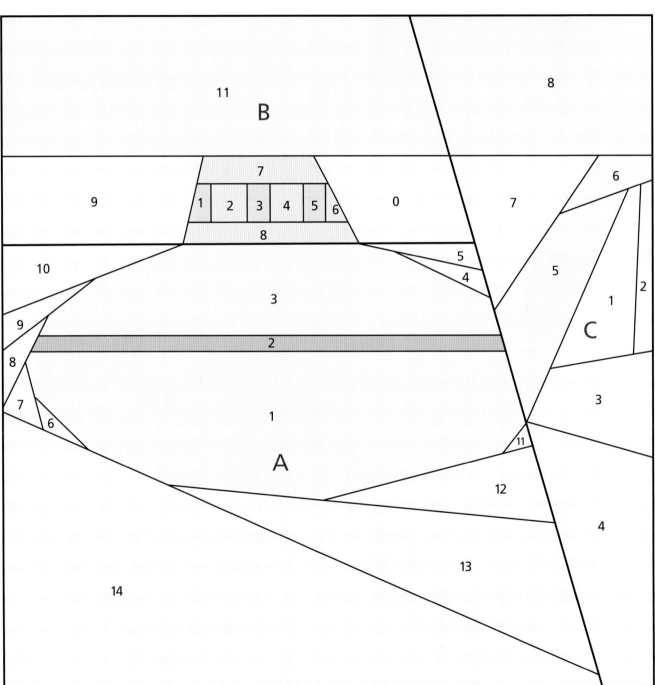

B

11

8

9

7

1 2 3 4 5 6

0

7

6

8

5

4

5

2

1

C

10

3

9

2

8

3

7

1

6

A

11

12

4

13

14

Windblown Flower

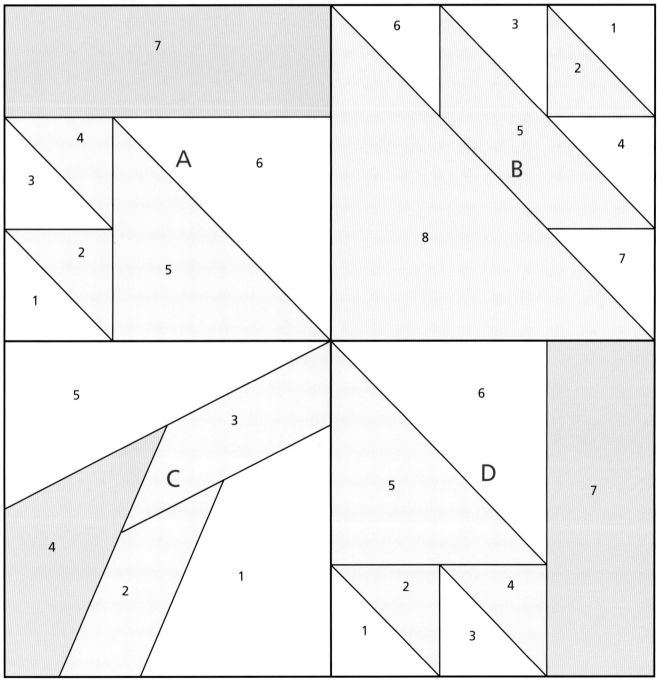

9

Amethyst — February Birthstone

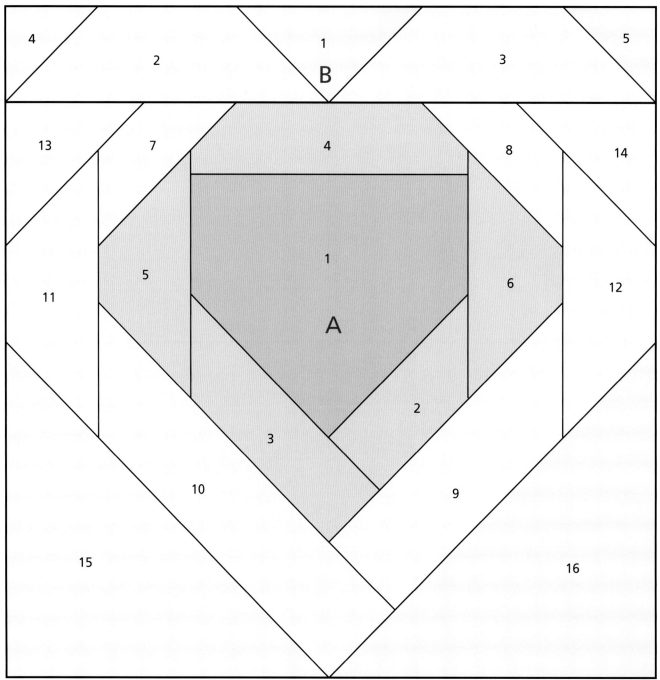

Bluebird of Happiness

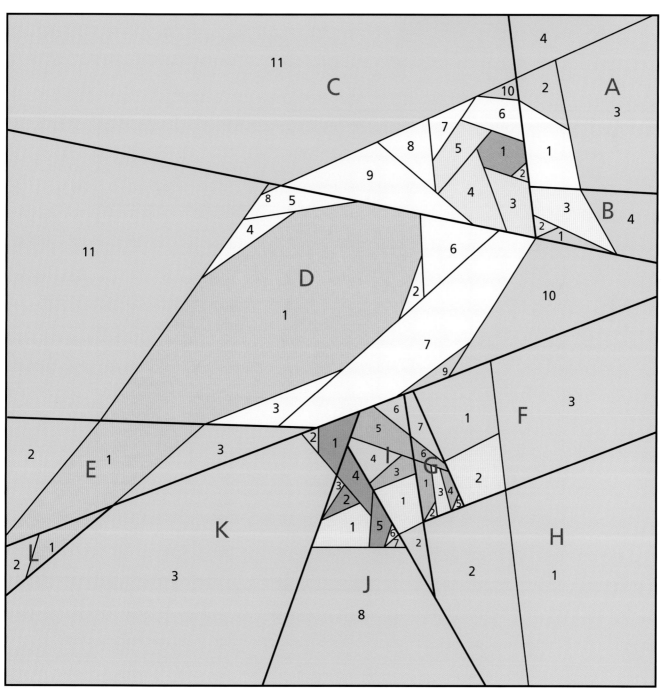

Courthouse Steps

February

12							

10   6   2   1   3   7   11

8

4

5

9

13

Log House —
Lincoln's Birthday

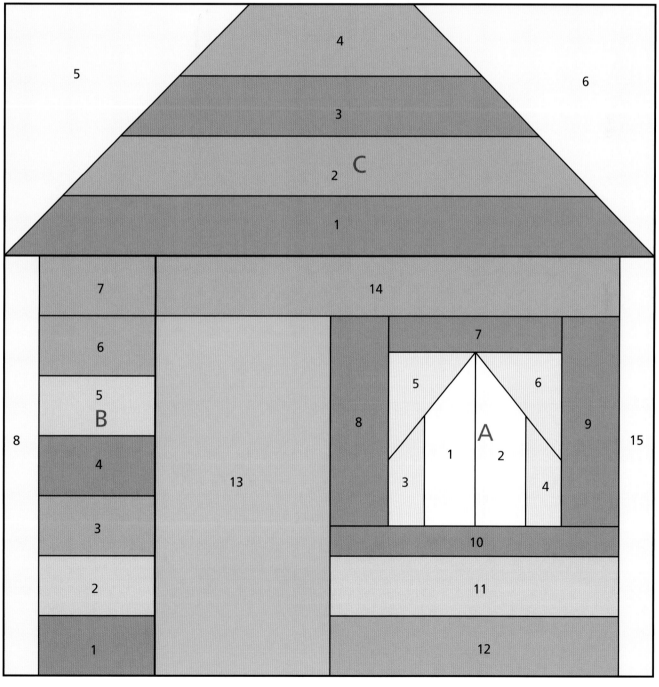

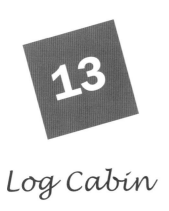

13

Log Cabin

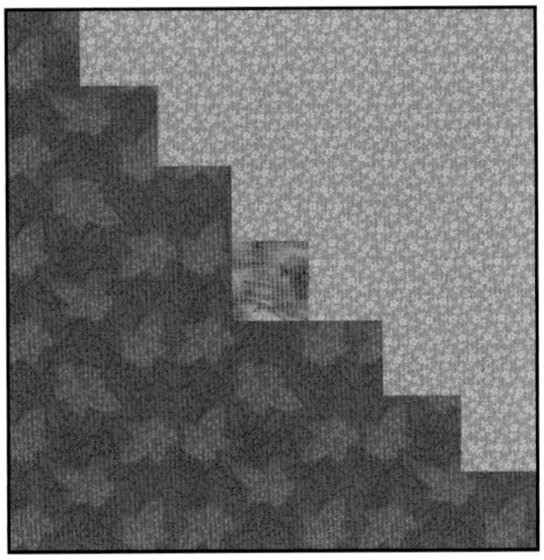

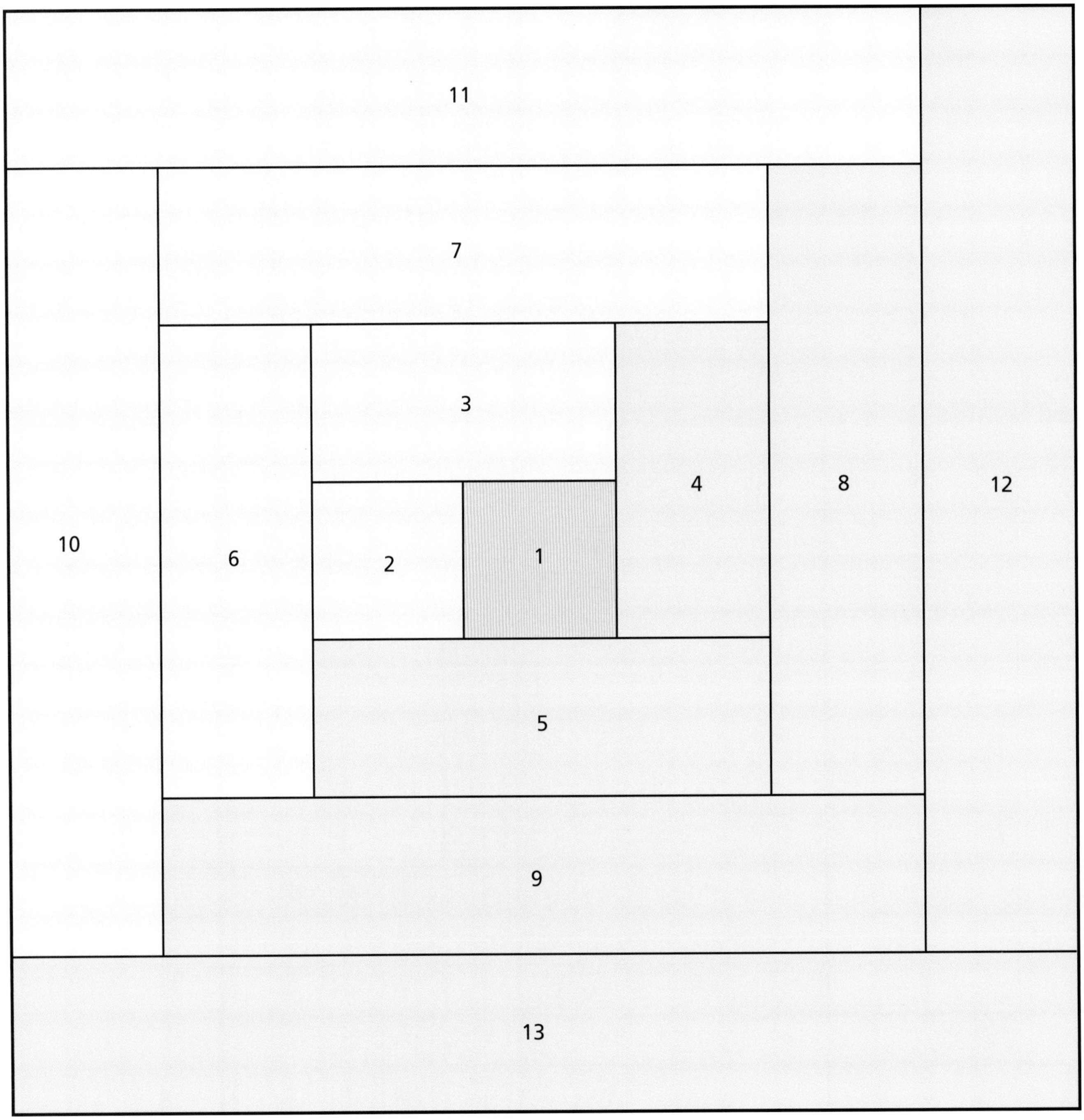
11
7
3
4
8
12
10
6
2
1
5
9
13

14

Valentine Angels

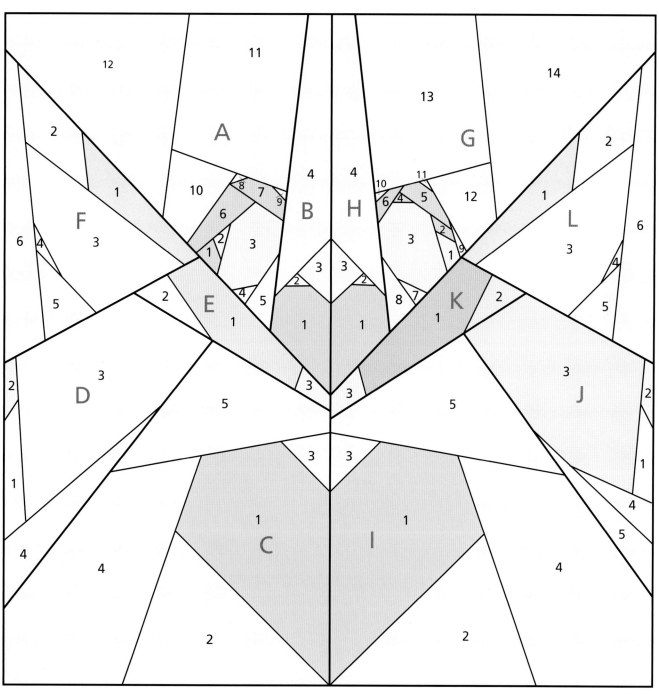

Violet –
February Flower

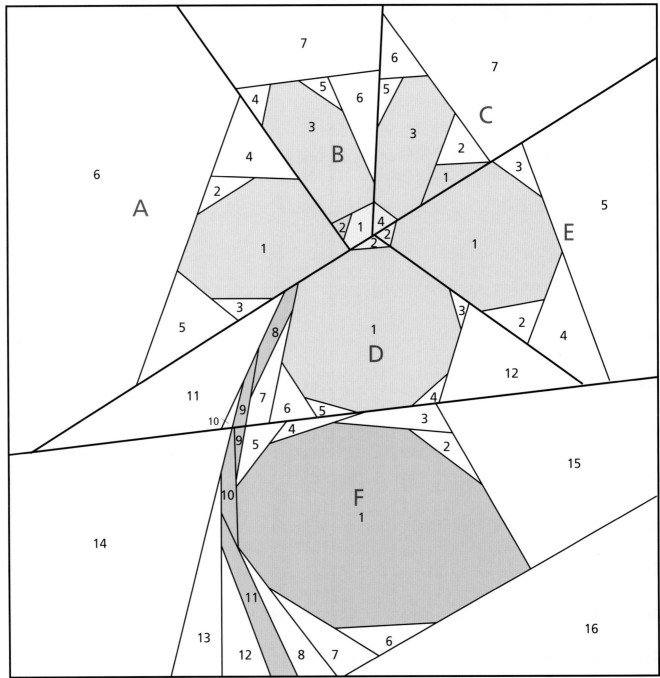

Semi-Truck

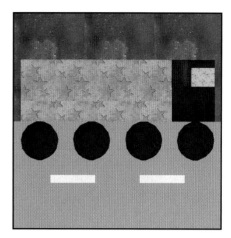

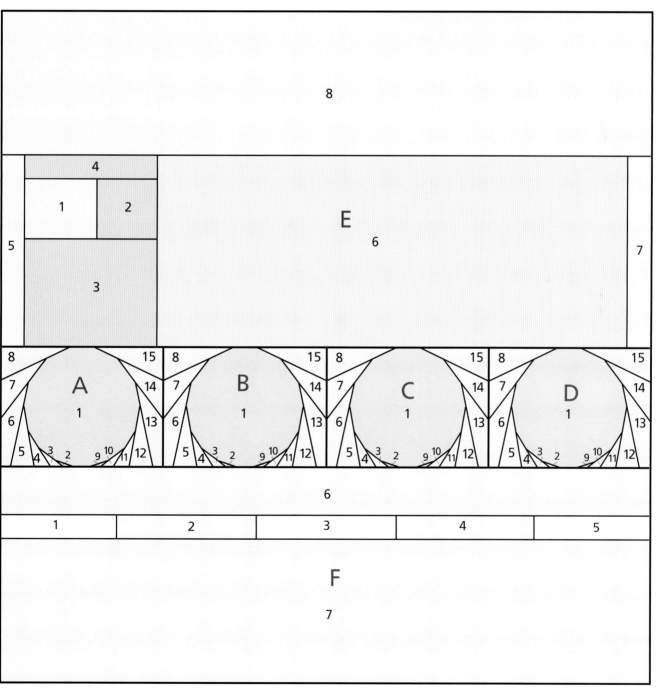

Broken Heart

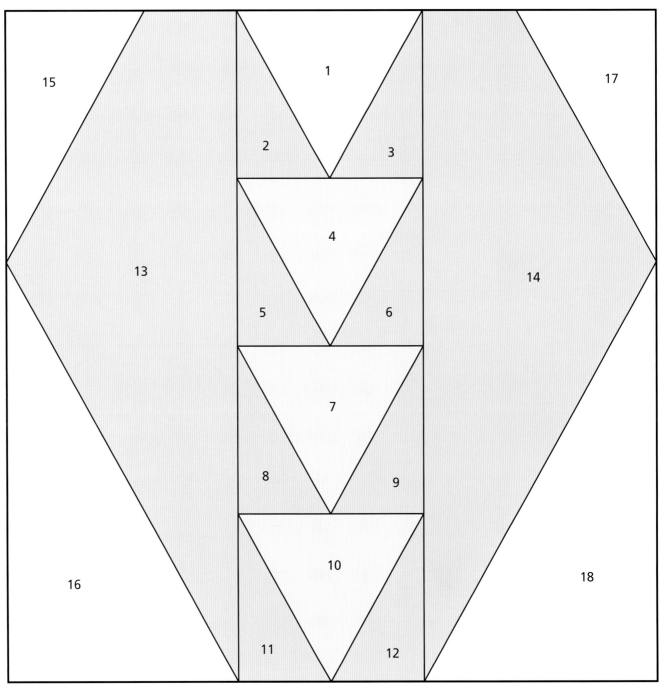

15

1

17

2

3

4

5

6

13

14

7

8

9

10

16

11

12

18

Log Cabin Star

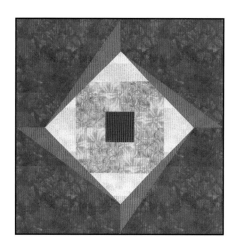

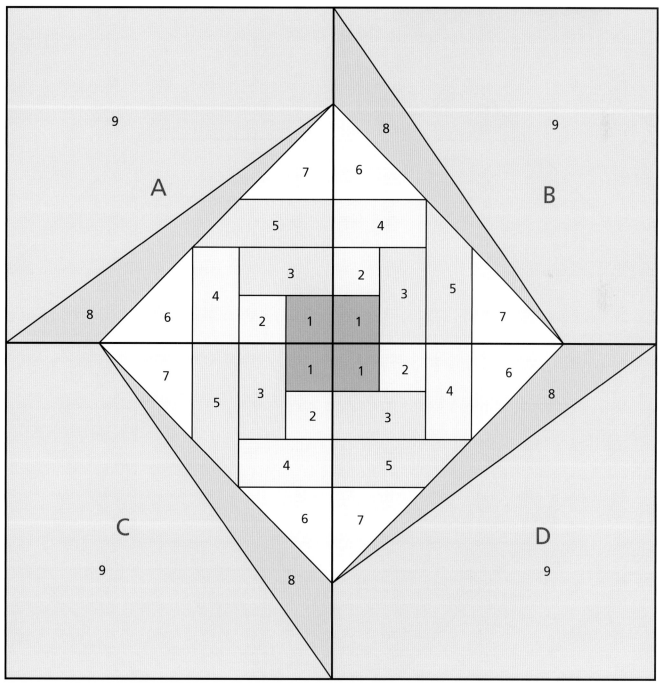

9

8

9

A

7

6

B

5

4

8

6

4

3

2

3

5

2

1

1

7

5

3

7

1

1

2

6

5

3

2

4

8

2

3

4

5

6

7

C

D

9

8

9

19

Square Dance

F 2
F 1
2
B 1
3
H 1
H 2

2
4
3
2

D 1
A 1
E 1

2
3
5
3

I 1
3
C 1
G 1
2
2
2

20

Pug

EMBELLISHMENT NOTE:
Use black felt for facial details.

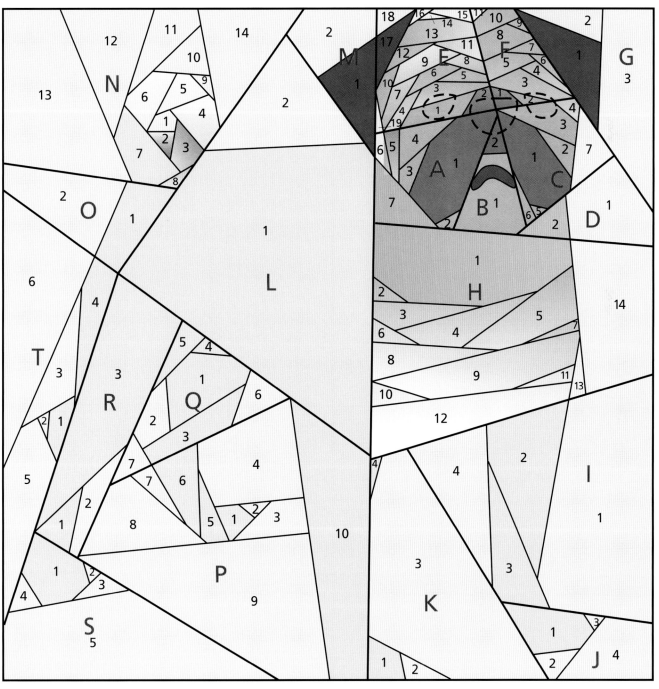

February

57

21

Southwest

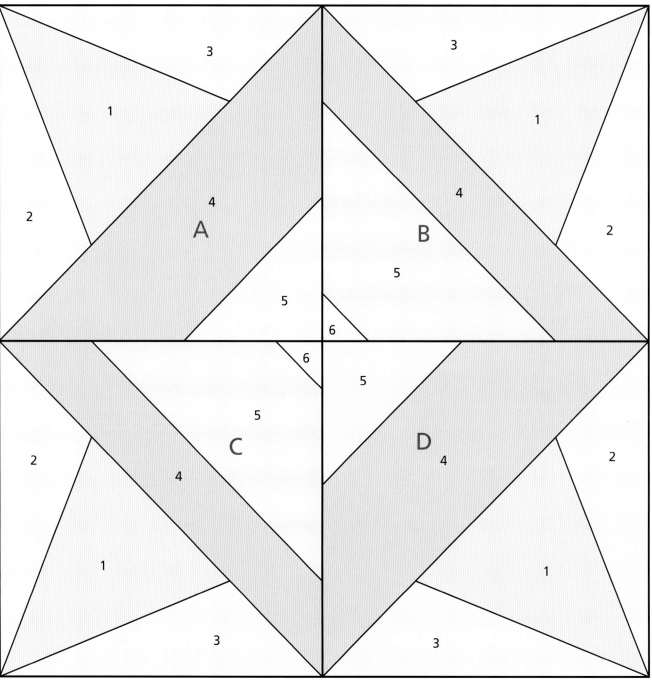

22

Cherries —
Washington's Birthday

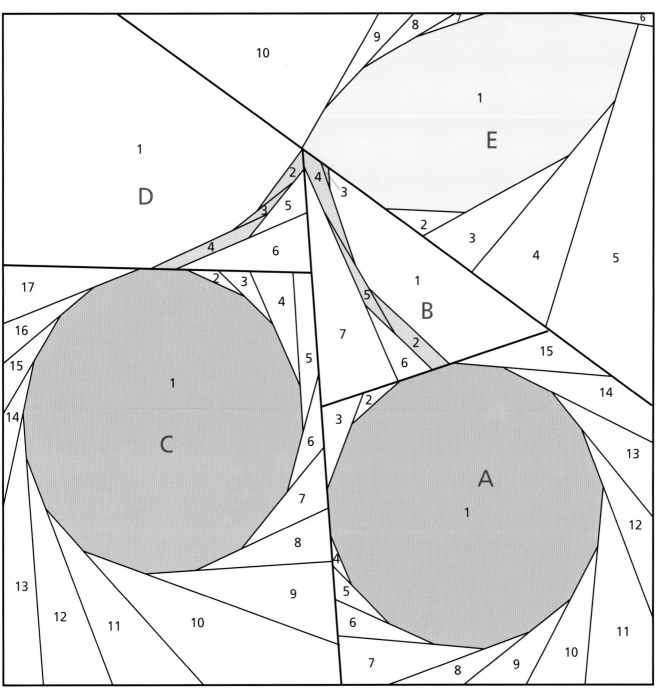

February

59

23

Flower Basket

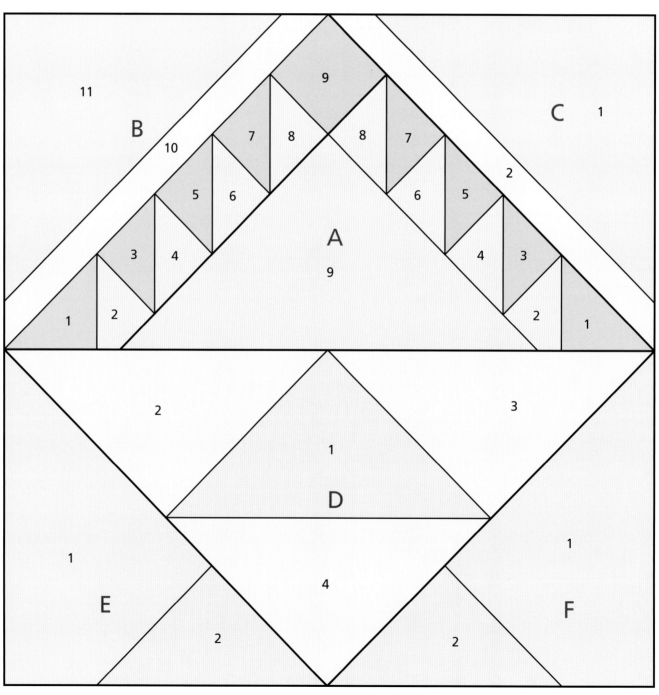

11

B

10

C   1

9

7   8   8   7

5   6   6   5

2

3   4   A   4   3

9

1   2   2   1

2   3

1

D

1

E   1   4   F   1

2   2

24

Flowering Fan

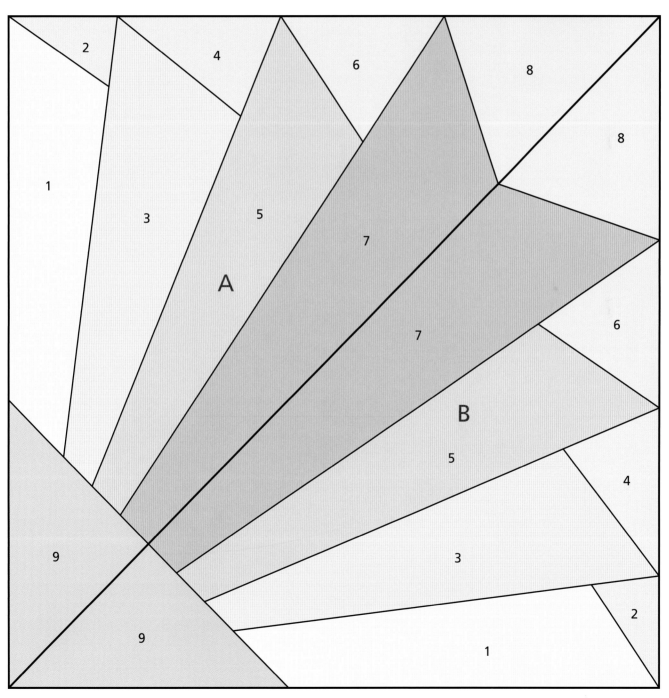

2

4

6

8

8

1

3

5

7

6

A

7

B

5

4

9

3

9

2

9

1

25

Radio Windmill

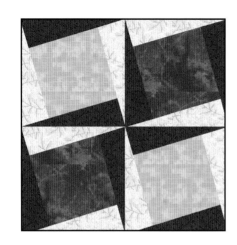

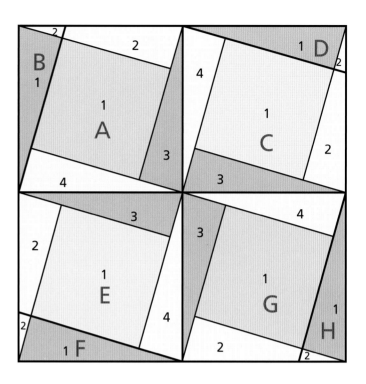

26

Candy

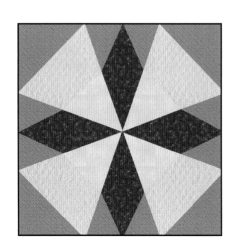

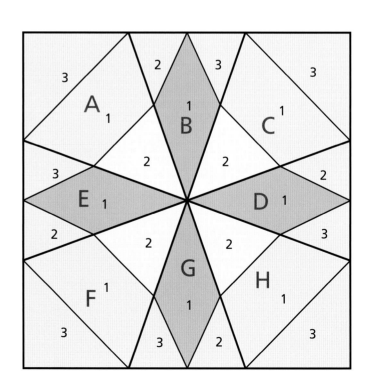

27

Gift Package

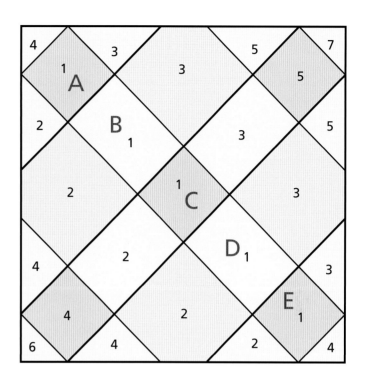

28

Pinwheel Hearts

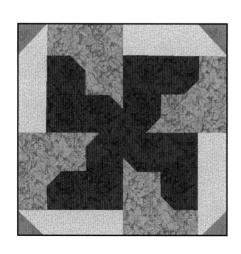

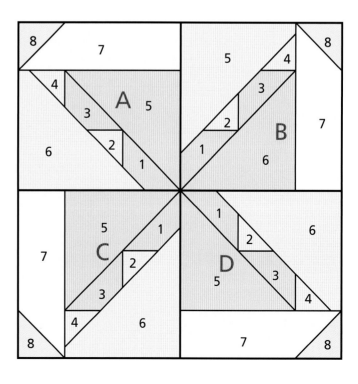

March

Celebrate the arrival of Spring by creating this quilt. Here are flowers, a red-breasted robin as well as a St. Patrick's Day shamrock. For fun in the park on a bright Spring morning, how about a charming sailboat or a tree with a swing hanging in its leaves. Add to it some of your favorite Spring mementoes; the quiltmaker added a musical note because March was always the month for the high school band concert. A sampler quilt like this one gives you a chance to try many different foundation quilt blocks. You won't get bored, and you're sure to have fun.

In Like a Lion

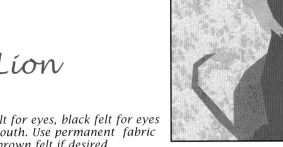

EMBELLISHMENT NOTE: Use white felt for eyes, black felt for eyes and nose and dark brown felt for mouth. Use permanent fabric markers instead of black and dark brown felt if desired.

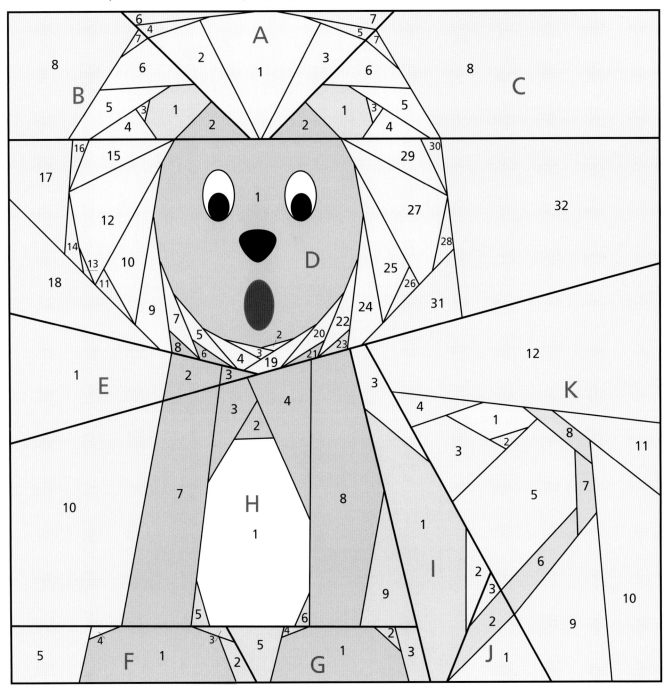

Jonquil — March Flower

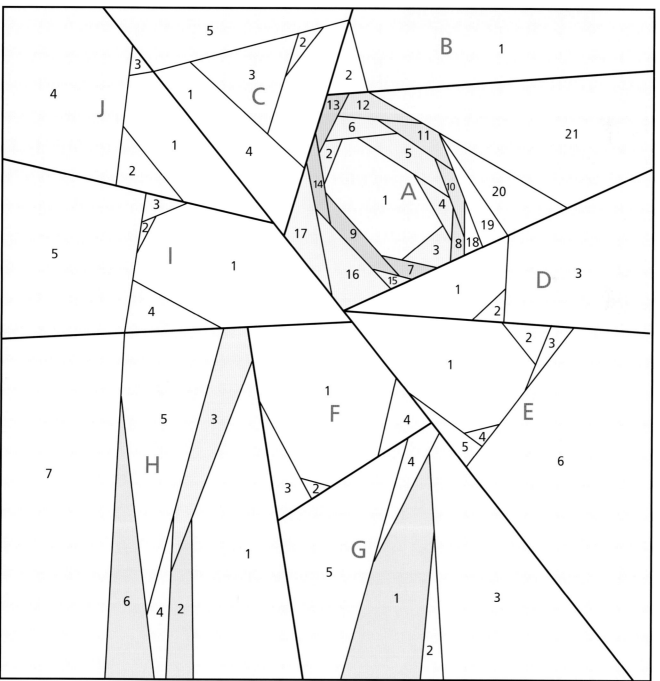

Log Cabin

		9		
8		5		10
	4	1	2	
		3	6	
	7			
	11			

Robin

EMBELLISHMENT NOTE:
Use permanent black fabric marker for eye.

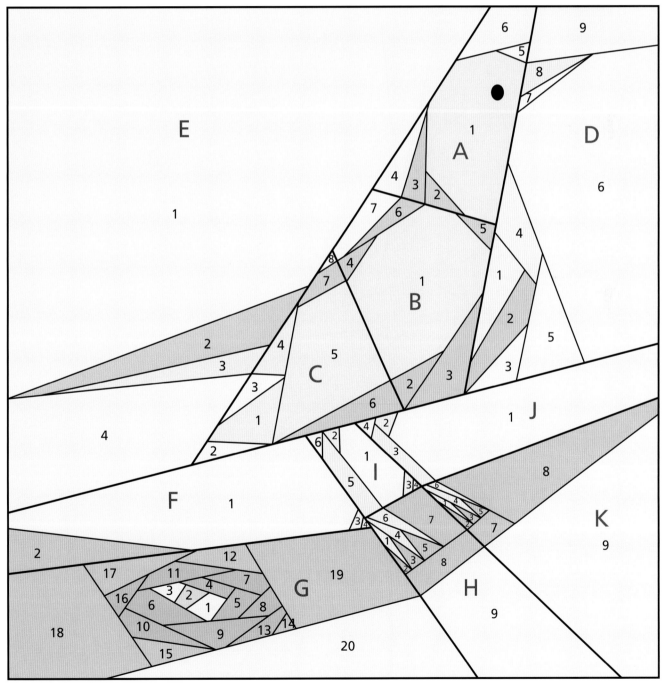

5

Angel

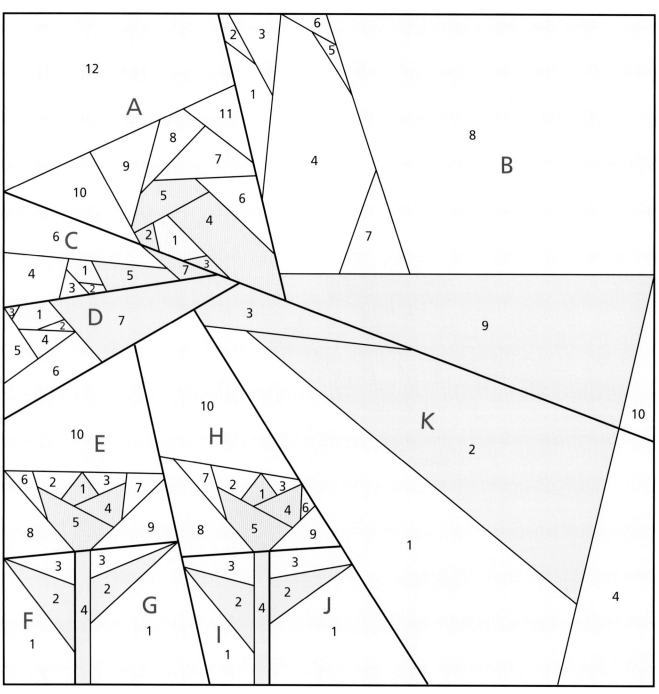

Lenten Cross

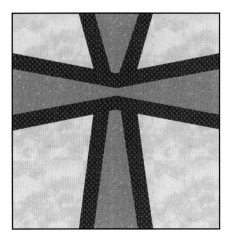

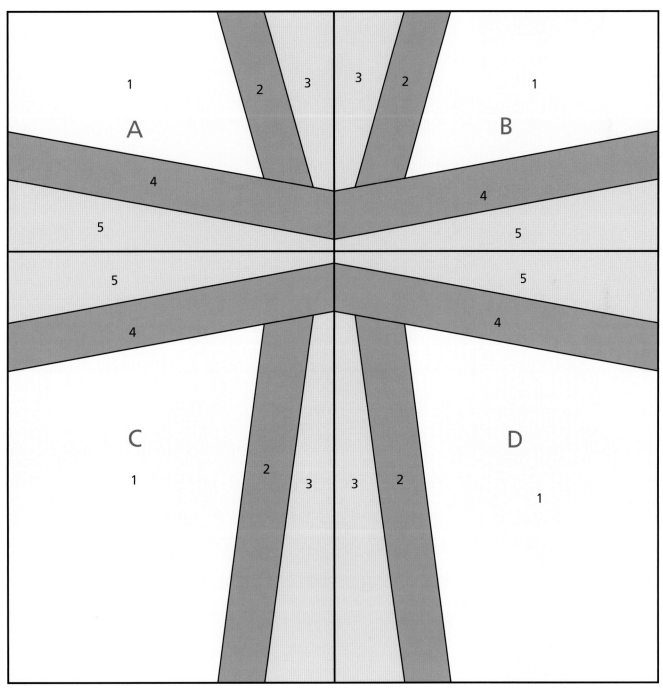

Telephone Invented by Alexander Graham Bell

EMBELLISHMENT NOTE:
Use a black permanent fabric marker to add phone cord.

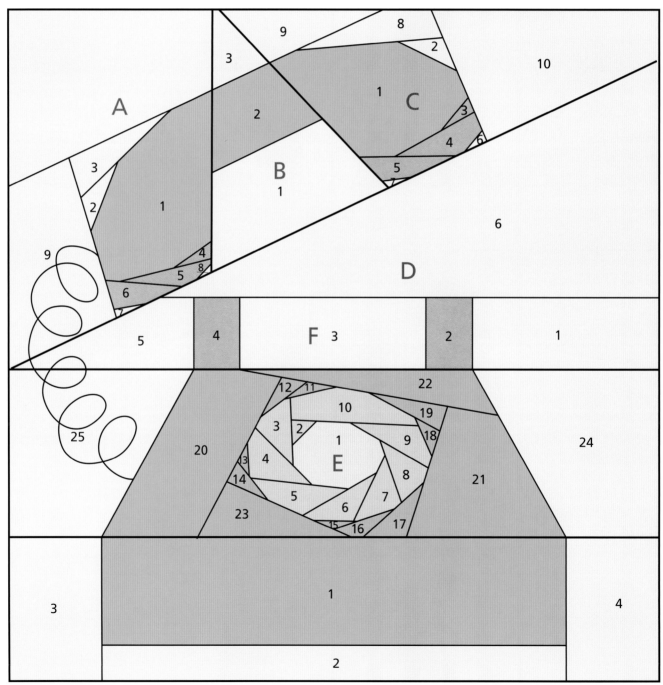

8

Musical Notation

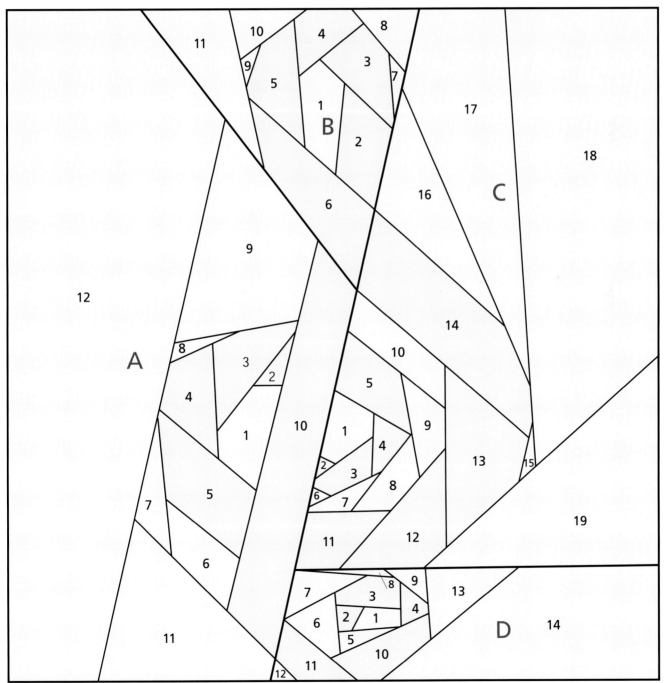

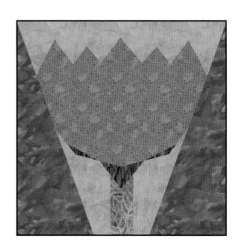

9

Flower

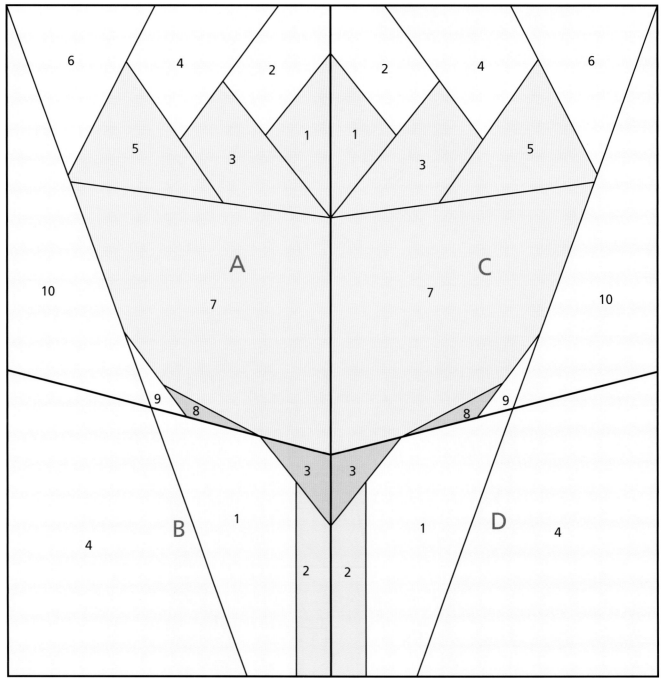

6   4   2   2   4   6

5   3   1   1   3   5

A   C

10   7   7   10

9 8   8 9

3   3

B   1   1   D

4   2   2   4

Flower

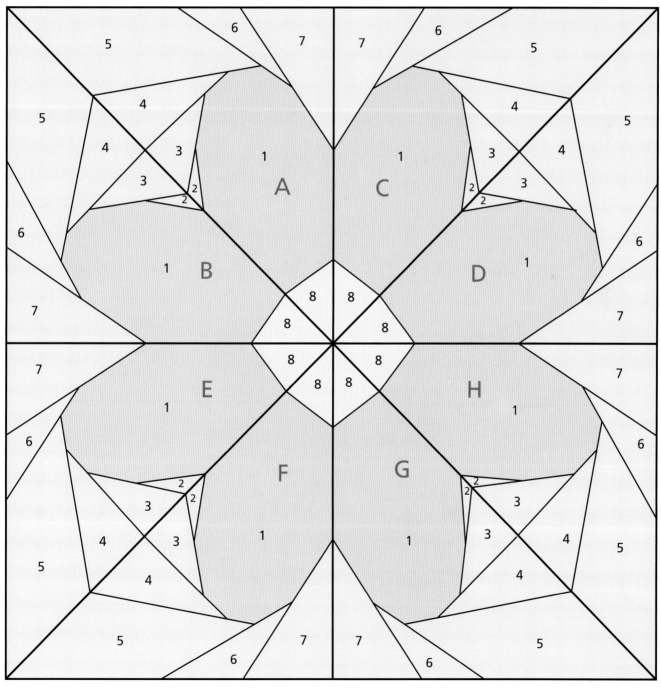

Tree

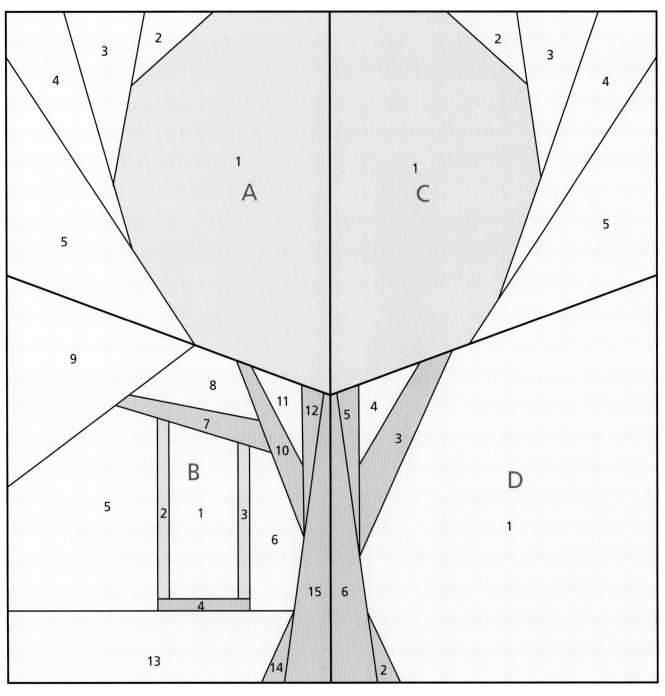

3

2

4

1

A

5

1

C

5

9

8

11 12 5 4

7

10 3

B

5 2 1 3

6

D

4

15 6 1

13

14 2

2

3

4

Seesaw

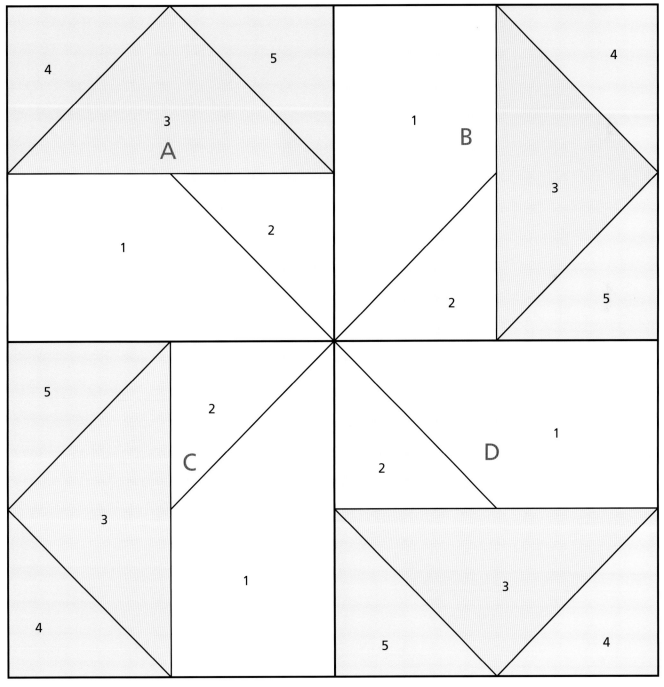

A

4 5

3

A

2

1

B

1

3

2

5

4

C

5

2

3

C

1

4

D

1

2

D

3

5 4

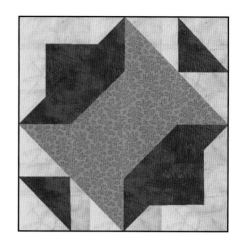

13

Kite

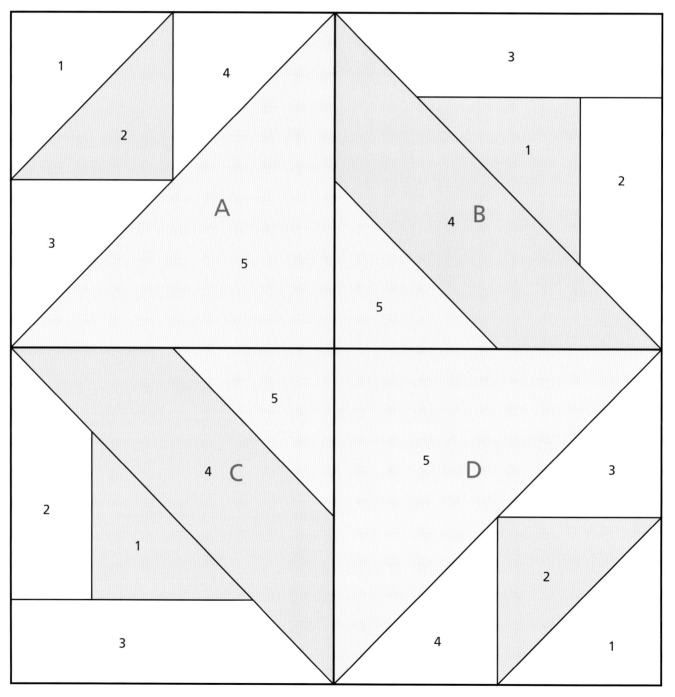

Aquamarine —
March Birthstone

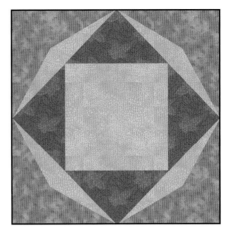

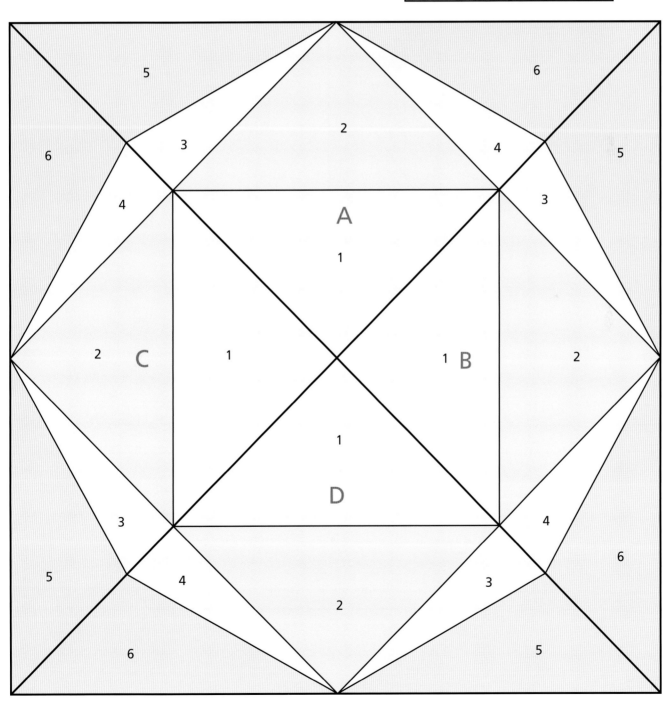

15

Sailboat

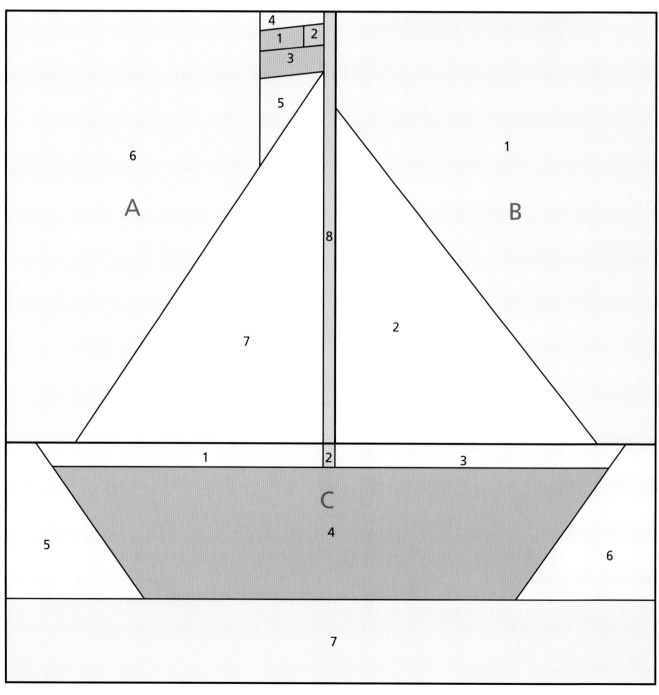

Tulip Pinwheel

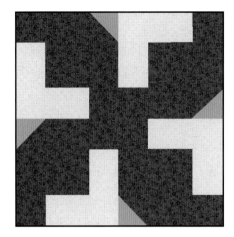

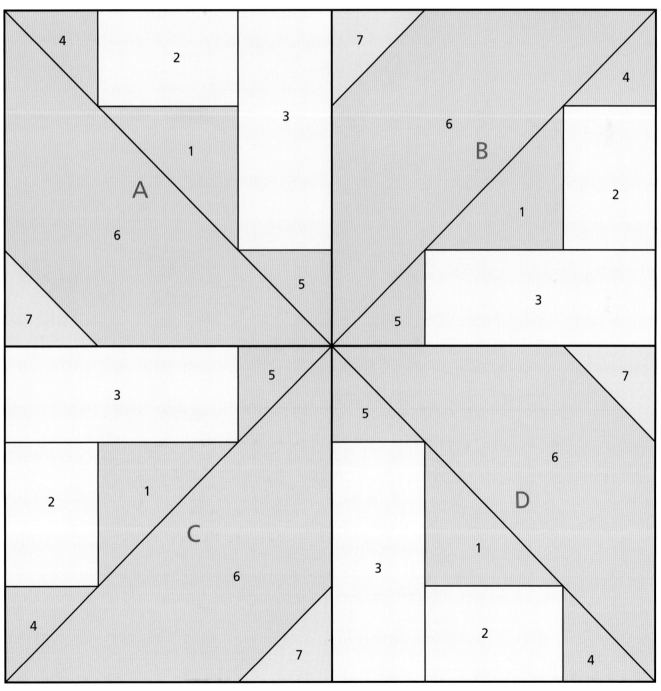

Shamrock –
Saint Patrick's Day

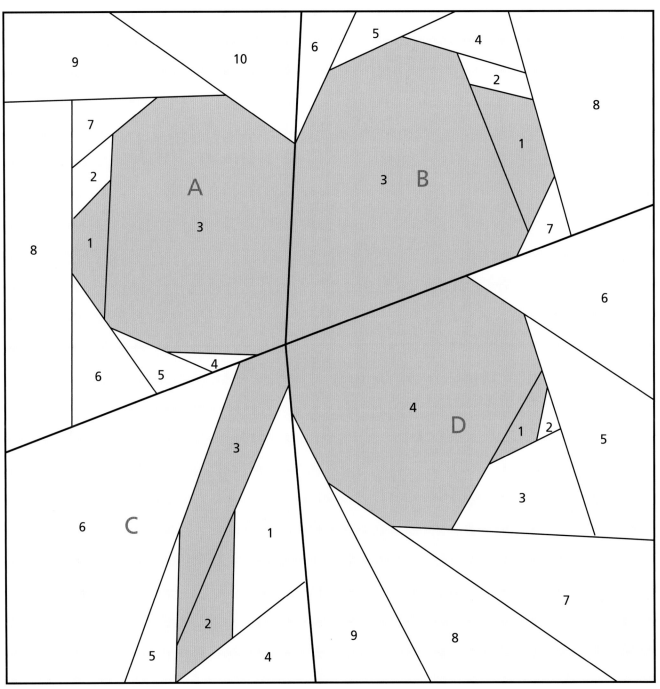

Star

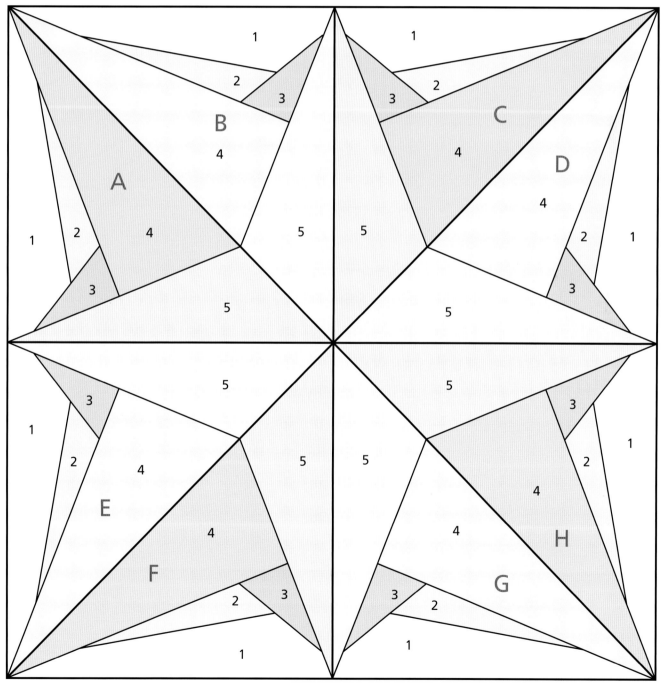

19

Joseph's Coat —
Feast of St. Joseph

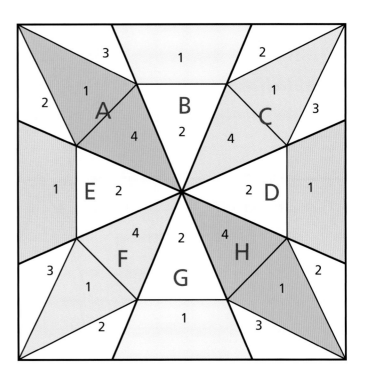

20

Lemoyne star

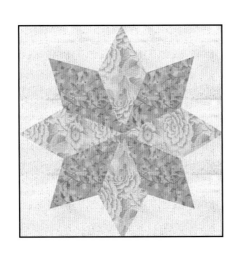

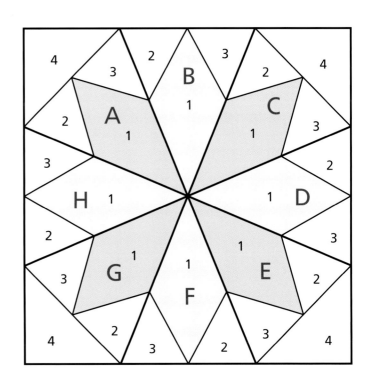

21

Butterfly

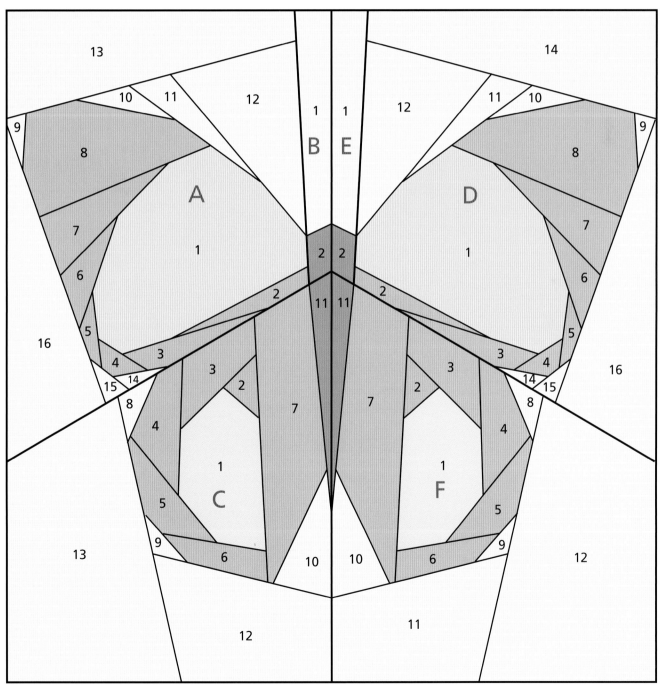

22

Small Flower

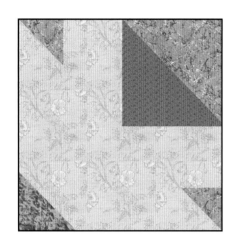

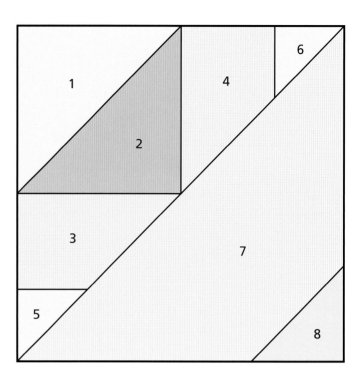

23

Squares and Diamonds

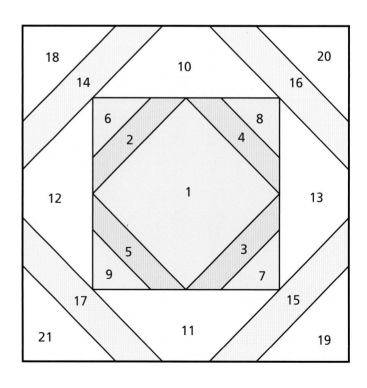

24

Birthday Cake

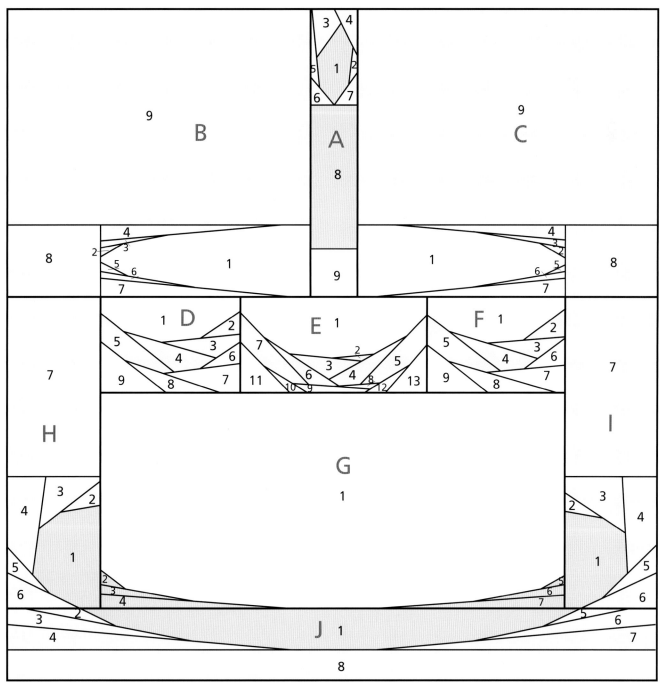

25

Log Cabin Skewed

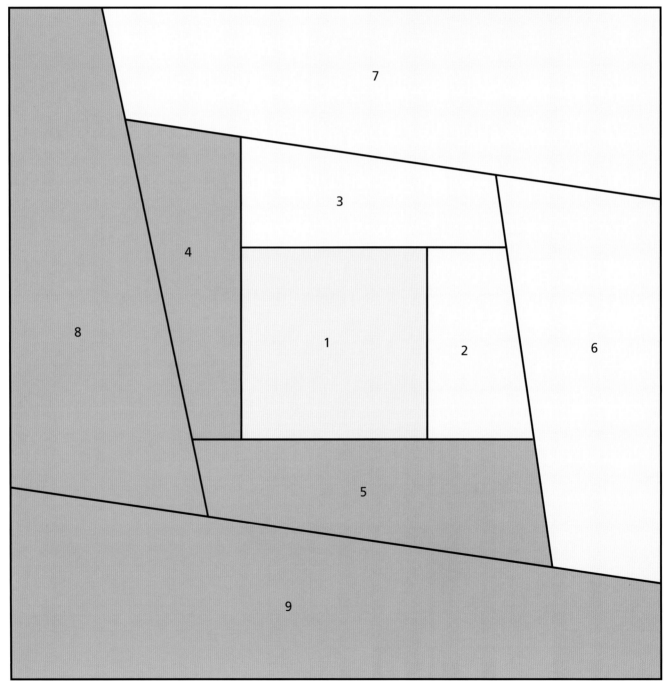

26

Beethoven's Birthday

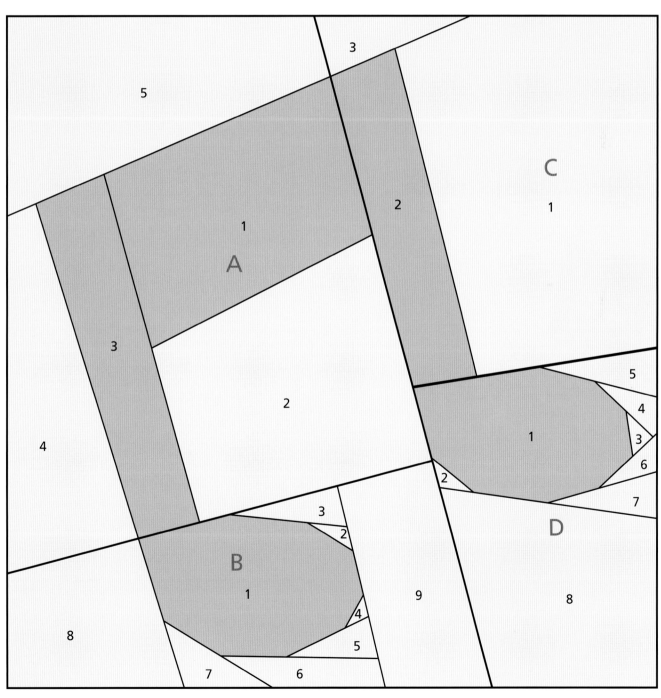

27

Uneven Log Cabin

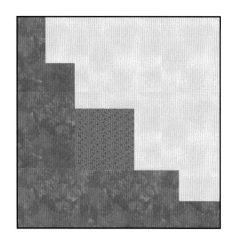

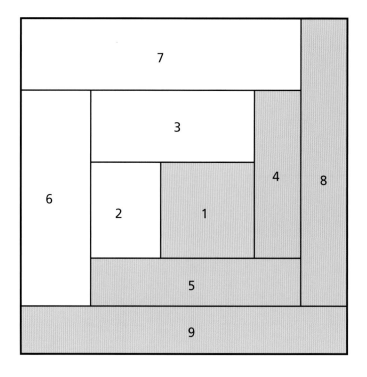

28

Sunny Flower

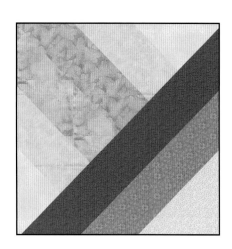

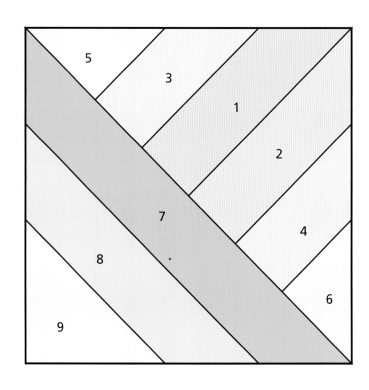

29

Perpetual Motion

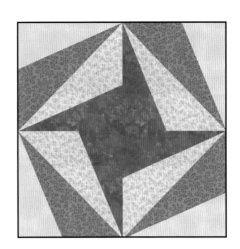

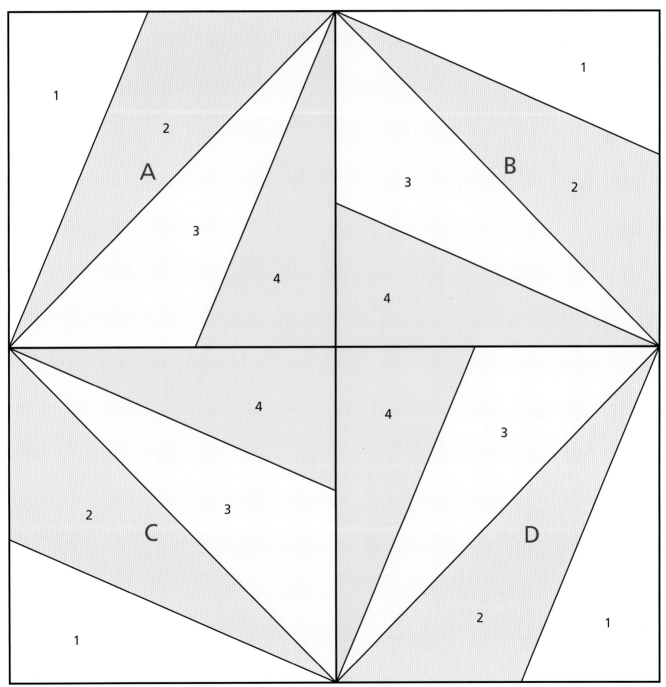

30

Out Like a Lamb

EMBELLISHMENT NOTE:
Use permanent black fabric marker for facial features.

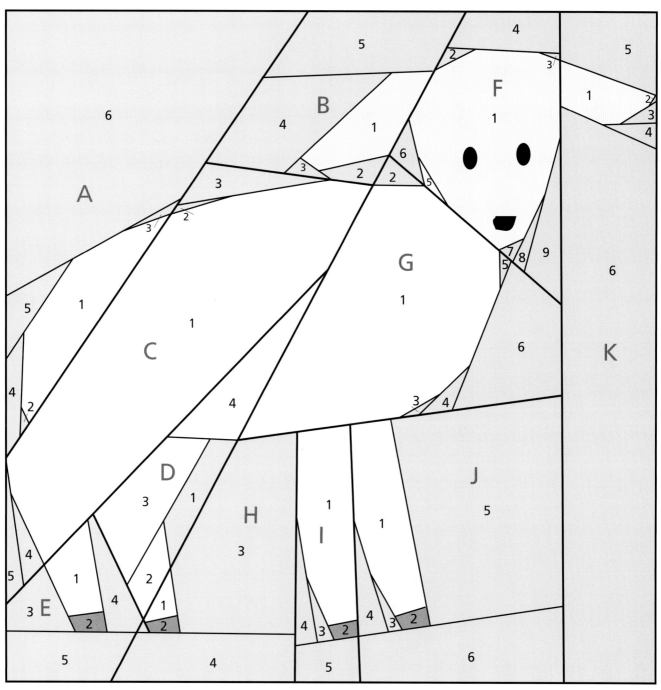

Eiffel Tower Built

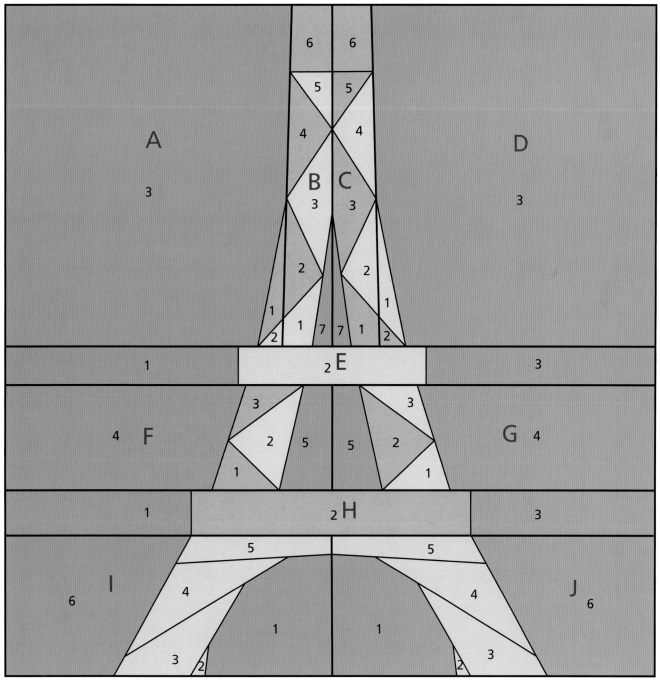

April

In its precision and beauty, the diamond has

no rival in nature, and the Diamond block can create

a quilt of great beauty as well. Diamonds are the

April birthstone, and here the Diamond block is

used to create a precious jewel of a quilt. The cen-

tral focal point is created with nine Diamond blocks,

sweetly set off with four small Flower blocks nestled

in the corners of the borders. This quilt is a shining

example of how to use the small blocks.

Easter Basket

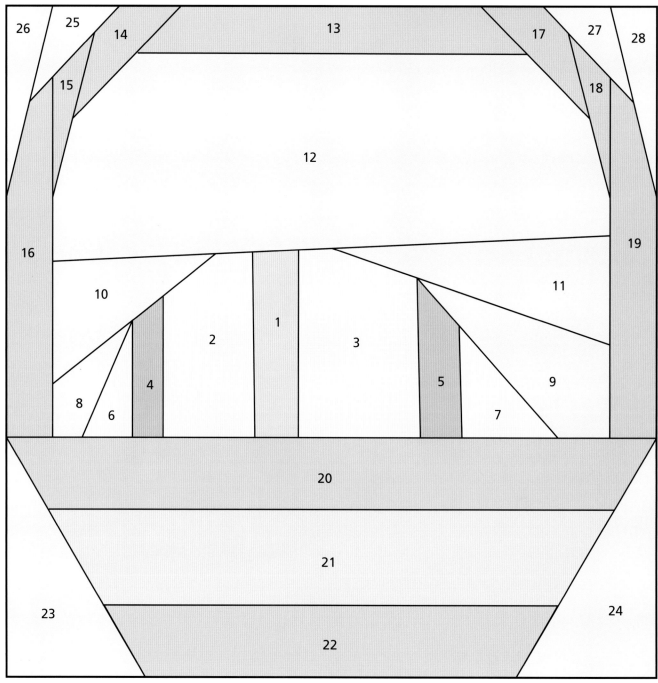

26 25 14 13 17 27 28
15 18
12
16 19
10 11
1
2 3
4 5 9
8 6 7
20
21
23 24
22

Easter Bunny

EMBELLISHMENT NOTE:
Use black and white felt for the eye and pink felt for the nose.
Permanent fabric markers may be used in place of felt if desired.

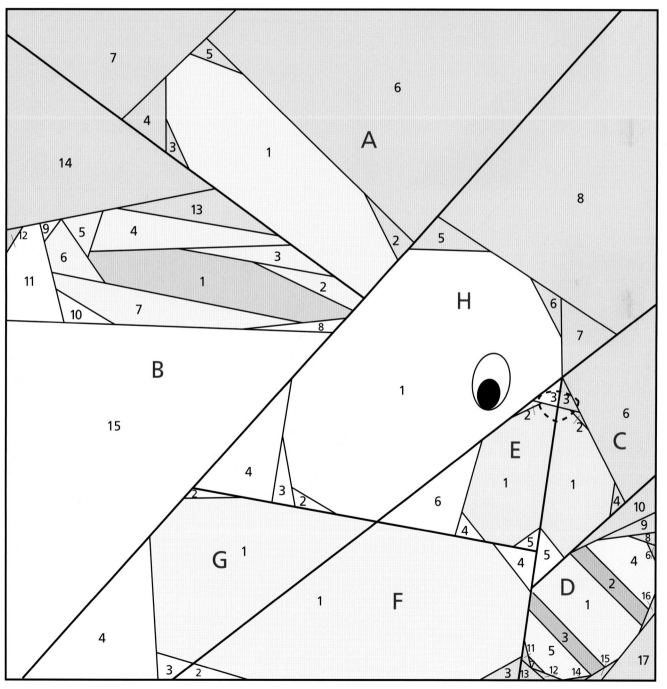

Symmetry

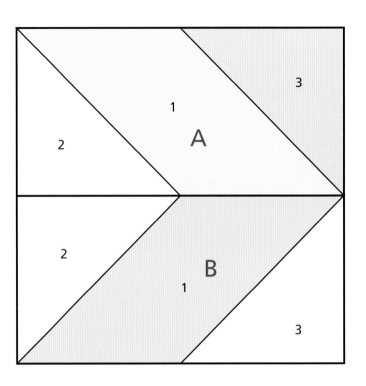

Windmill

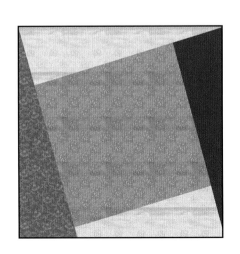

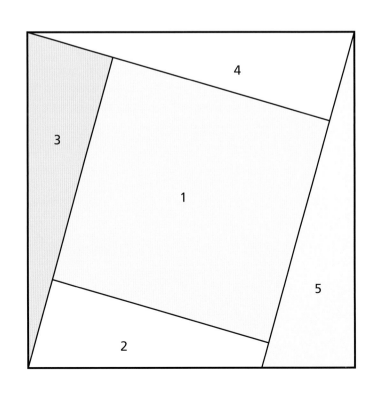

5

Follow the Leader

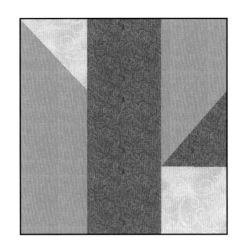

1

A

2

4

2

3

2

B

1

Circle of Ovals

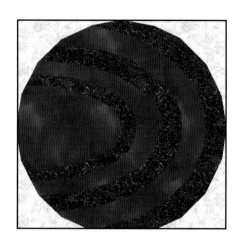

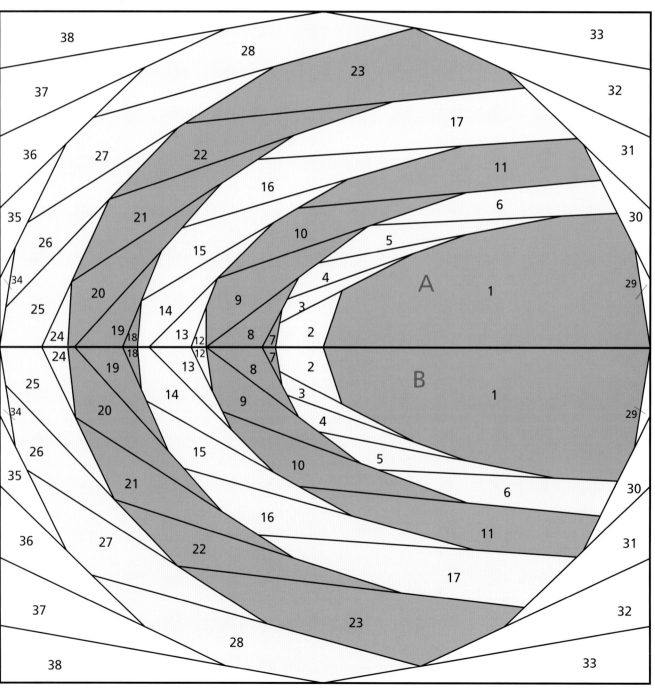

7

Tulip

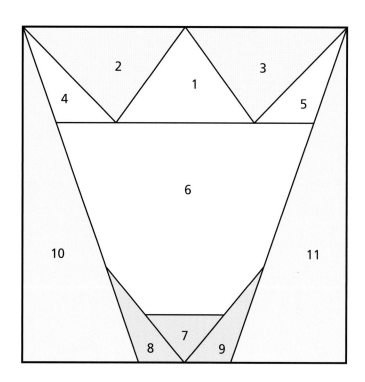

8

King's Cross

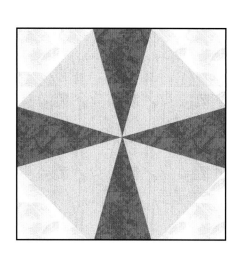

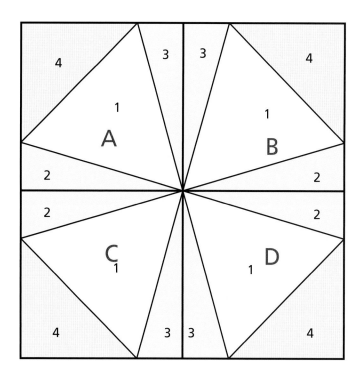

Daisy

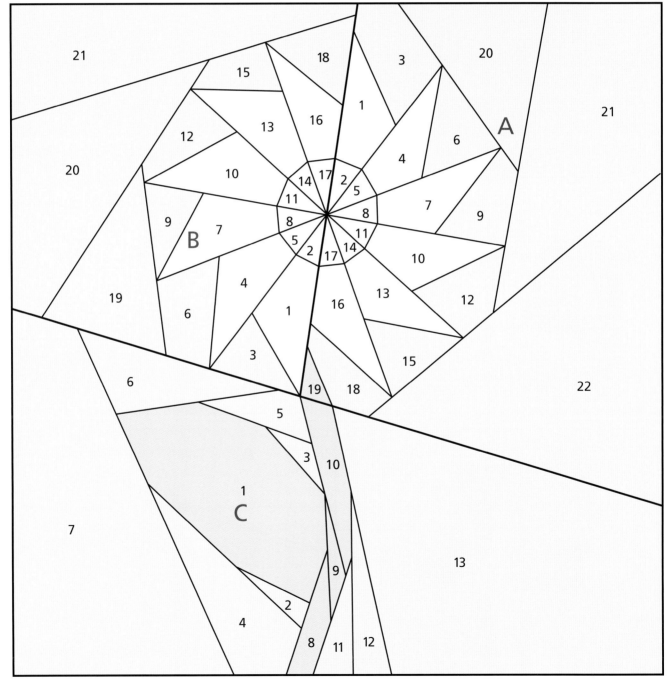

10

Log Cabin Flower

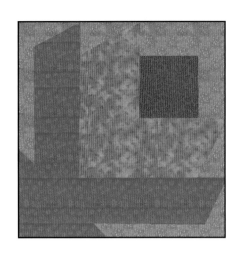

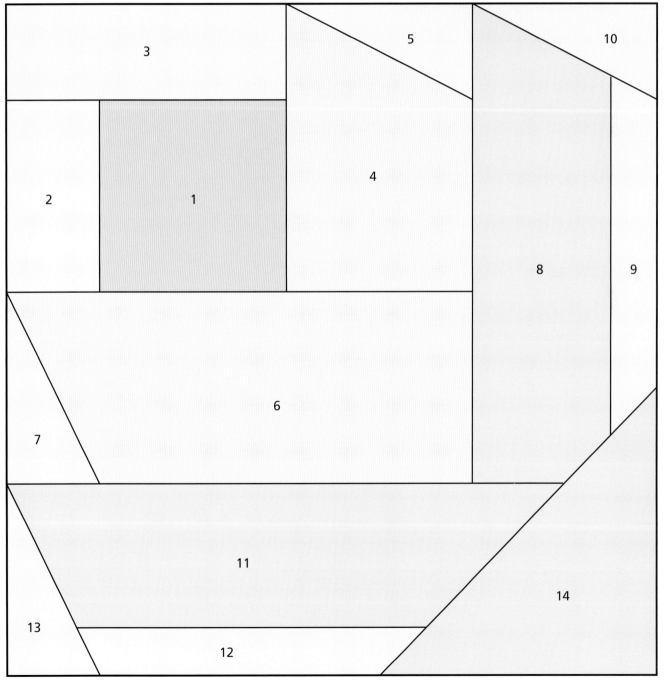

3

5

10

2

1

4

8

9

6

7

11

14

13

12

11

Pinwheel

5	3	4	5
4	A 2 1	B 1 2	3
3	2 C 1	2 1 D	4
5 4		3	55

12

Star

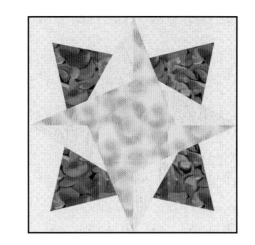

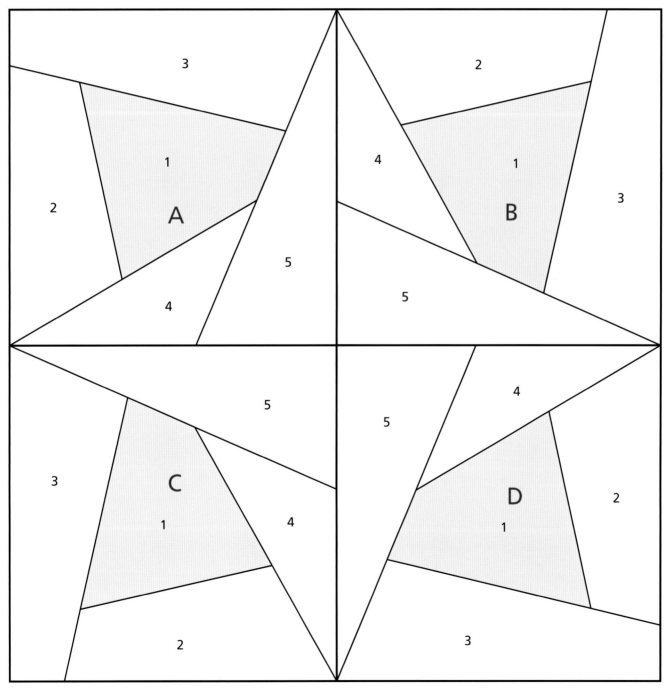

A
3
1
2
4
5

B
2
4
1
3
5

C
3
1
2
4
5

D
4
5
1
2
3

13

Baby Chick

EMBELLISHMENT NOTE:
Use a permanent black fabric marker to add eyes.

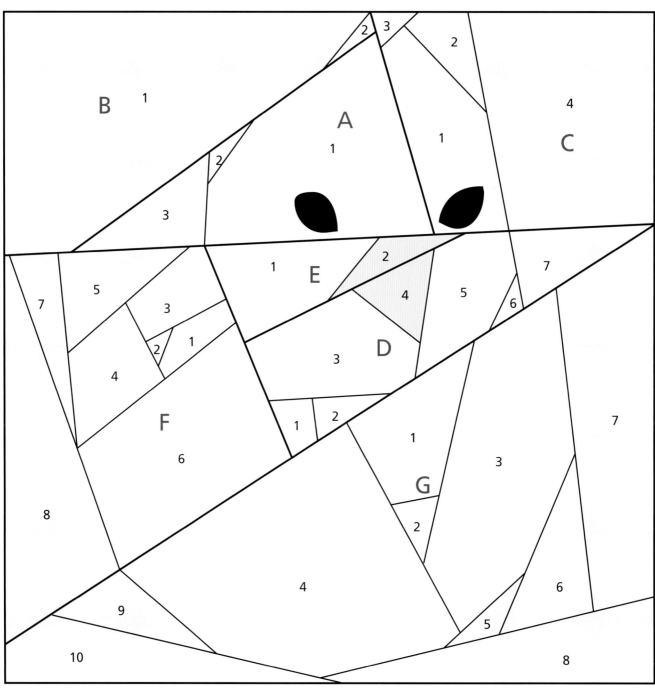

Angel

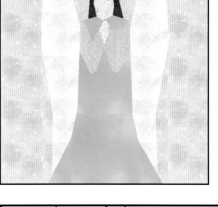

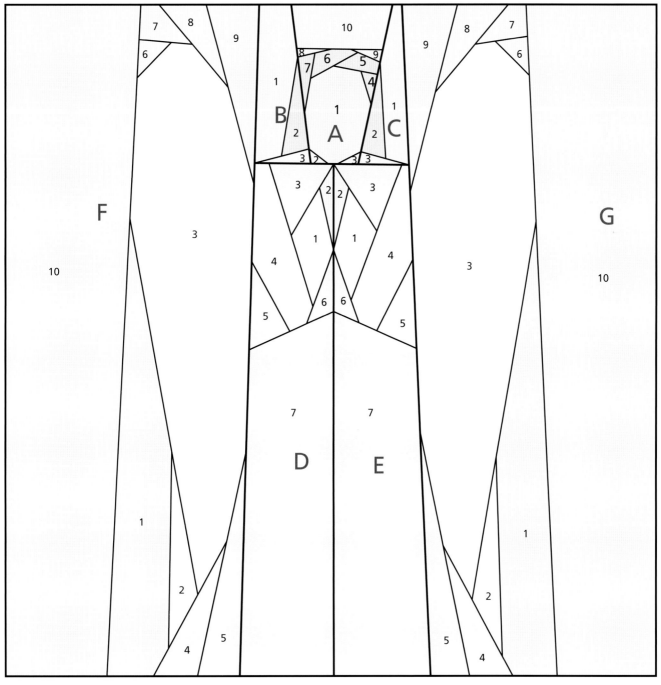

15

Tax Day

EMBELLISHMENT NOTE:
Use a black permanent marker to add dollar signs.

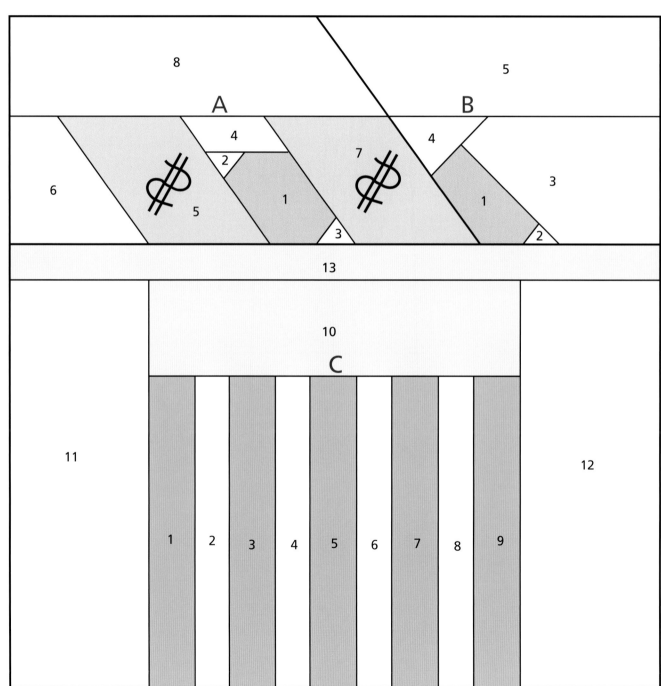

16

Anniversary

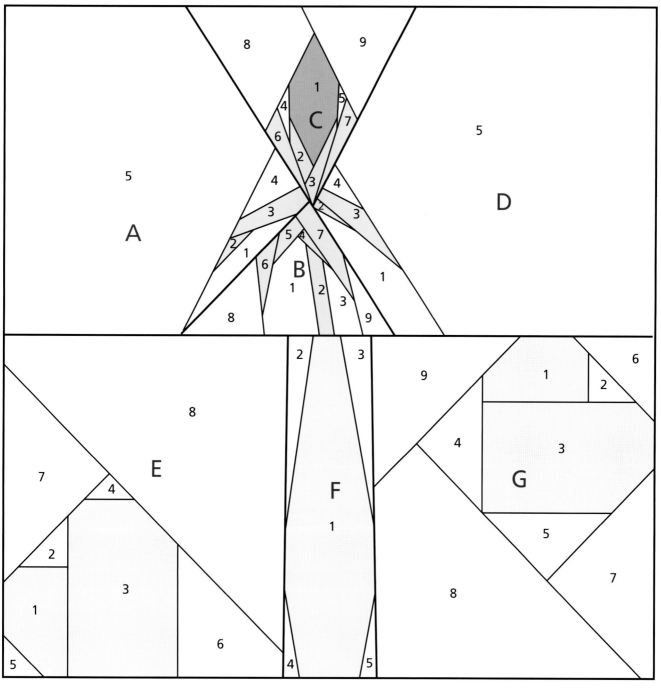

17

Passover

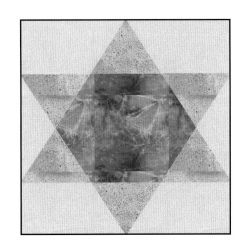

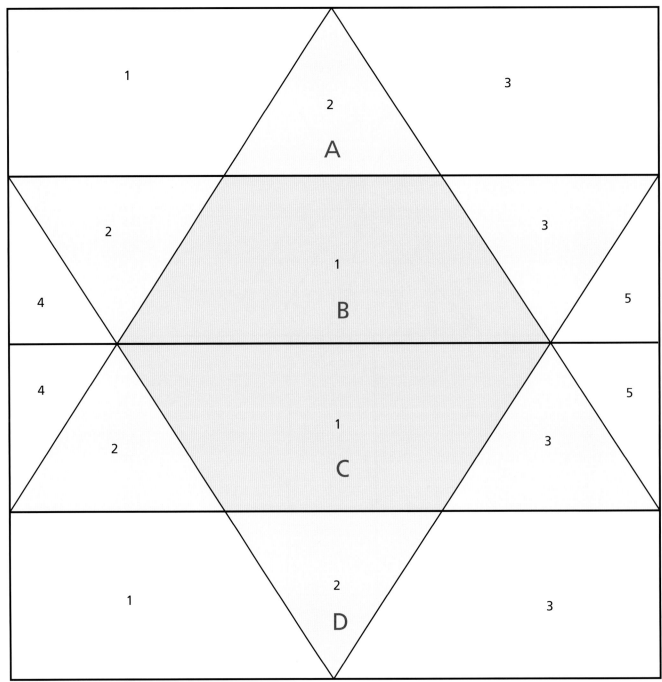

18

Diamond —
April Birthstone

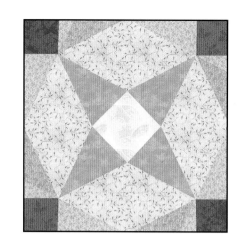

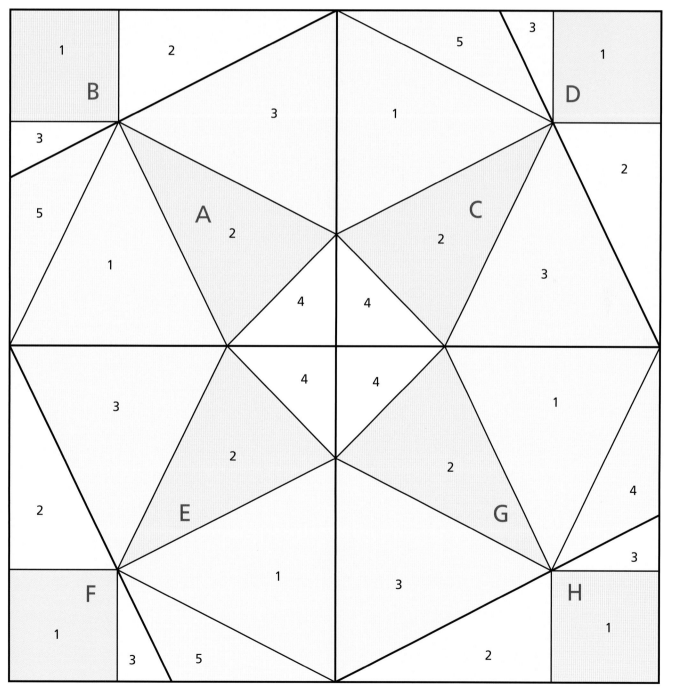

Cracked Log

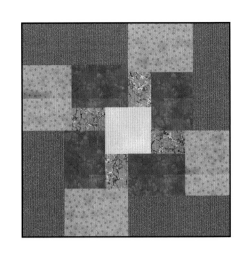

A
4

5

B
4

3

2

3

1 1 2

5

2 1 1

4

3

C 3

2

D

5

5 4

20

Daffodil

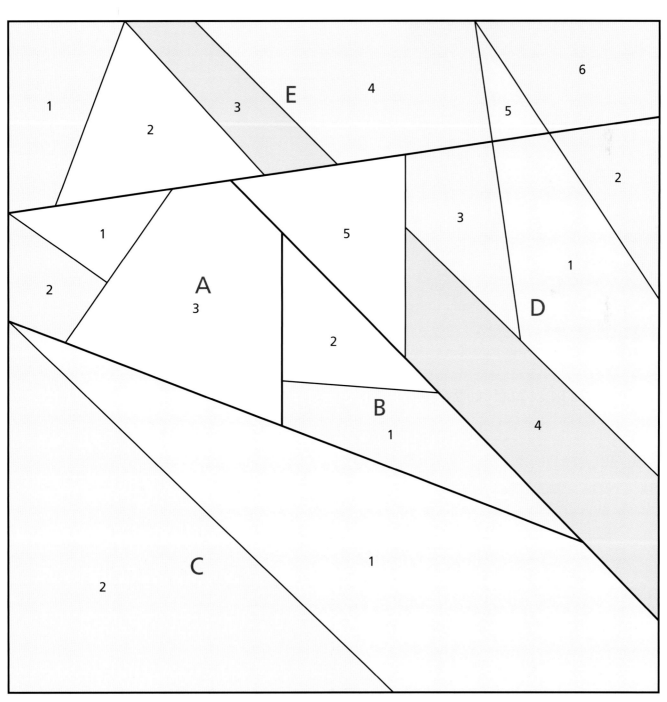

1

2

3

E

4

5

6

1

2

1

2

A

3

5

3

2

1

D

2

B

1

4

C

1

2

21

Springtime Bud

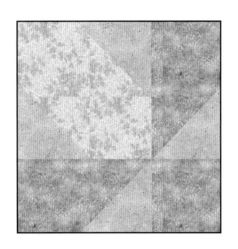

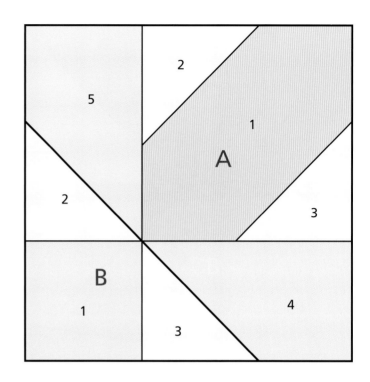

22

Springtime Geese

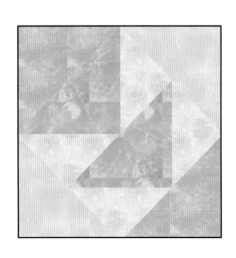

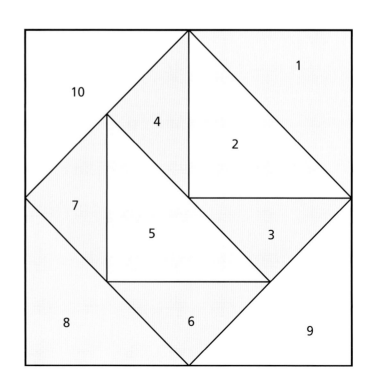

23

Springtime

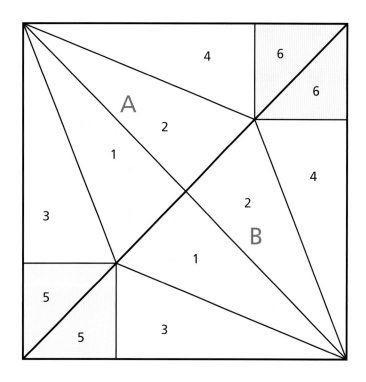

24

Flower

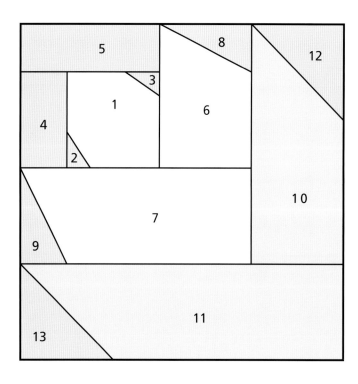

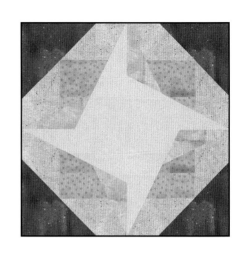

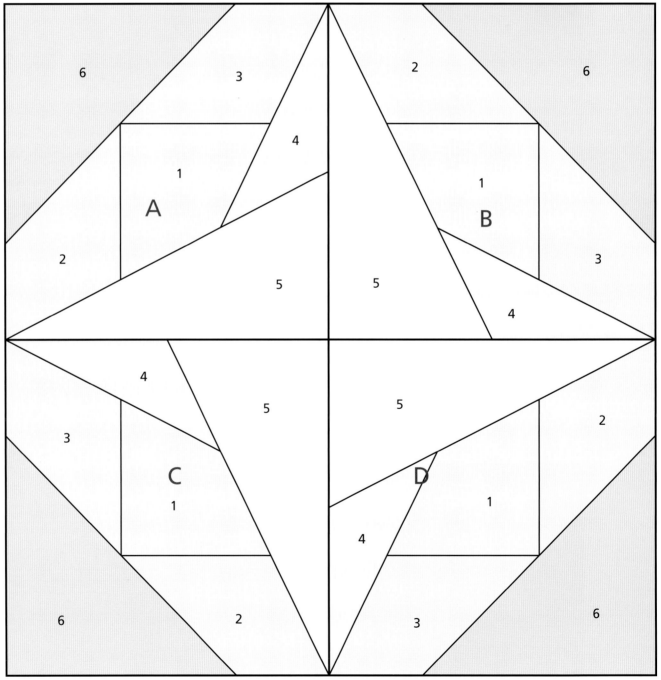

26

April Showers

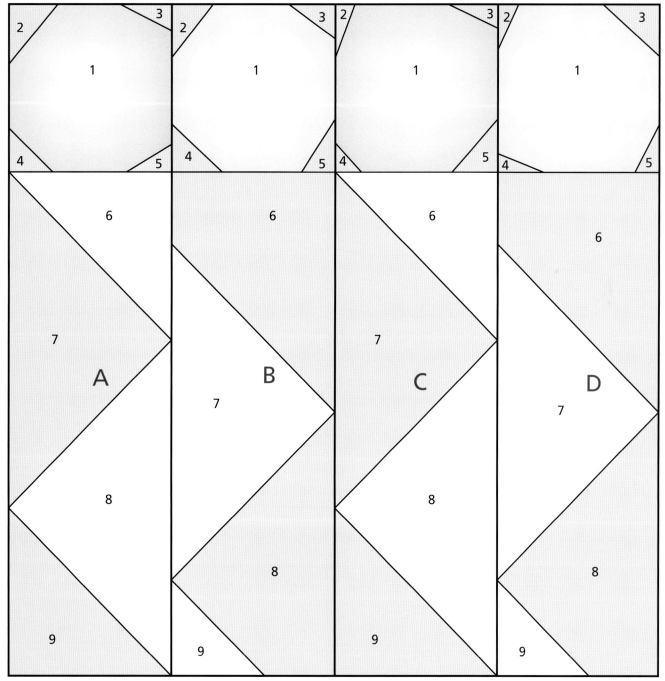

Basket

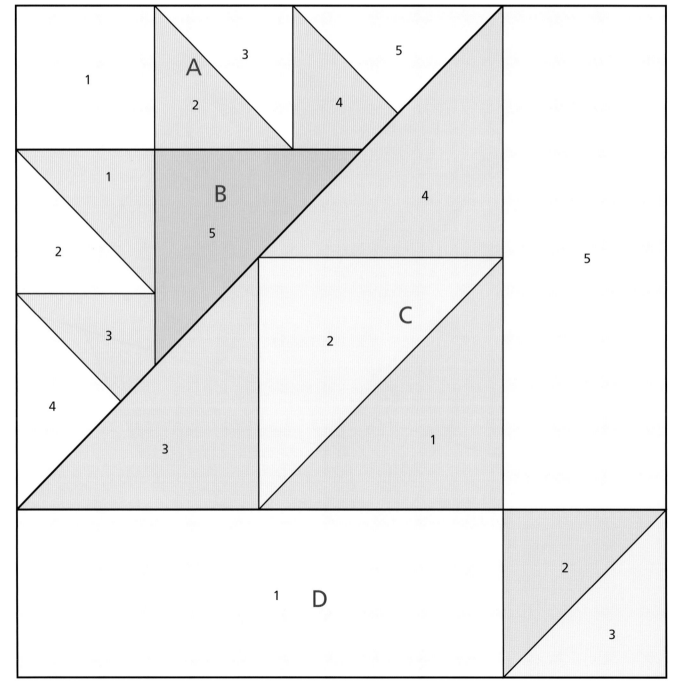

28

Orbit

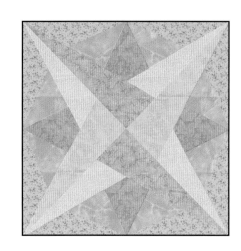

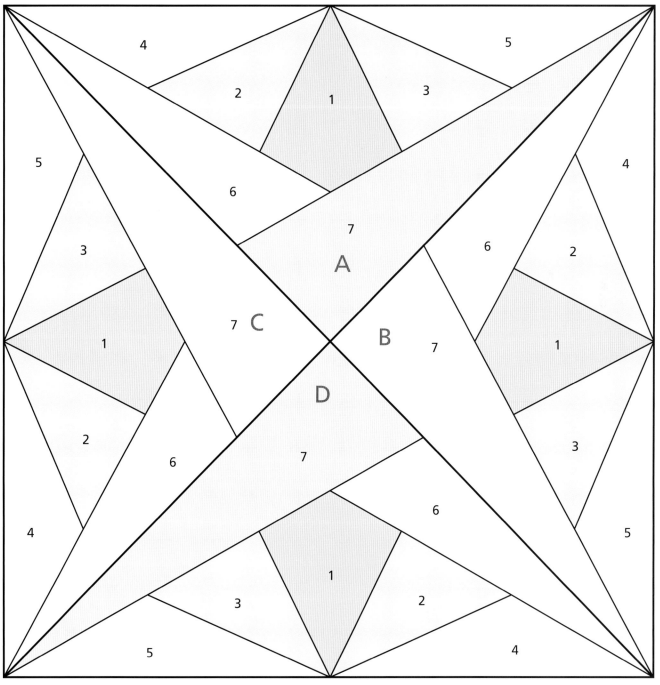

Tumblers

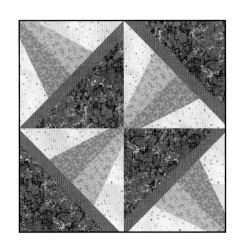

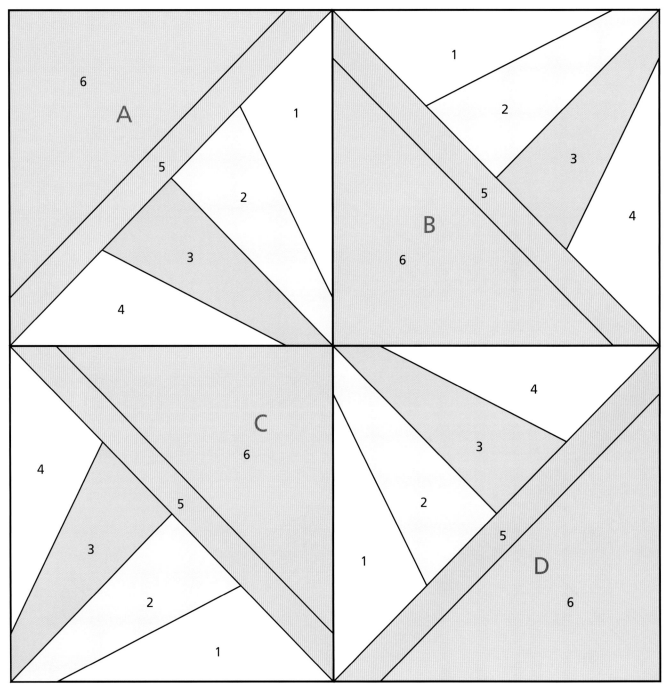

30

Diamond in the Rough

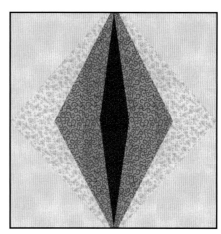

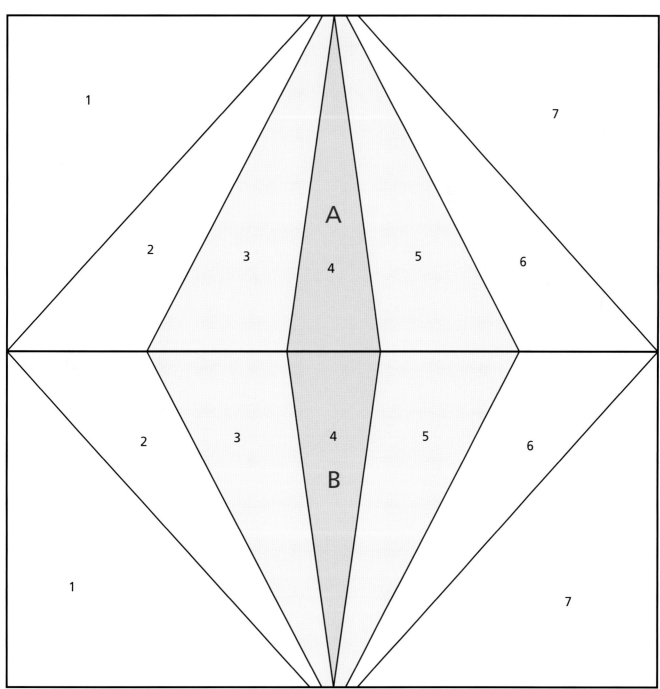

May

With just two blocks, the Four Square block and the Tulip block, this quilt has the look of a most complicated design, but it is easy to construct. Foundation pieced with Spring fabric, the quilt glows with the freshness of springtime. Note the clever use of the Tulip blocks hiding in the corners of the border and adding a Spring fragrance to the entire quilt.

1

May Day

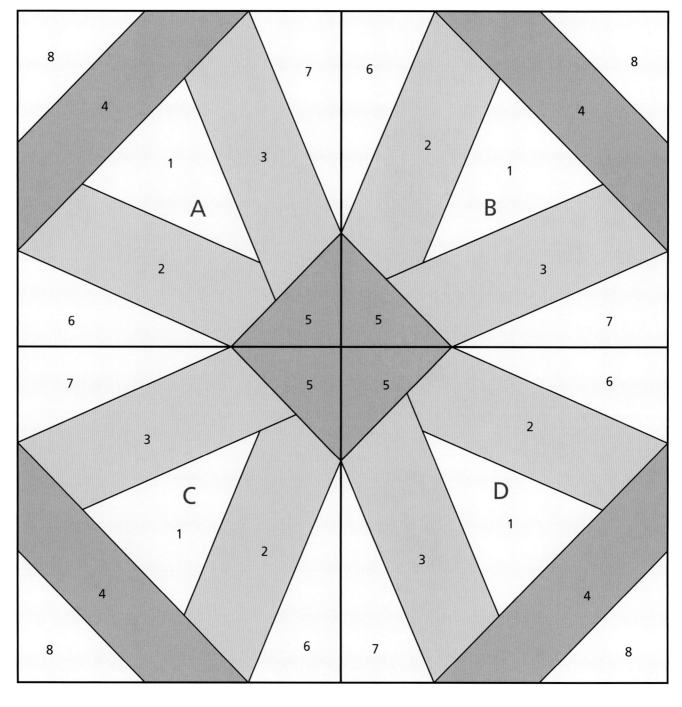

Four Square

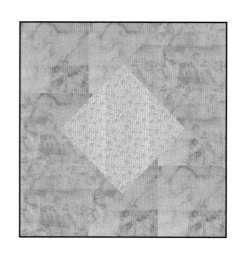

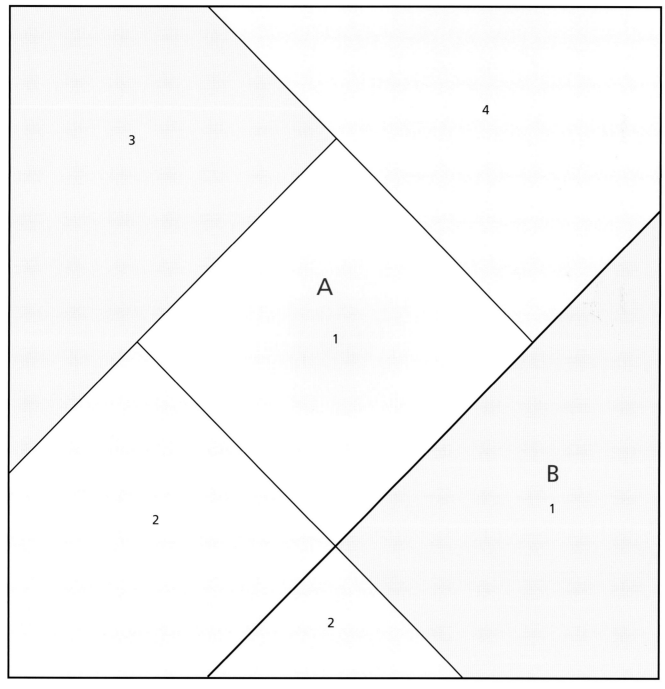

3

4

A

1

2

B

1

2

3

Lily of the Valley —
May Flower

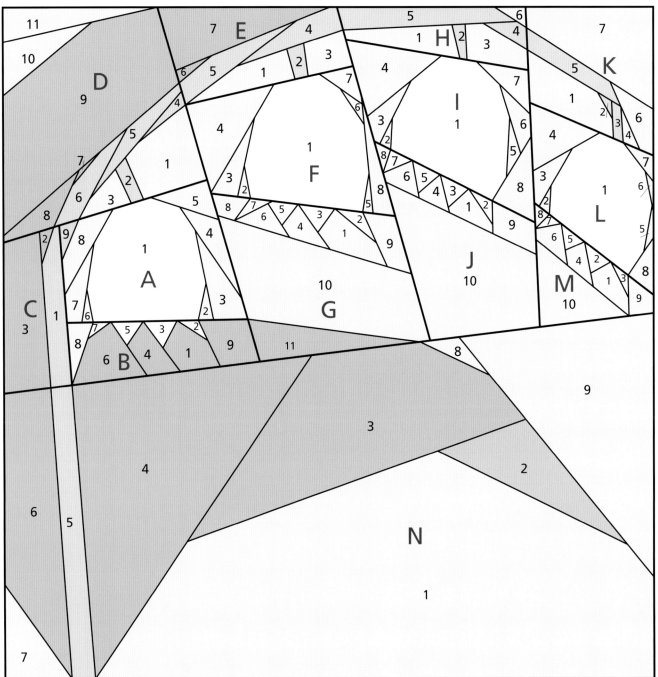

4

Ladies Aid

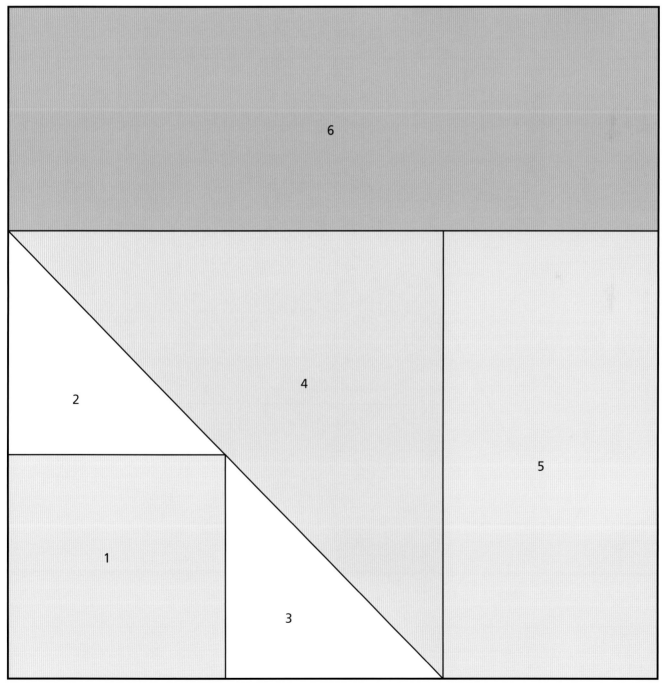

Cinco de Mayo

3

2 D

1

5

5   2   5   3   4

1

C

5

3 2

10   8   7   6

4   9

1   11   12

16   14   13   15

18   17   4

3
2

A

B

19   1

6

21   20   6

1

2 E

3

6

Tulip

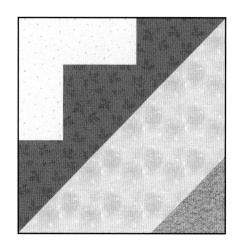

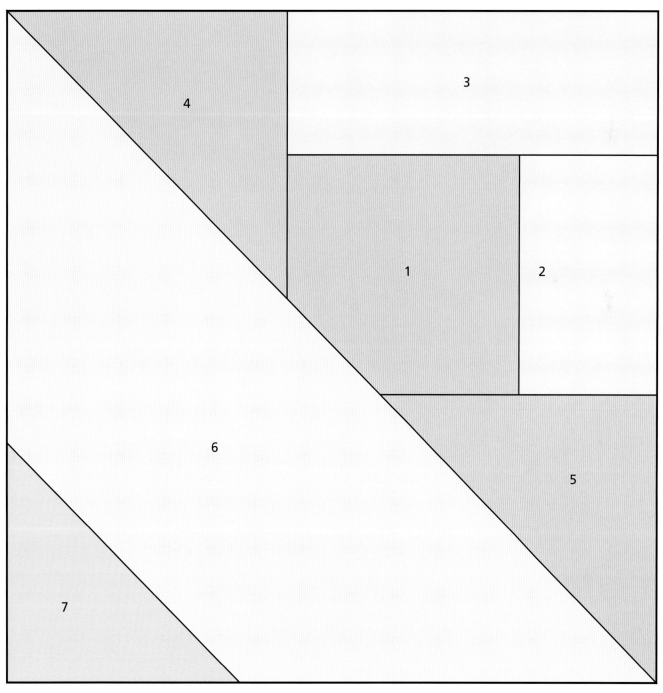

4

3

1

2

6

5

7

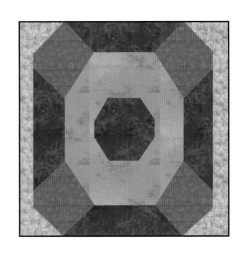

Emerald — May Birthstone

A
5   3
6
1
A
4
2

8

6

E
3   5
1
6
E
4
2

B
3
2   B   1

D
2   3
1
D
4   5

F
1   F   2   3

C
2   4
C
1
6
5   3

7

9

G
4   2
G
1
6
3   5

VE Day

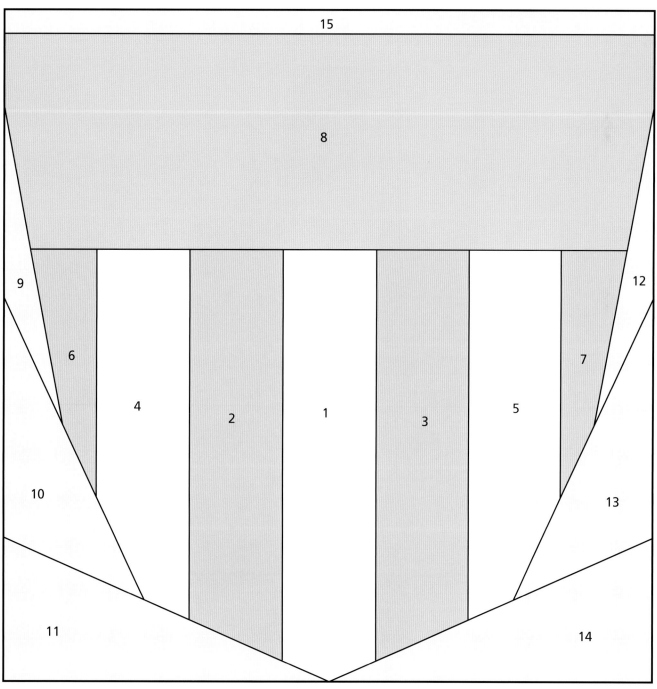

Hummingbird

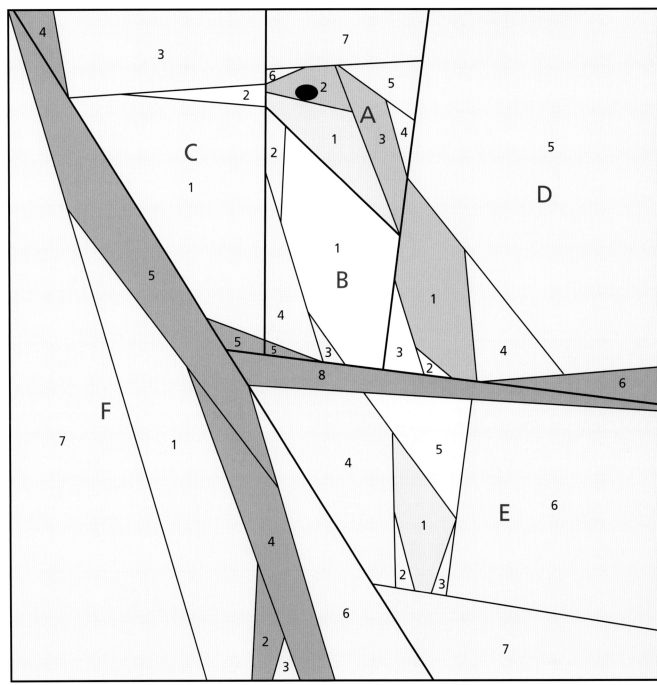

Log Cabin

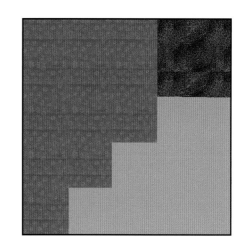

1	3	5	7
2			
4			
6			

Angel

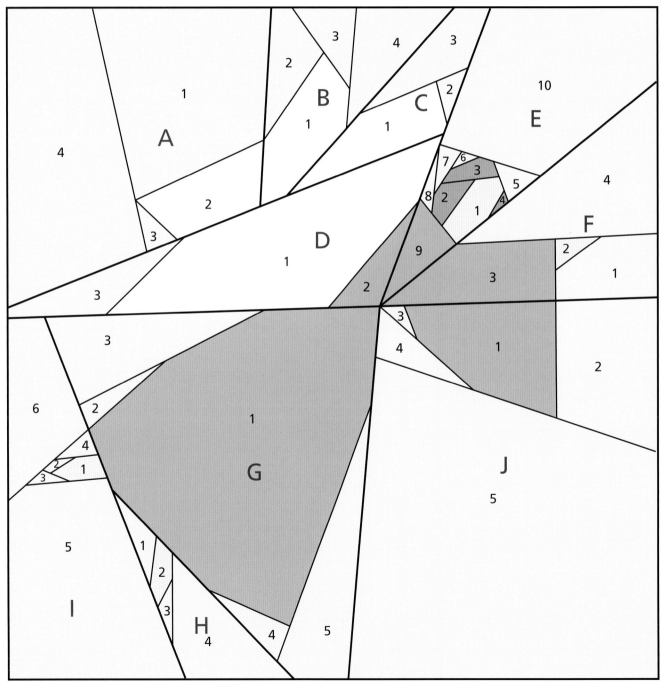

12

Star

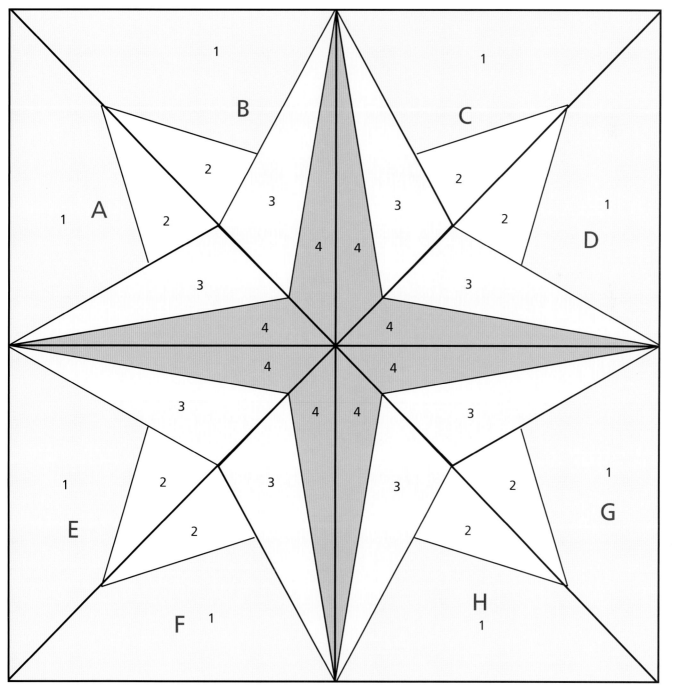

13

Mother's Day

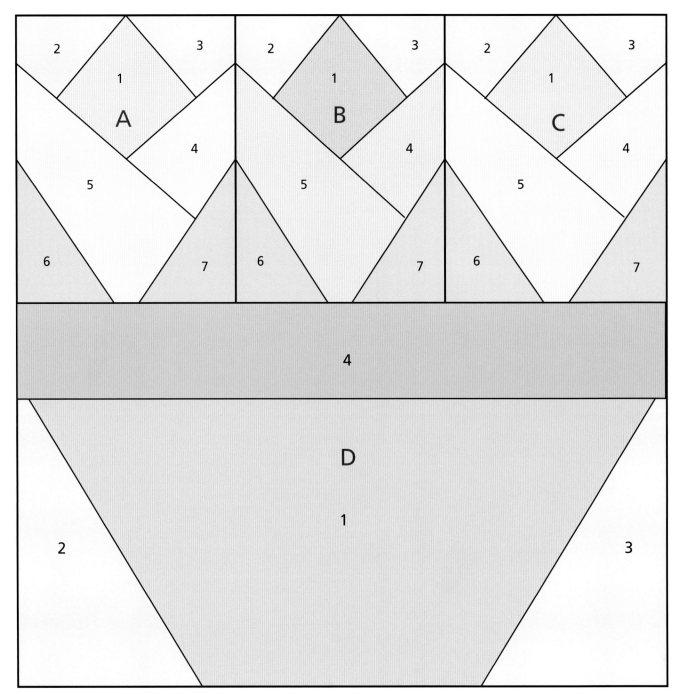

14

Butterfly

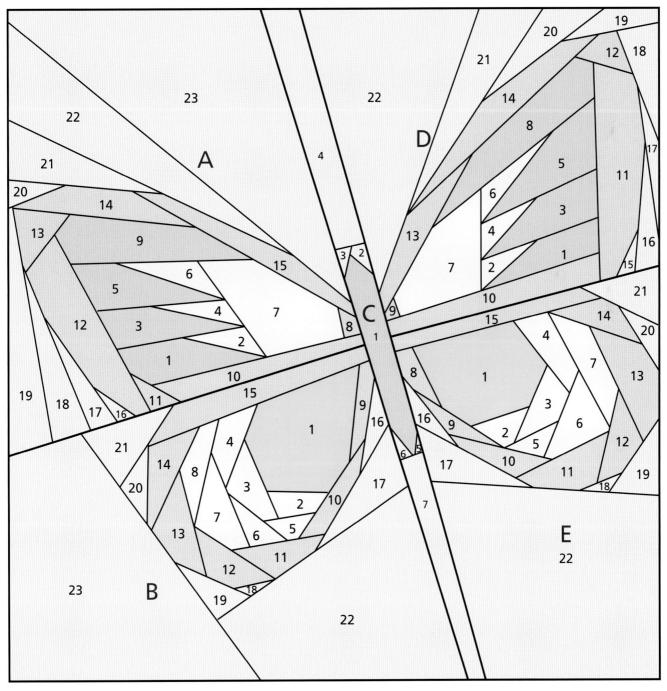

Sampler Quilt

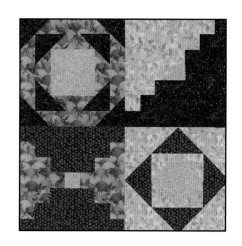

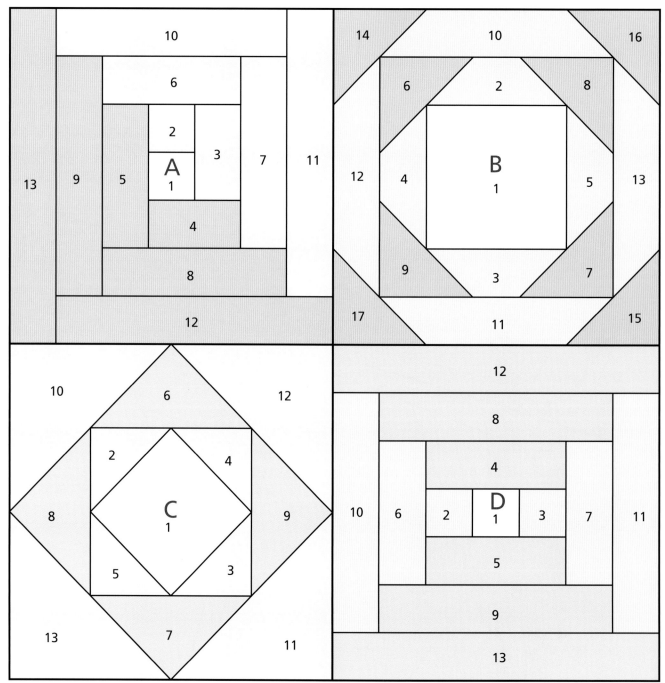

16

Easy Star

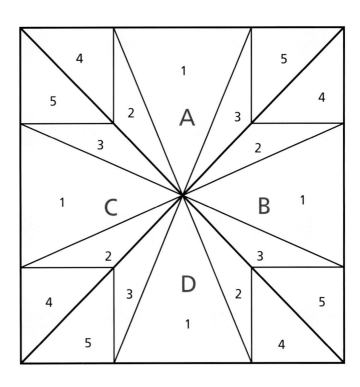

17

Tulip Star

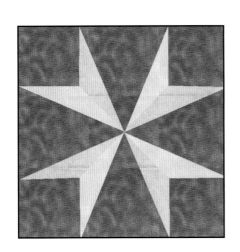

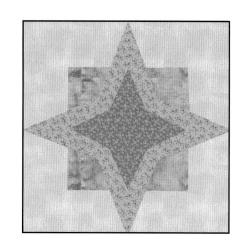

Star

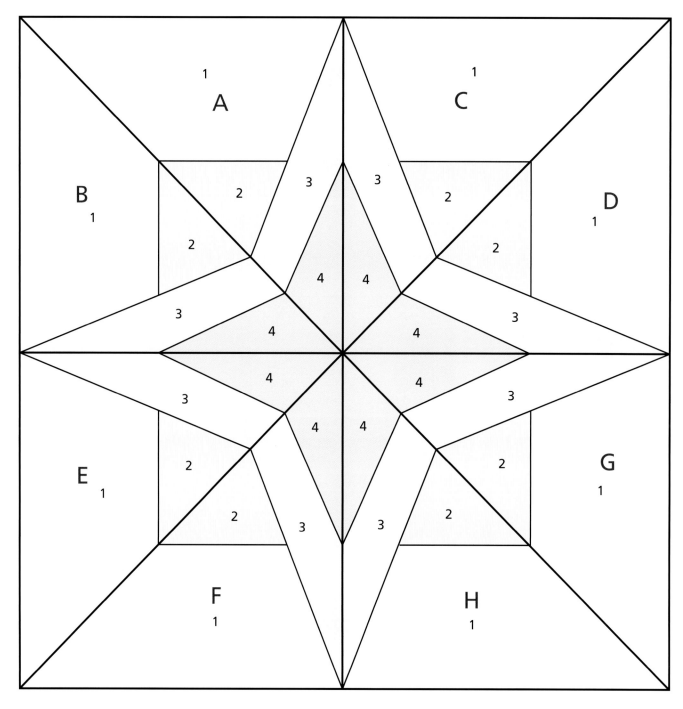

19

Circus Clown — Barnum and Bailey Circus Opens

EMBELLISHMENT NOTE:
Use white and black felt for eyes. Use red felt for nose and mouth.

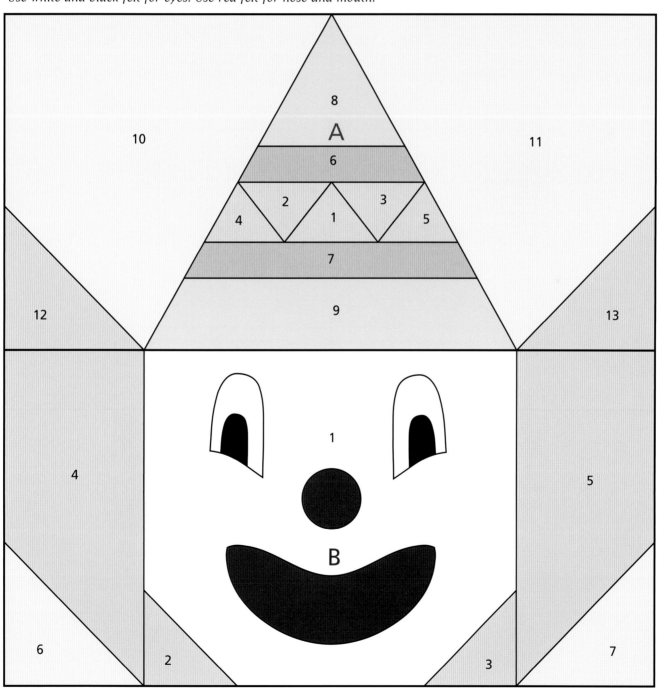

20

Tulips

2	3
1	
4	5

6

A

7   8

2	3
1	
4	5

6

B

7   8

2	3
1	
4	5

6

C

7   8

2	3
1	
4	5

6

D

7   8

The Red Cross is Established

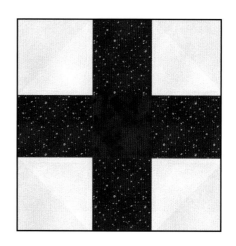

4	1	5
2	A	3
1	2	3
	B	
2	1	3
4	C	5

Whirlpool

5

6

6

A

4

2 2

B

4

5

1 1

3 3

2 1 1 2

5

4

C

3 3

D

4

6

6 5

23

Log Cabin Twist

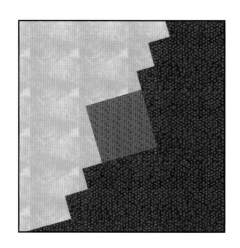

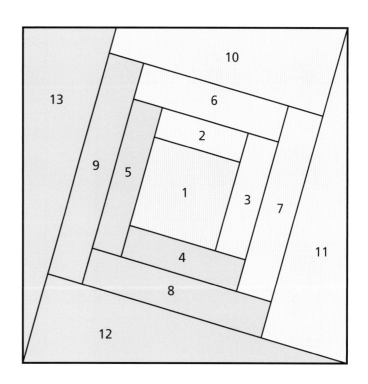

24

Four Square

25

Pinwheel Tulips

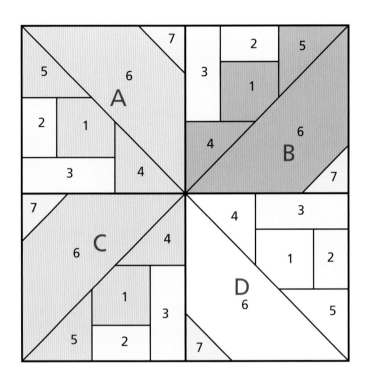

26

Gift Package

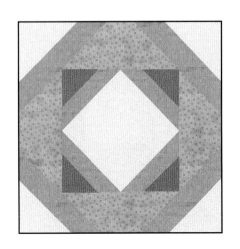

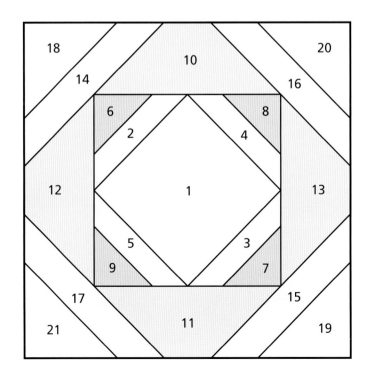

Double Zigzag

A
4
3
2
1

B
4
1
2
3

C
3
2
1
4

D
1
2
3
4

28

Golden Gate Bridge

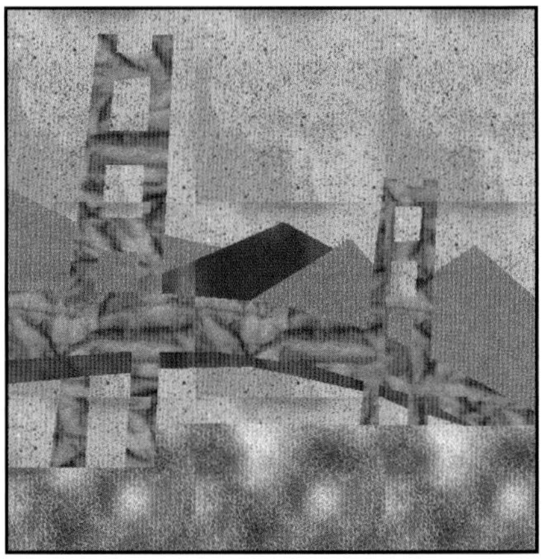

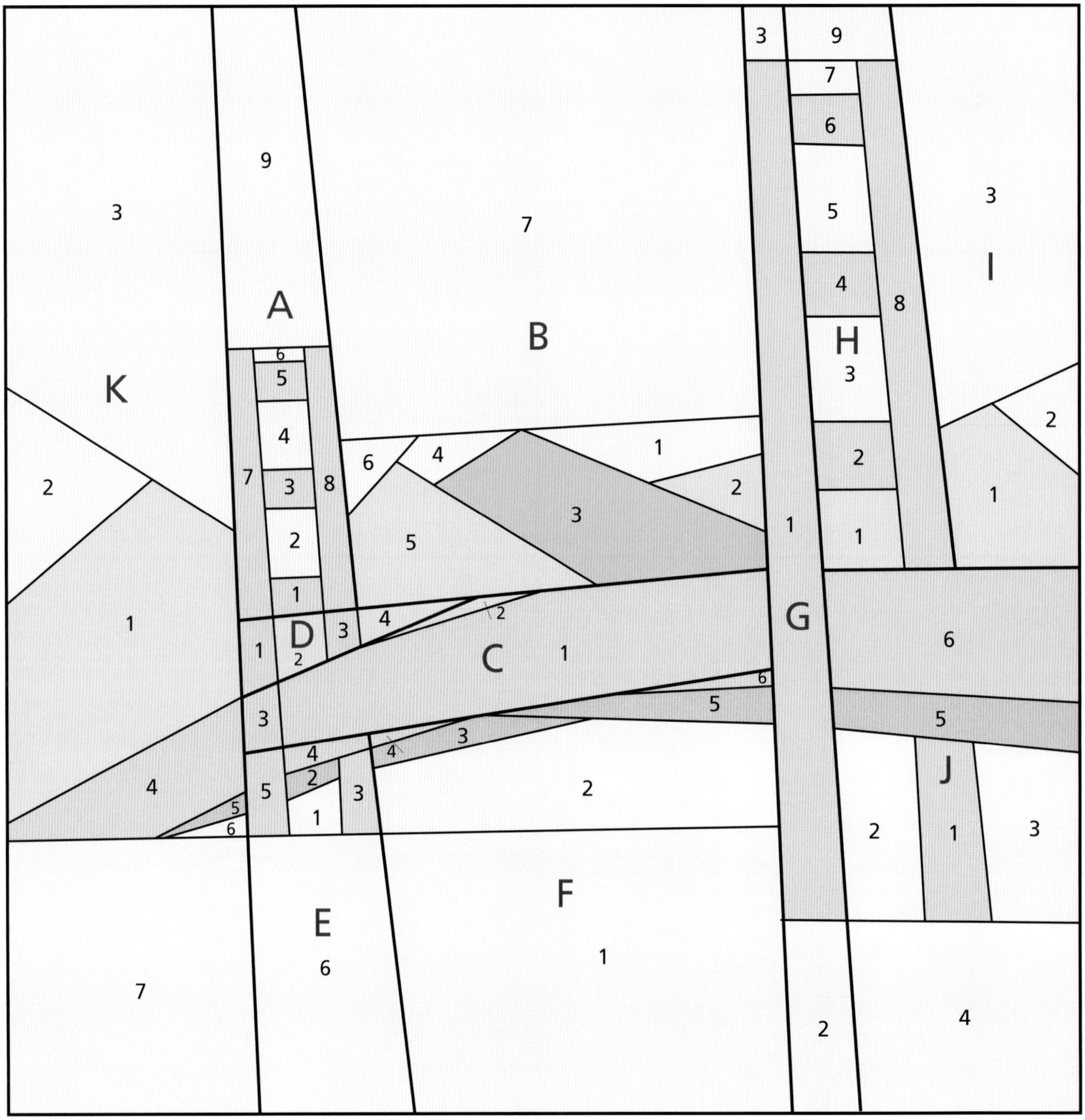

29

Spring Cottage

6

D

| 1 | 2 | 3 | 4 | 5 |

10　　　　　　　　　　　　　　　　　　**11**

9

C

7　　**5**　　**3**　**1**　**2**　　**6**　　**8**

4

A

2　1　3

6　　　　7　8　6　　　2　**B**　1　3　　7

4　　　　　　　　　　4

5　　　　　　　　　　5

Carnival

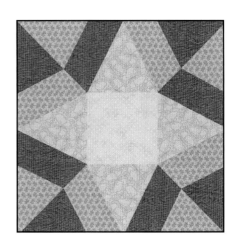

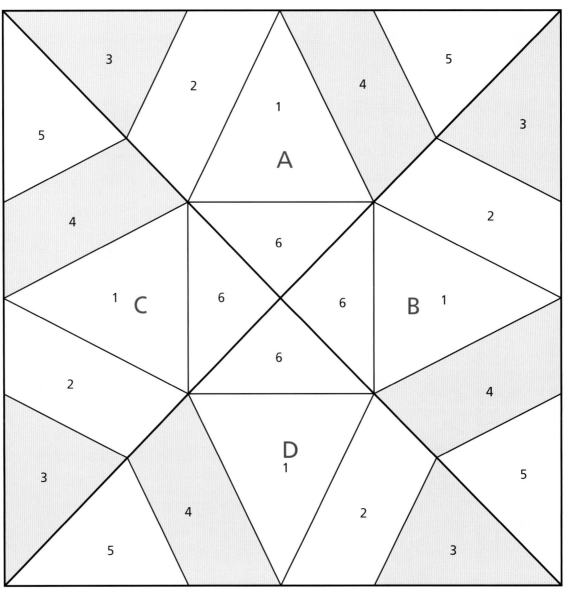

Memorial Day

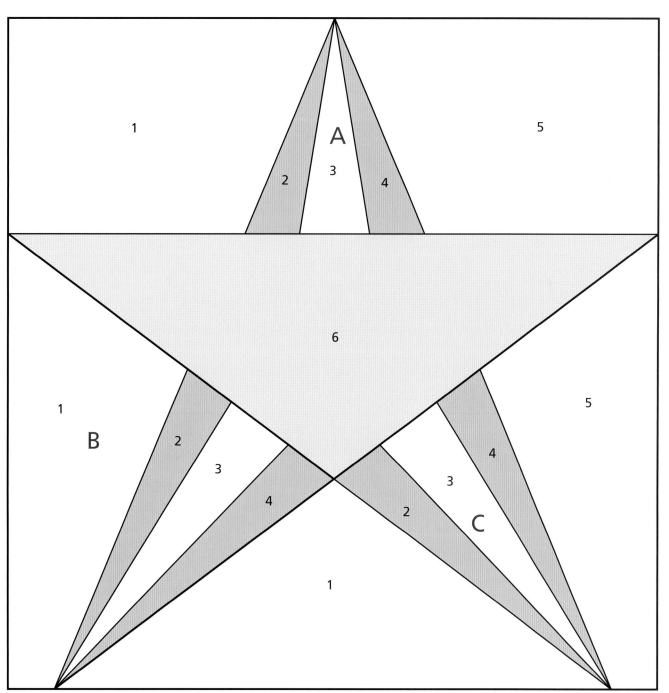

June

The rose is the queen of flowers, and June is the month when roses burst into bloom, so, of course, roses reign in this lovely quilt. Rose fabric is used for the borders, and three of the small Rose blocks are used in the quilt. The large Rose block is used in the center while two of the small Rose blocks are used to create a rose border. Only a royal rose garden could mirror the beauty of this quilt.

1

Star

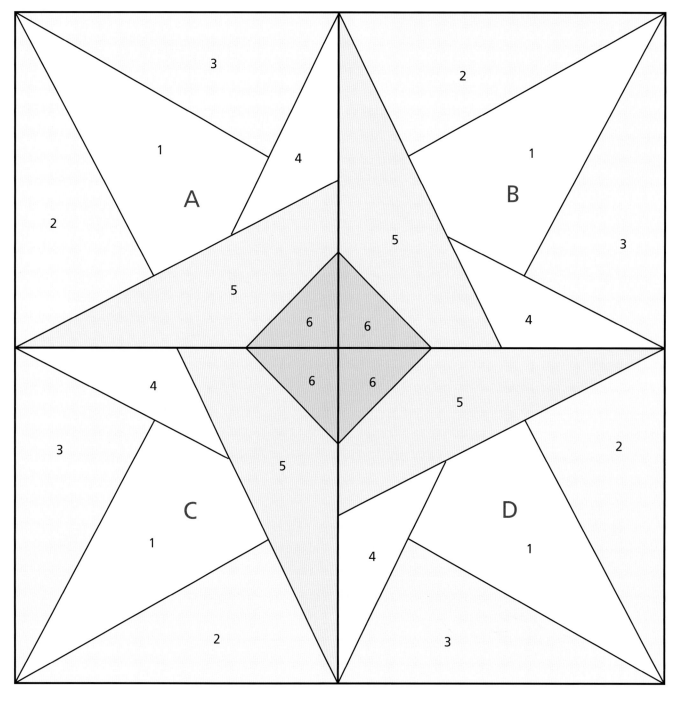

Doves

EMBELLISHMENT NOTE:
Use a black permanent fabric marker to add eyes.

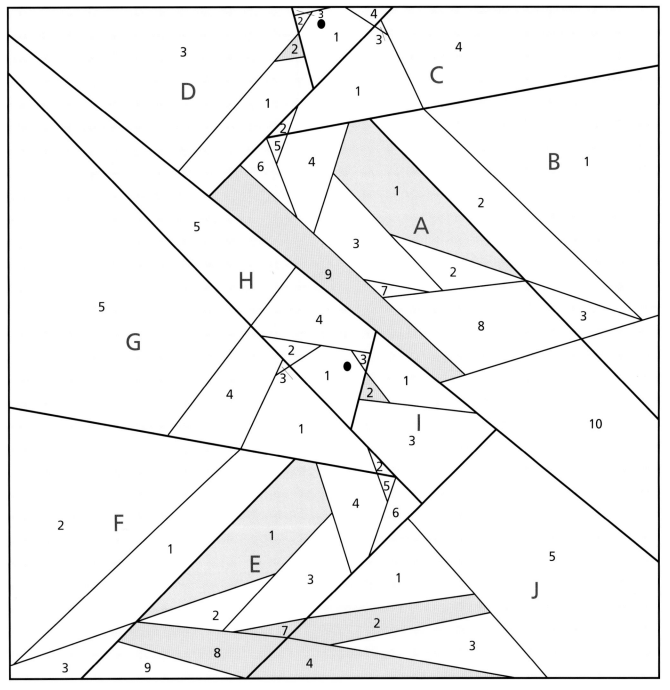

3

Pearl —
June Birthstone

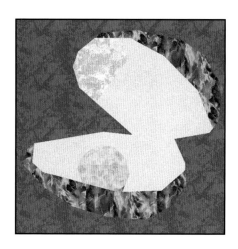

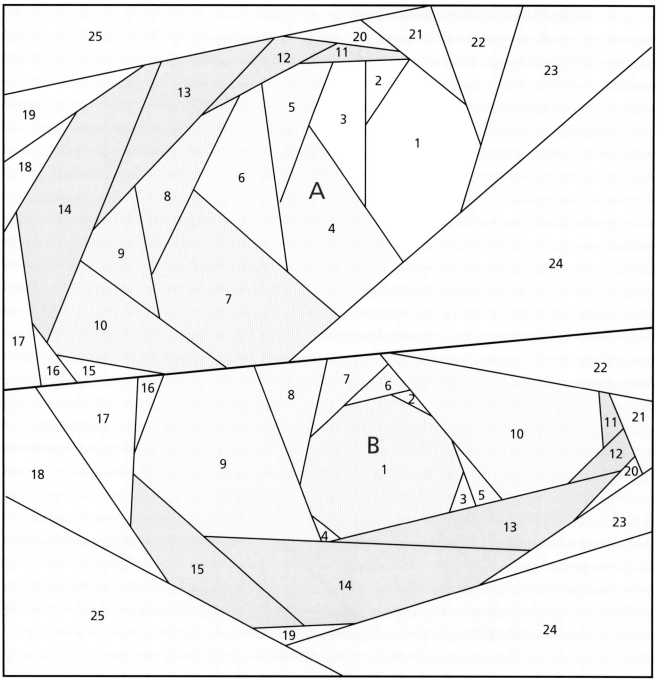

Graduation

EMBELLISHMENT NOTE:
Use black felt or a black button in center of mortar board.

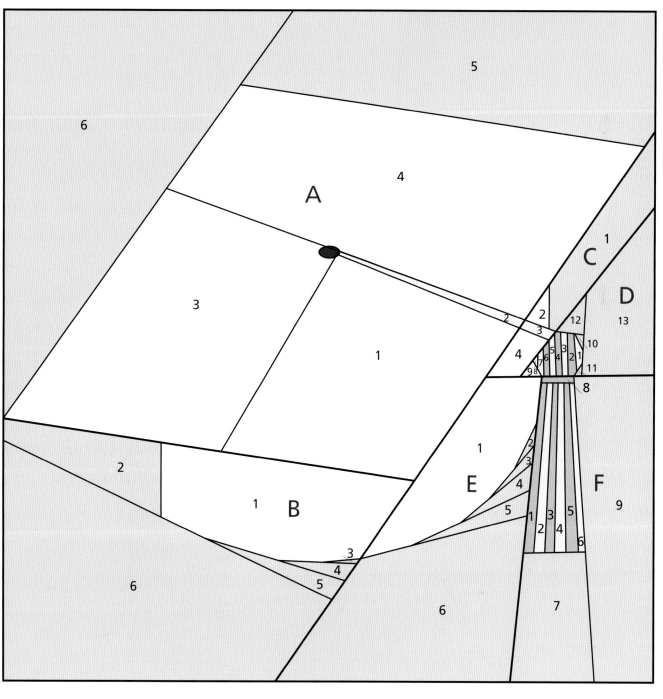

5

Diploma

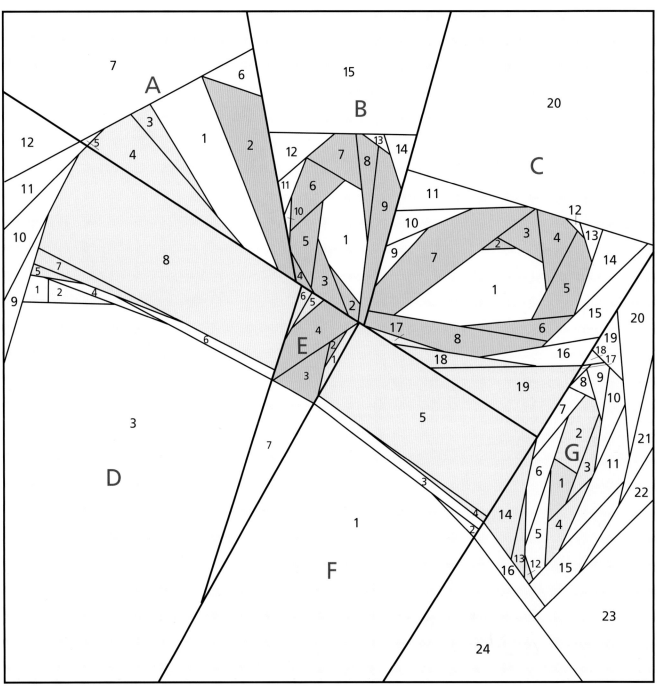

6

Rose –
June Flower

4 reds/pinks
1 green
background

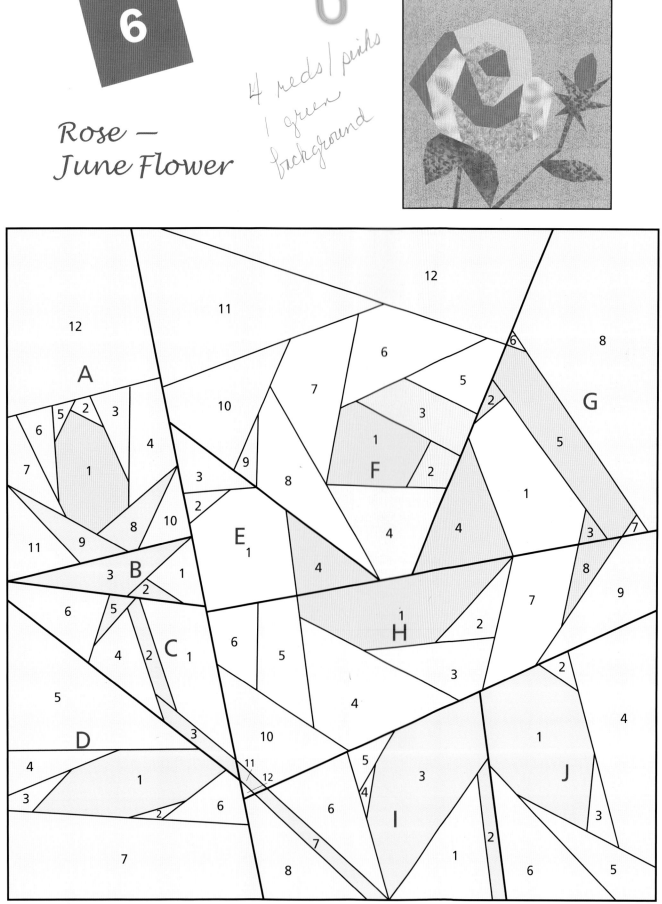

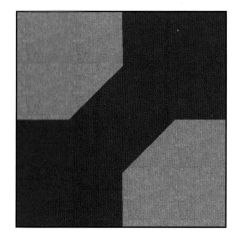

7

Bowtie

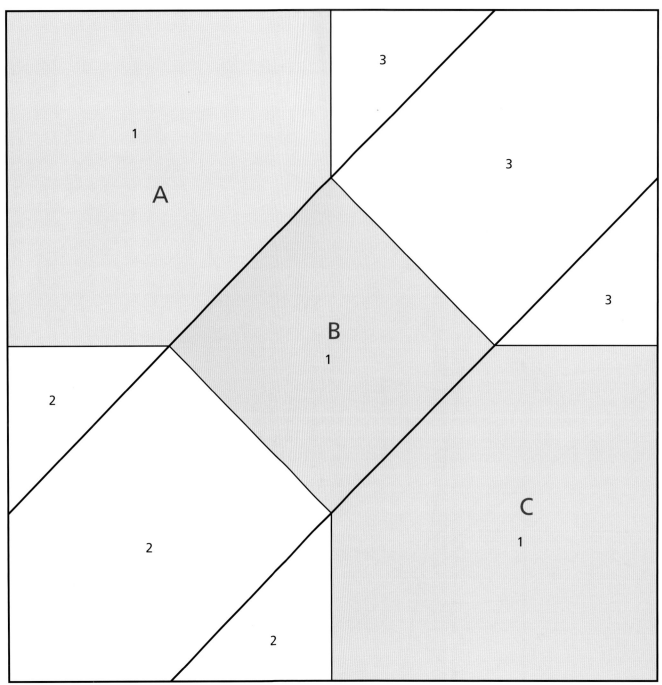

8

Military Star

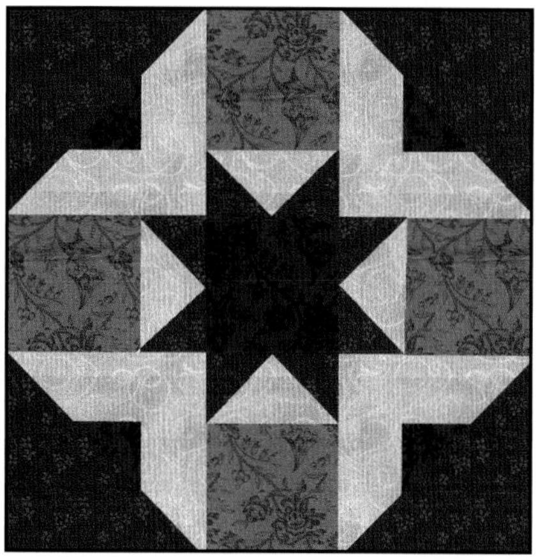

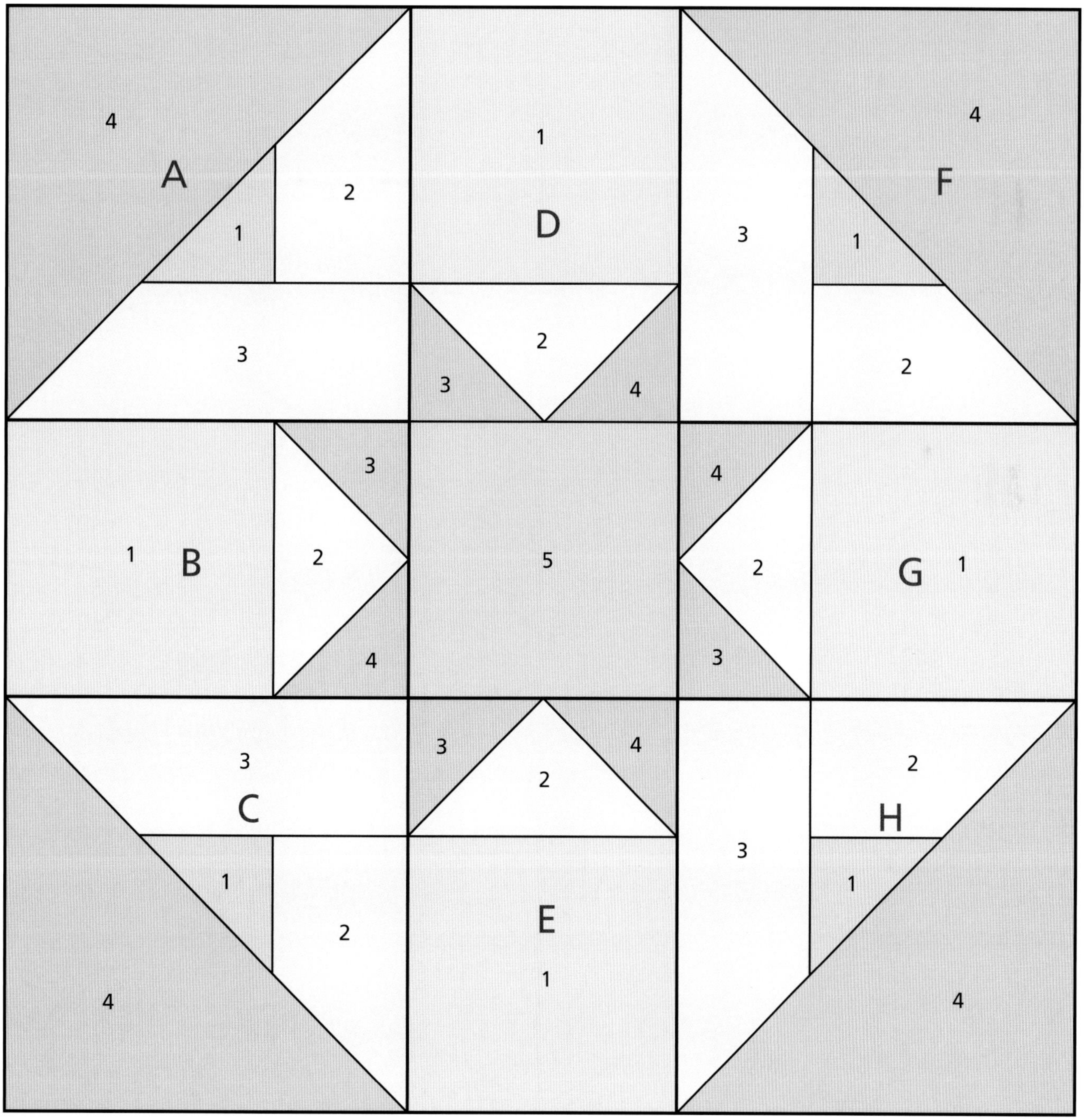

9

Whirligig

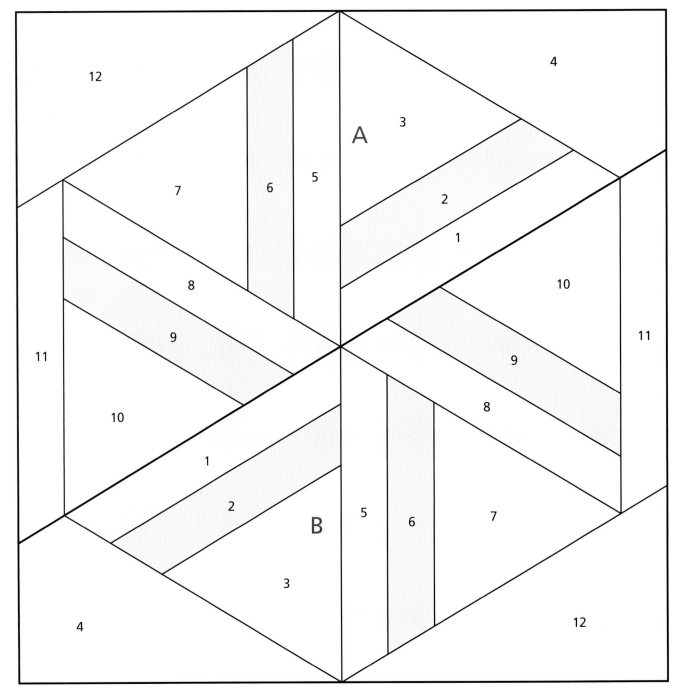

10

Benamin Franklin's Birthday

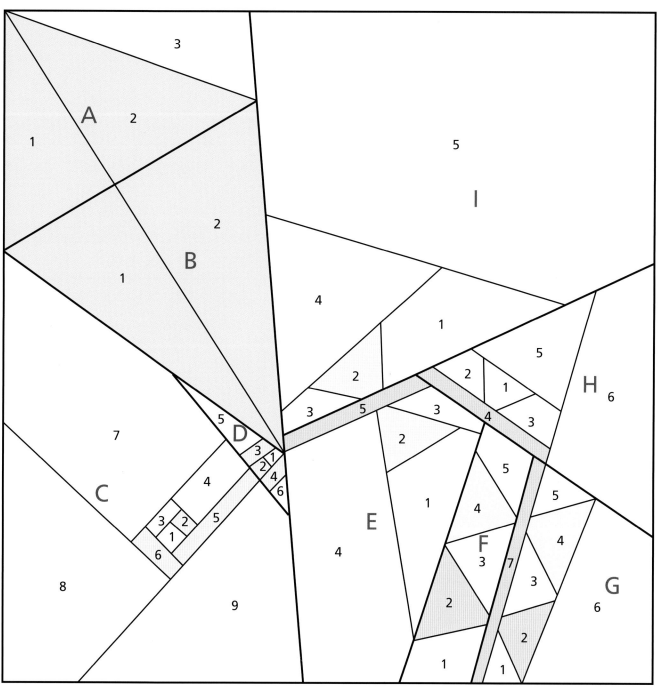

Wedding Ring

G 1 2 3 4 5 4 6 B 1 2 C 1 2

F 1 3 2 4 A 3 3 4

4 9 5 2 1 3 7 5 4

D 4 3 3 5 H 2 3 1

E 2 2 8 4 2 1 1 4 5 I 4 3 1

12

Corner Rosebud

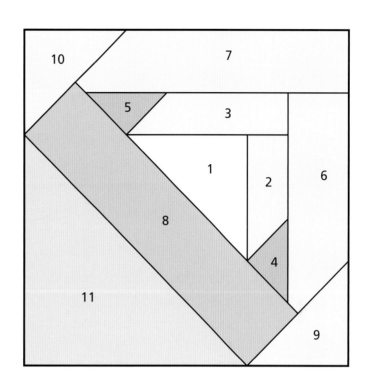

13

Long Rosebud

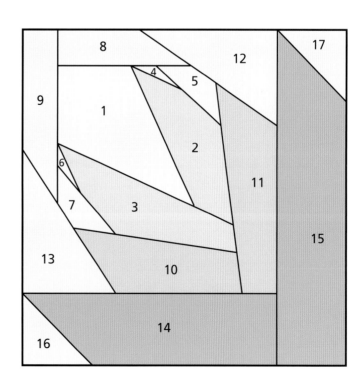

14

Flag Day

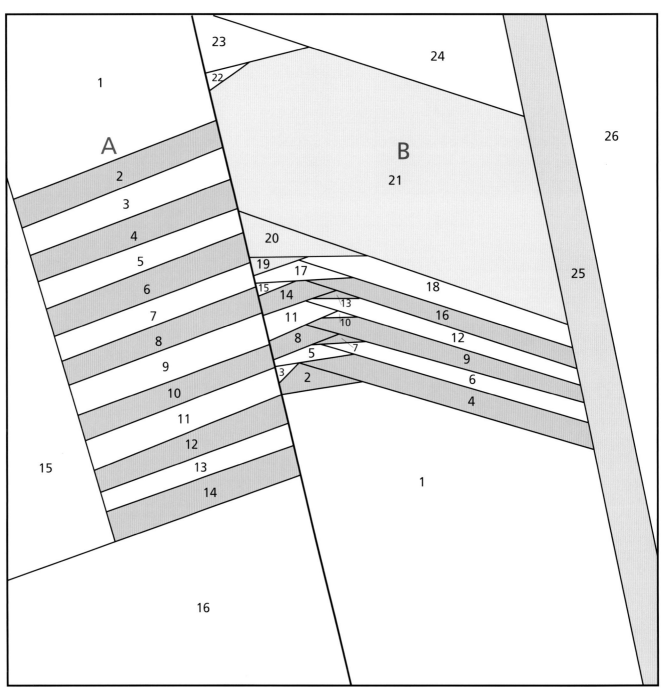

23

24

1

22

A

26

2

3

4

5

20

6

19

17

25

7

15

14

18

8

11

13

9

8

16

5

10

12

10

3

7

11

2

9

12

6

13

4

14

15

1

16

15

Pinwheel

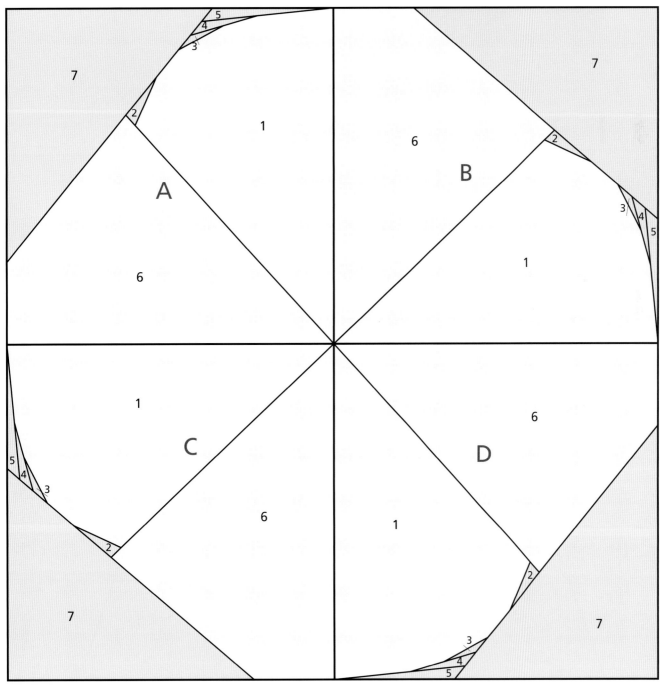

7

5
4
3

2

1

A

6

6

B

2

3 4
5

1

1

C

5
4
3

6

2

6

D

1

7

7

2

3
4
5

16

Angel

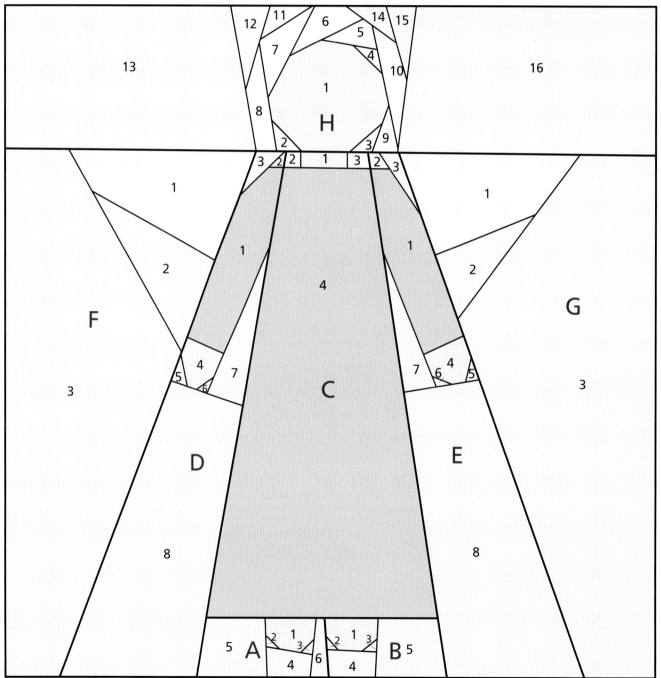

17

Statue of Liberty Comes to U.S.

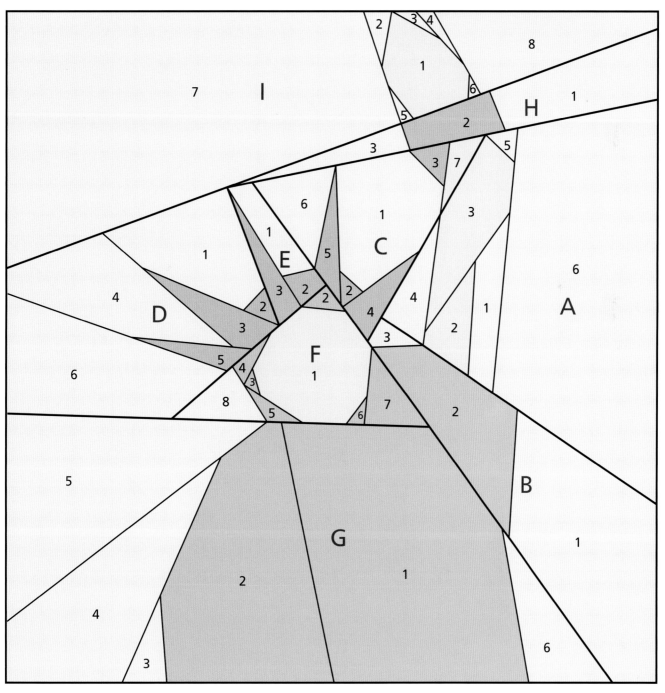

18

June Wedding Bouquet

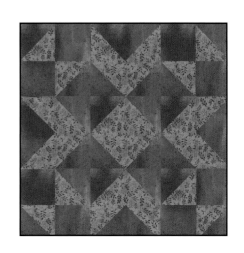

June

170

8	6		4		1	2	G		3		5		9	7

8

6

4

2 G

3

5

9

7

4

2

4

2

4

4

A
1

B
1

2

5

3

5

3

2

1 **E**

4

2

F 1

3

2

4

2

4

C
1

D
1

3

5

3

5

3

5

3

5

5

6

2

7

8

4

H
1

3

5

9

19

Father's Day Ties

| 6 | 4 | 2 | 1 A | 3 | 5 | 7 |

| 6 | 4 | 2 | 1 B | 3 | 5 | 7 |

| 6 | 4 | 2 | 1 C | 3 | 5 | 7 |

20

Snail's Trail

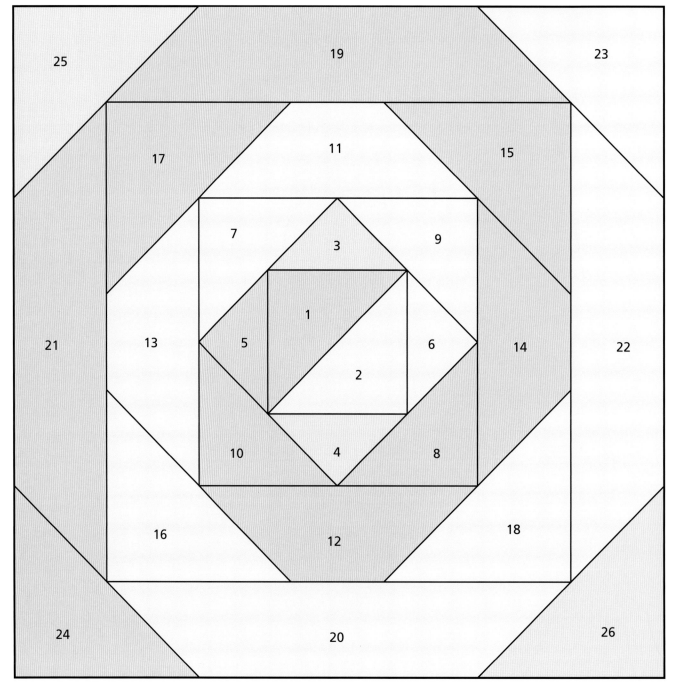

21

It's Summer

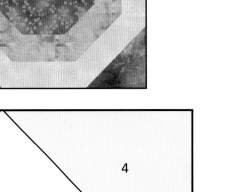

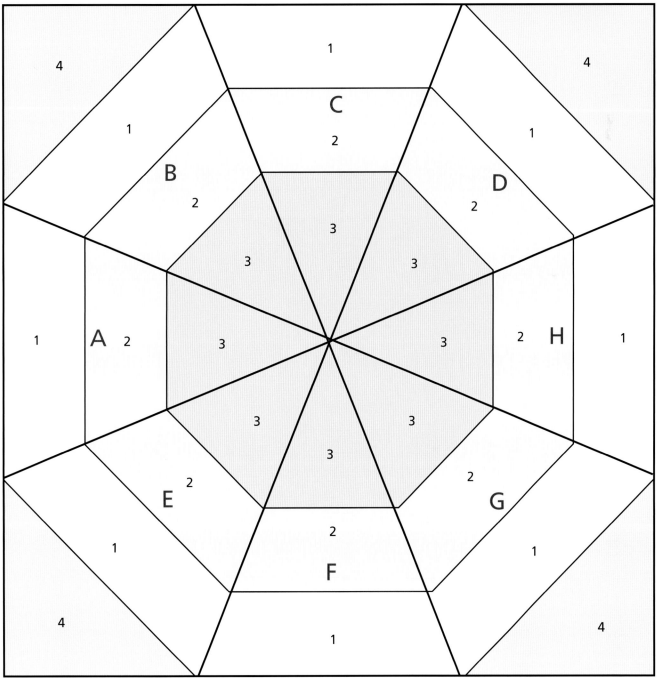

Navy Ship

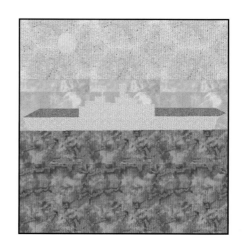

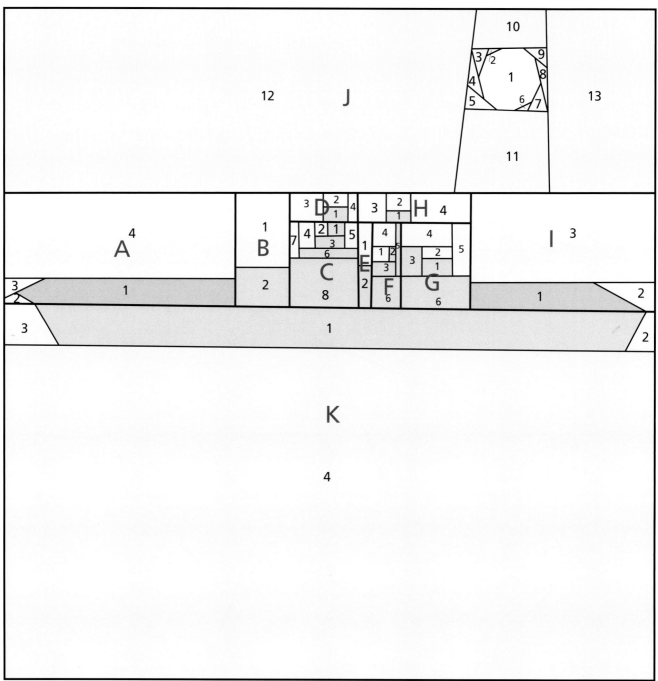

23

Weather Vane

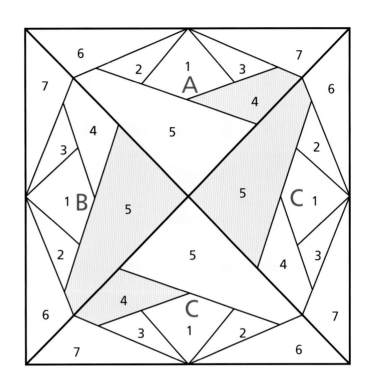

24

Simple Kaleidoscope

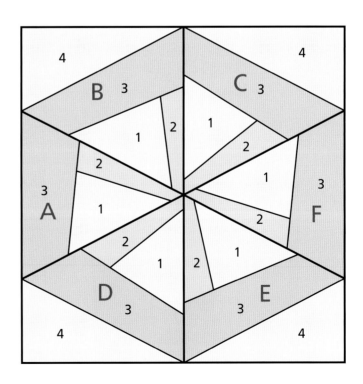

25

Grandmother's Fan

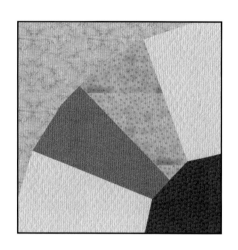

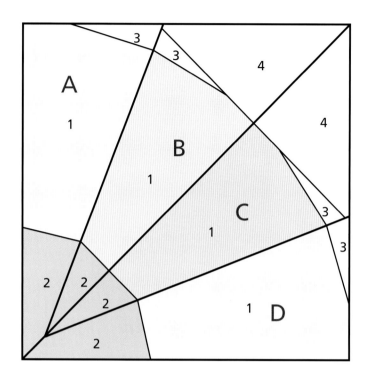

26

Garden Maze

27

House

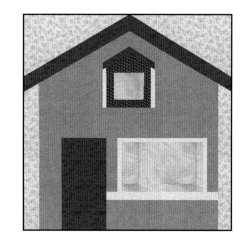

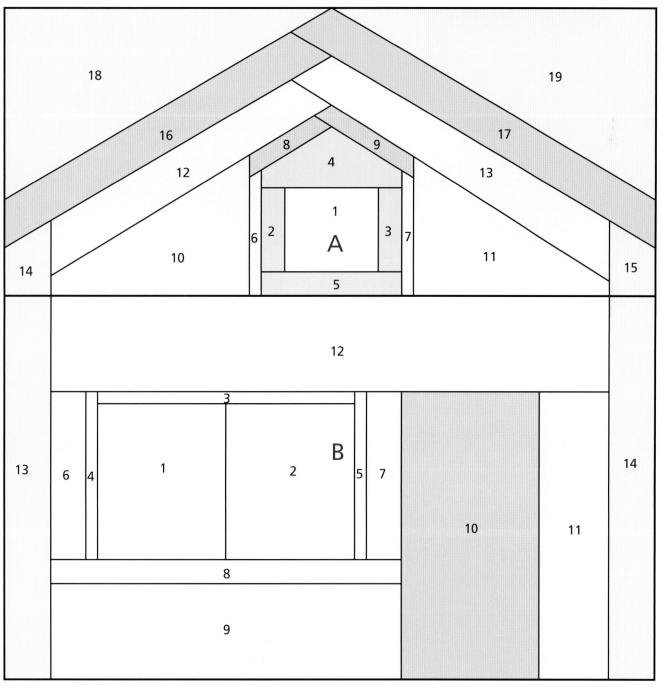

18

19

16

8   4   9

17

12

13

1

10   2   **A**   3   7   11

6   5

14   15

12

3

13   6   4   1   **B**   2   5   7   14

10   11

8

9

28

Bird House

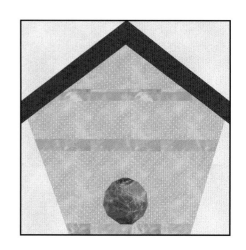

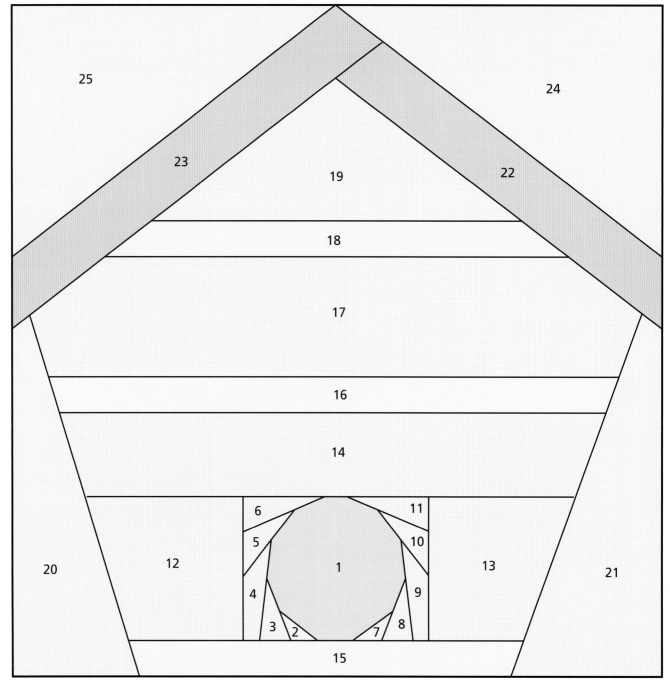

29

Prism

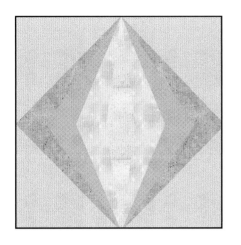

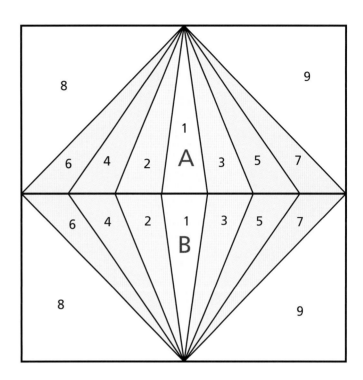

30

Geometric

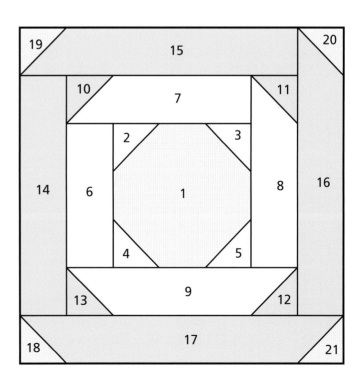

July

Speeches, fireworks and potato salad: that's the way we observe our country's birthday on the fourth of July. Add to the celebration by creating this patriotic red, white and blue wall hanging. Choose a patriotic fabric for the center square, then surround it with 12 foundation-pieced Stars and Stripes blocks. And to create the starry border, alternate the two 3¹/2" blocks, Small Star and Little Star. Now stand back for the compliments, all of which will be patriotic, of course.

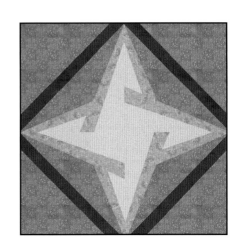

1

Golden Star

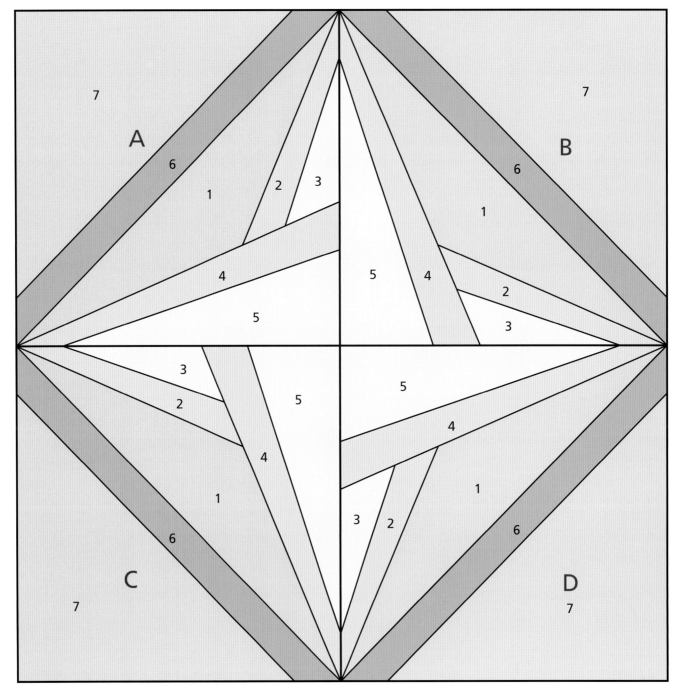

7

A

7

B

6

1   2   3

6

1

5   4

4

5

2

3

3

2

5

4

5

5

4

1

3   2

1

6

6

C

D

7

7

2

Small Star

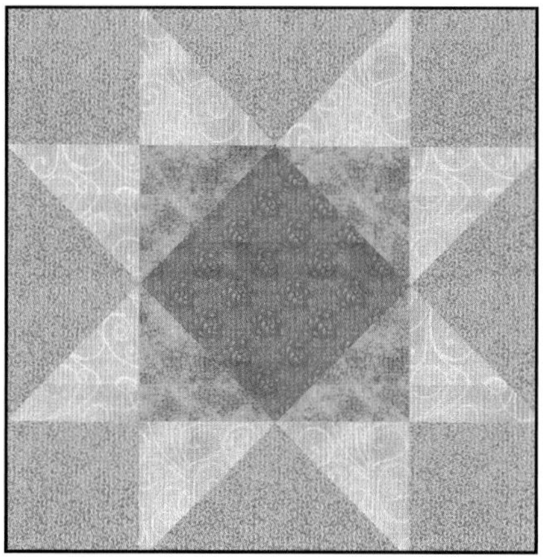

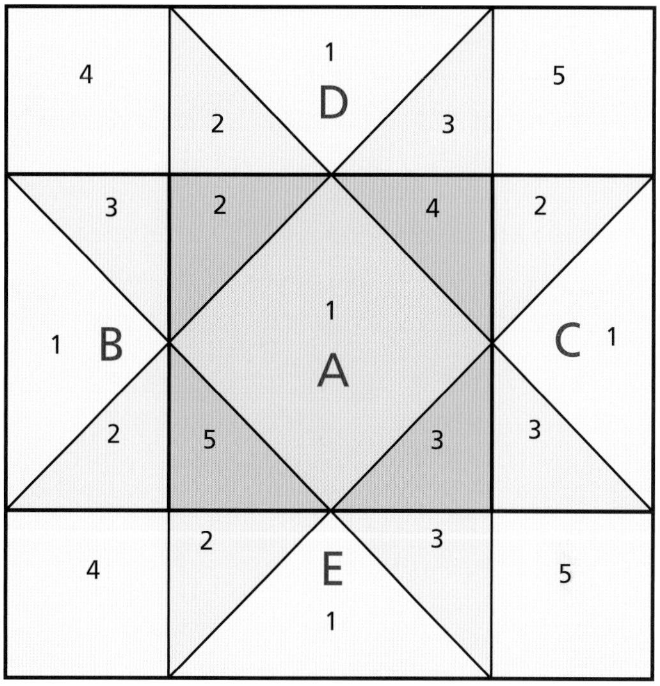

3

Petite Star

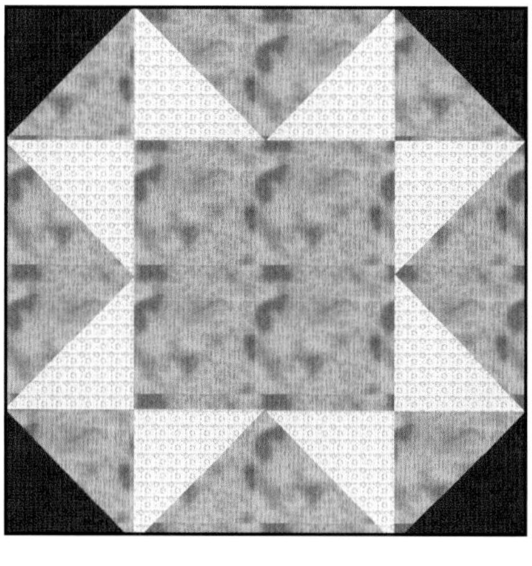

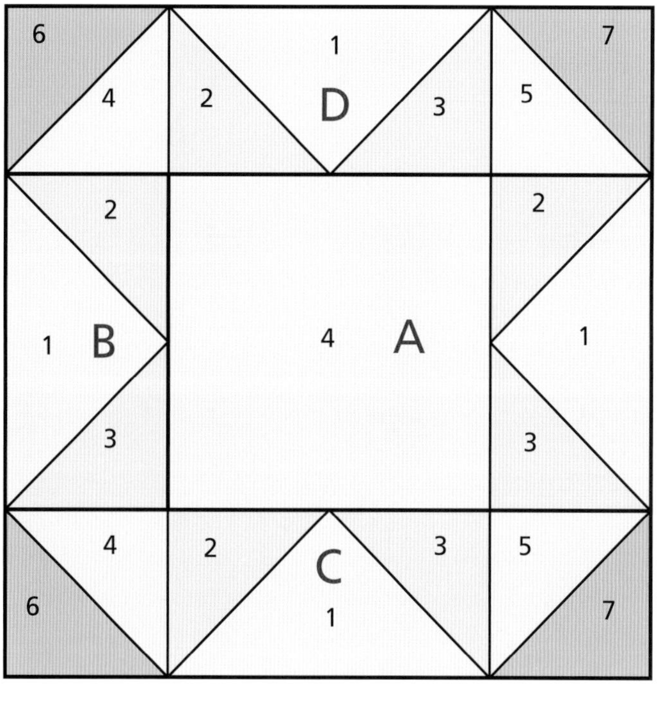

Stars and Stripes

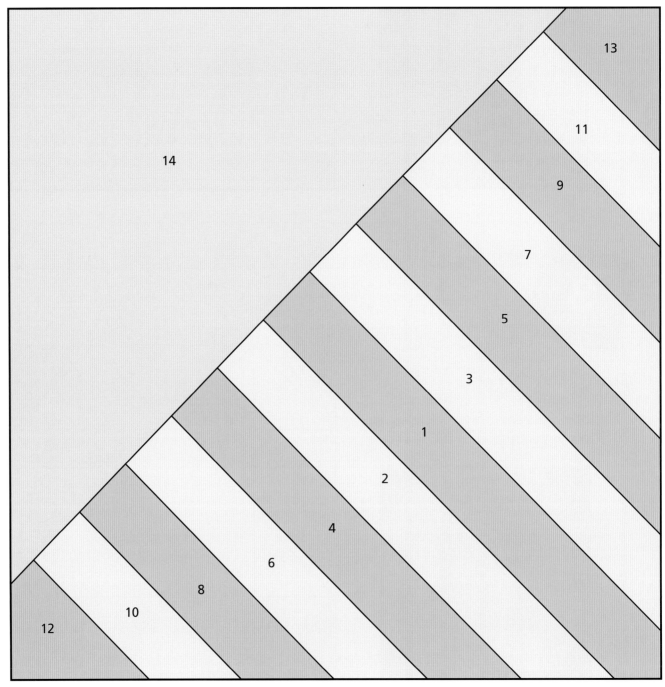

Little Star

Petite Star

7

Water Lily —
July Flower

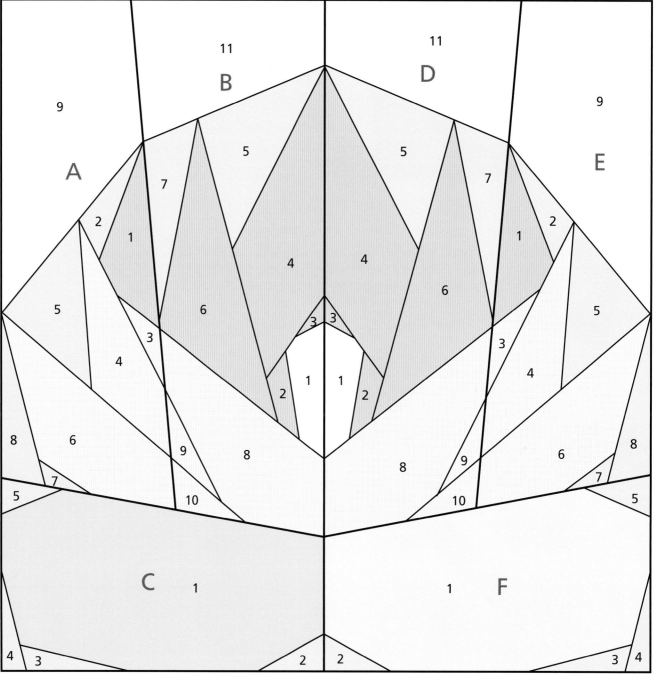

8

Ruby —
July Birthstone

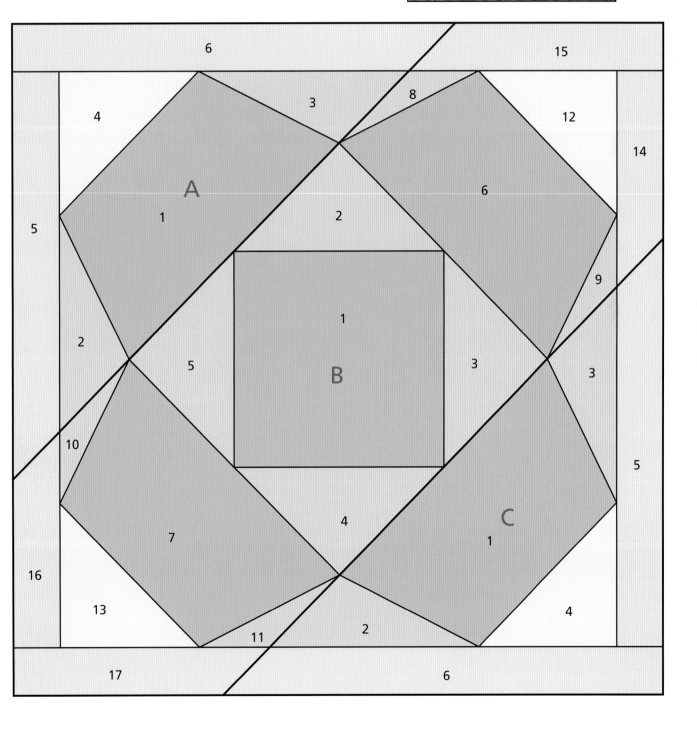

American Bandstand

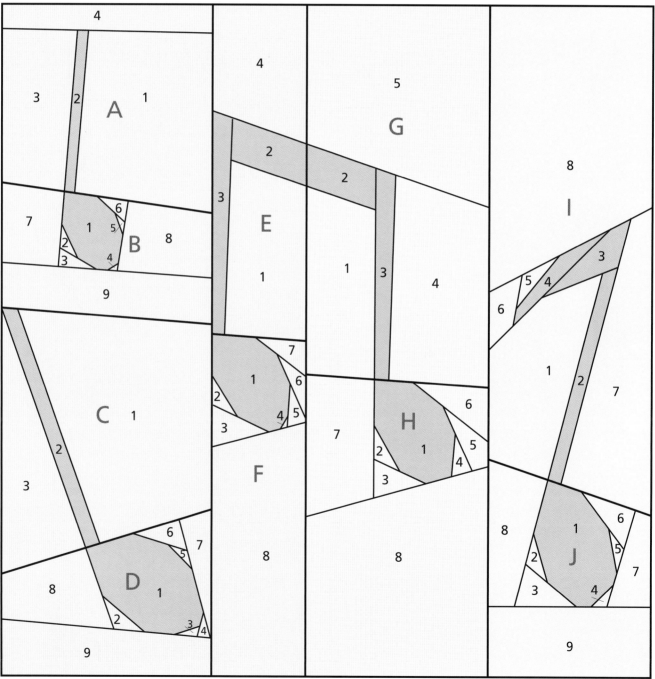

10

Patriotic Star

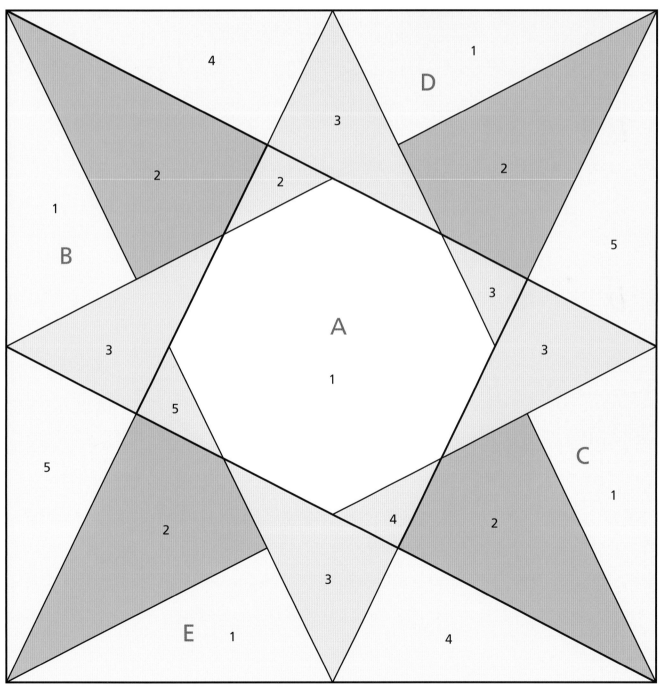

B

1

2

4

3

D

1

2

2

5

A

1

3

3

3

5

3

C

1

5

2

E

1

3

4

4

July

189

11

American Eagle

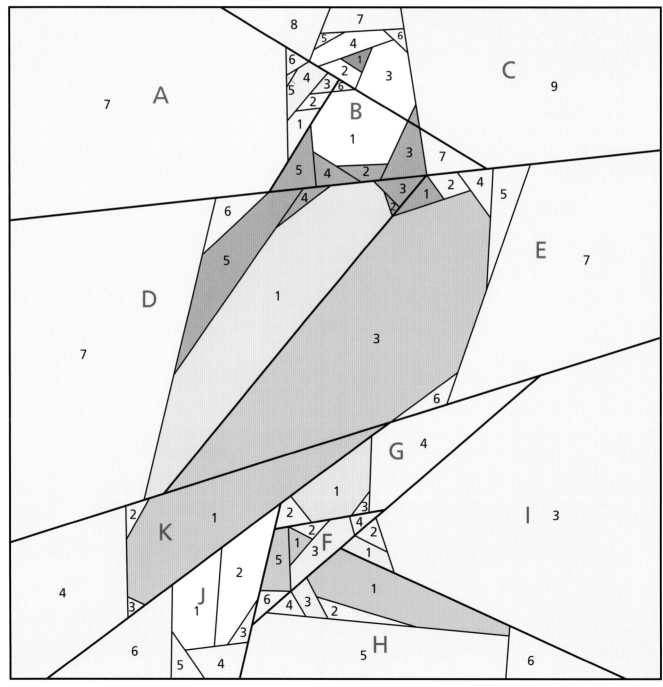

A 7

C 9

B 1

E 7

D 7

K 1

J 1

F

G 4

I 3

H

Log Cabin

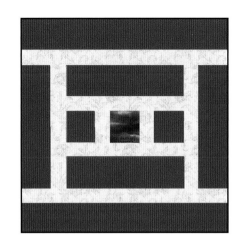

16										
14										

12	10	8						11	13
		6							
		4	2	1	3	5			
		7							
		9							

| 15 |
| 17 |

Angel

EMBELLISHMENT NOTE:
Use a black permanent fabric marker to add eyes.

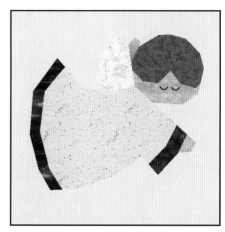

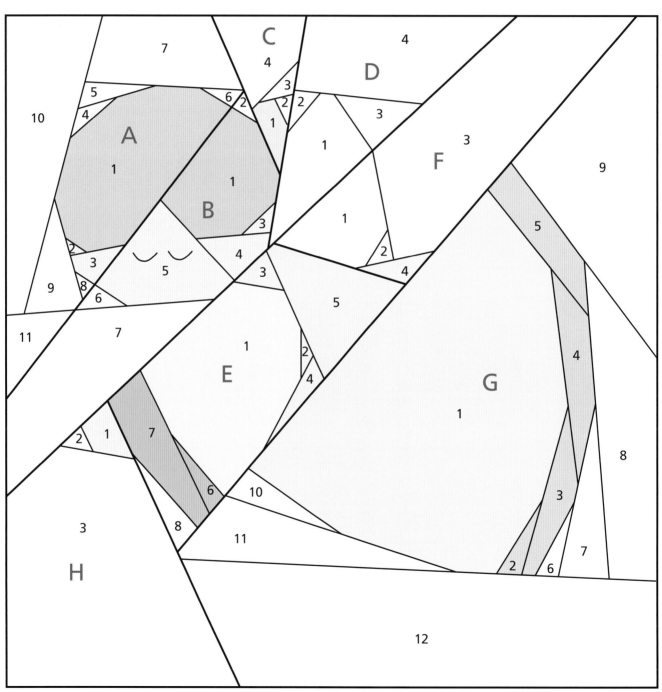

Pinwheel Stripes

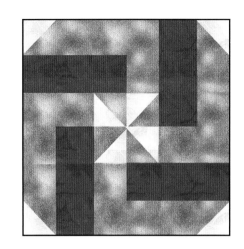

6

4

A

5

1

6

5

B 4

2

3

3

3

2

1

2

1

3

3

2

4 C

4

5

D

1

5

5

6

6

15

Twirling Roses

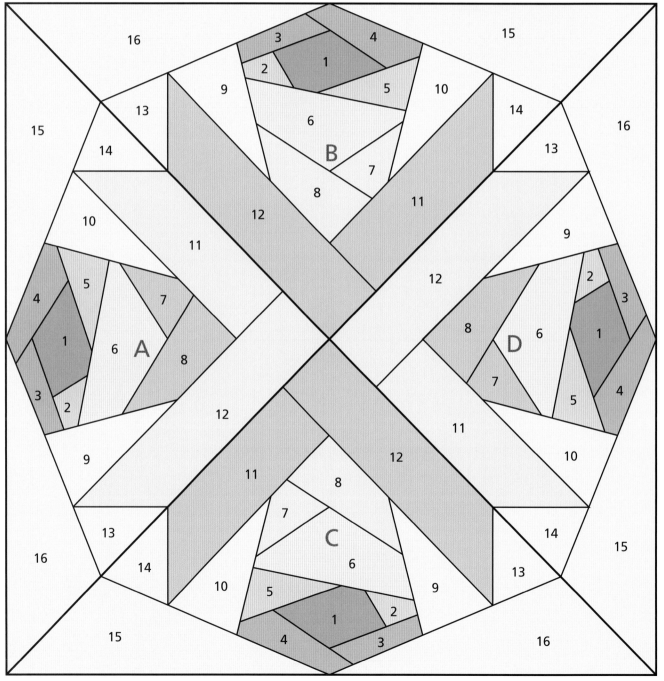

16

Lighthouse

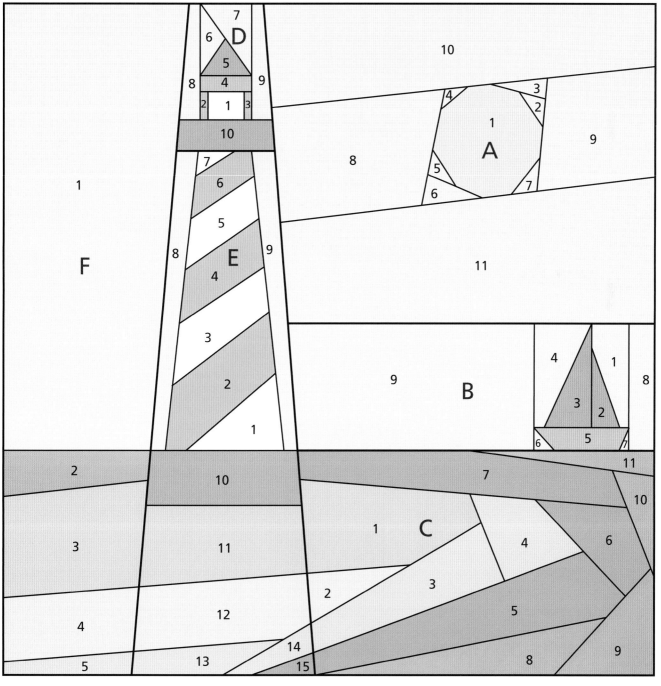

17

Disneyland Opens

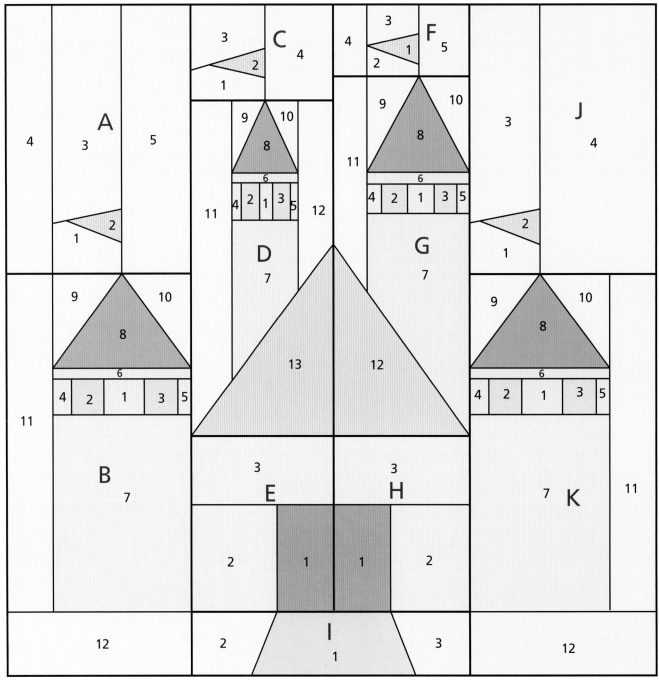

Whirling Dervish

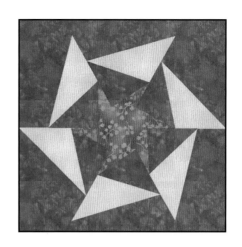

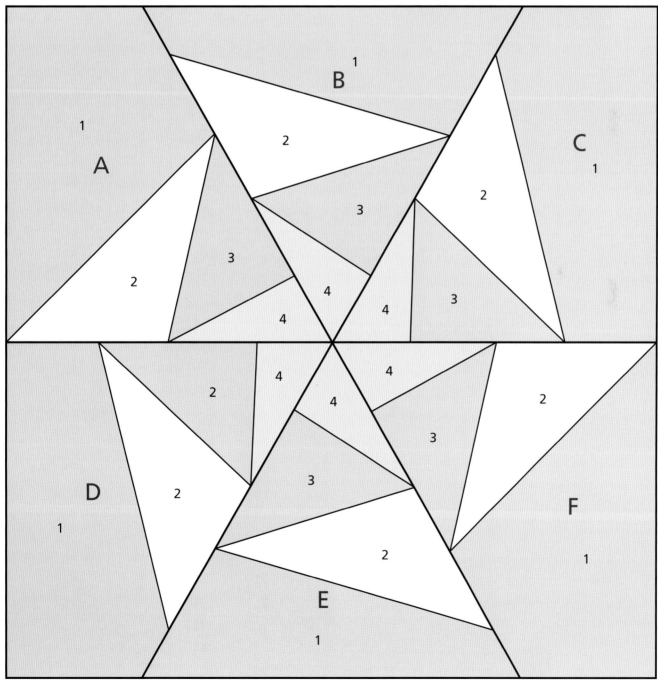

18

B ¹

A ¹

2

2

3

3

2

3

3

4

4

4

4

C ¹

2

2

4

4

4

3

2

D ²

2

3

3

2

2

1

3

F

1

E

1

2

19

Basket of Flowers

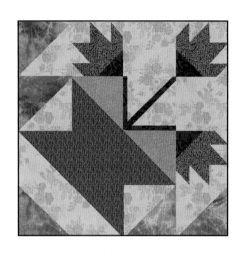

A 1 2 3 4 5 6 7 8 9 10

B 11 9 5 7 1 3 2 4 10 6 8

1 2

C 11 1 3 4 5 2 6

D 7 8

E 3 4 5 6

8 6 10 4 2 3 7 1 5 9

F 1 2 3 4 5 6 7 8

20

Moon Landing

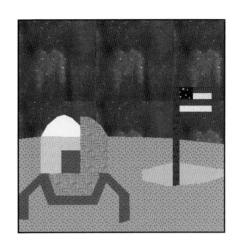

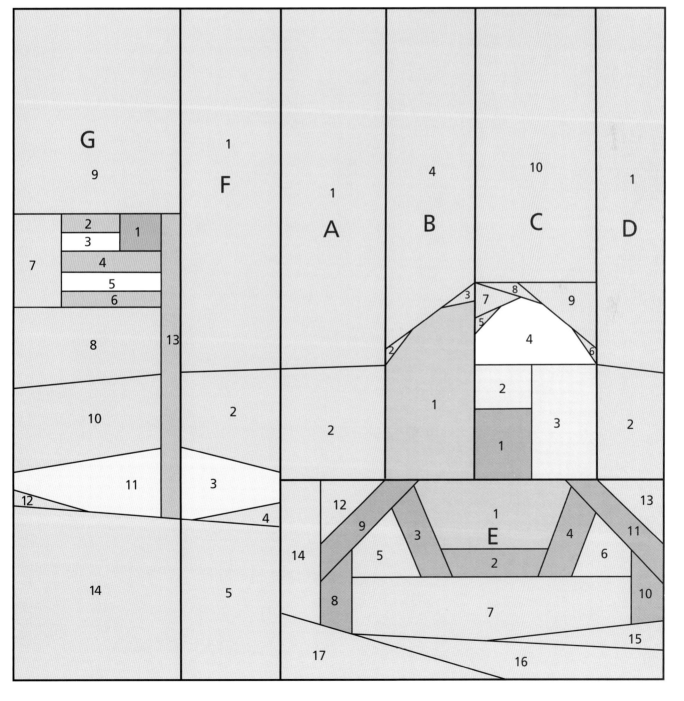

G
9

F
1

A
1

B
4

C
10

D
1

7
2
3
1
4
5
6

8

13

10

11

12

14

2

3

4

5

3
7
8
2
5

9
4
6

2
3
1

2

12
9
14
8

1
3
5

1
2
7

4
6
10

13
11
15

17
16

E

21

Playing Cards

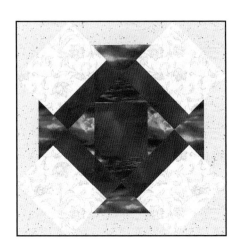

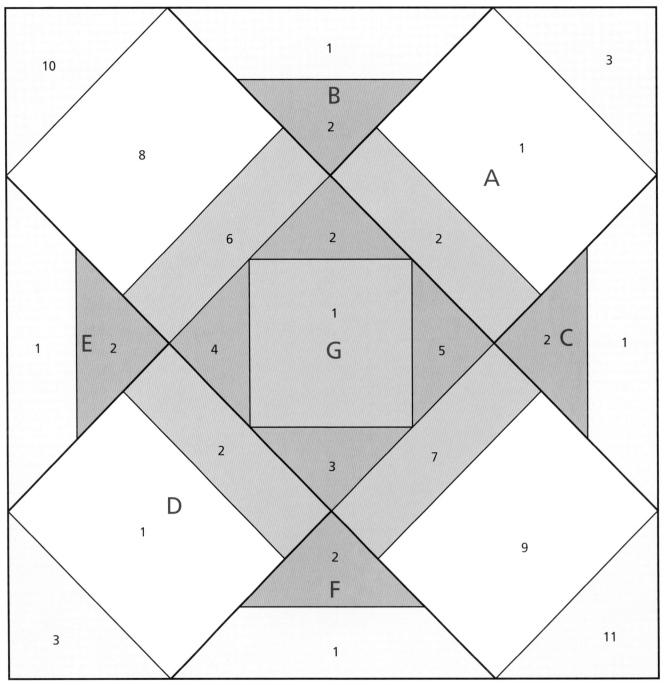

10

1

3

B

2

8

A

1

6

2

2

1

1

E 2

4

G

5

2 C

1

2

3

7

D

1

2

9

F

3

1

11

22

Winding Ribbons

1

2

A 3

2

1

B

3

2

3 C

2

1

1

2

D 3

2

1

E

3

3 F

2

1

1

2

G 3

2

1

H

3

2

3 I

2

1

1

2

J 3

2

1

K

3

2

3 L

2

1

23

Sunbonnet Sue

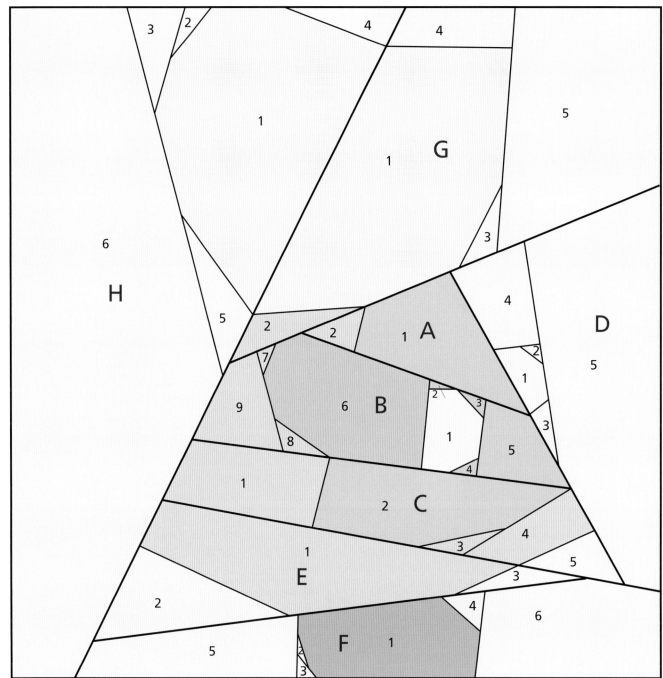

24

Overall Sam

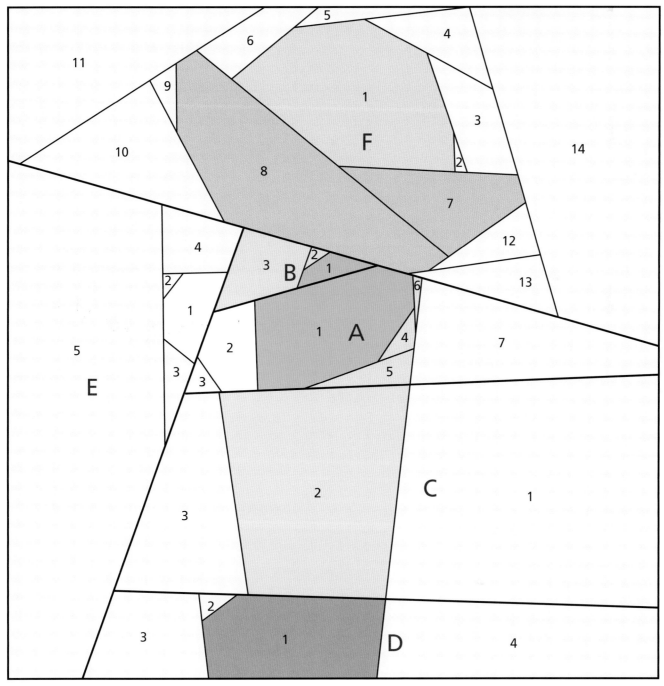

Summer Cottage

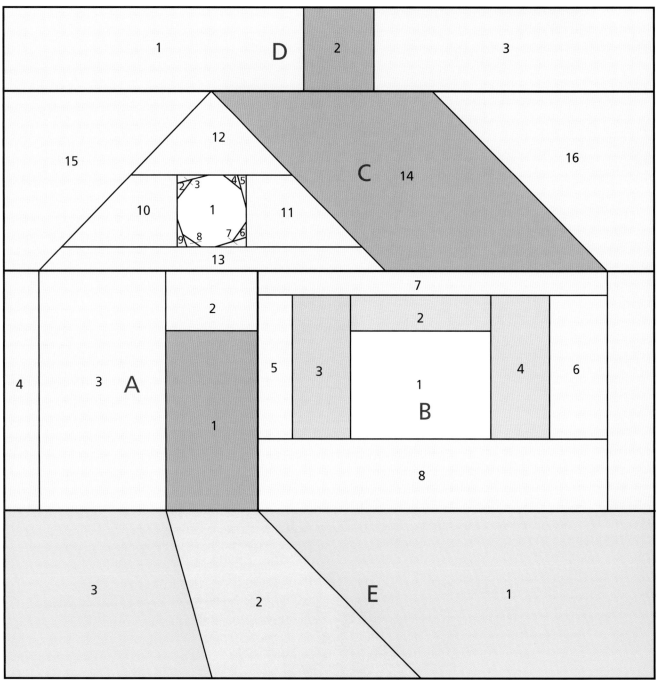

26

Rainbow Pinwheel

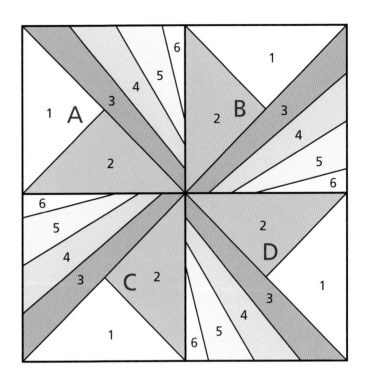

27

Patriotic Heart

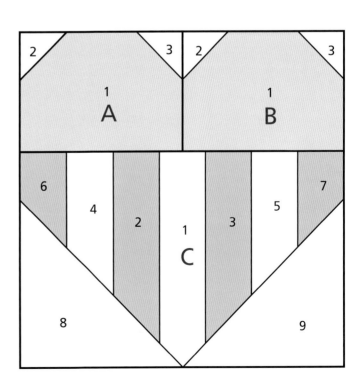

Summertime Carousel

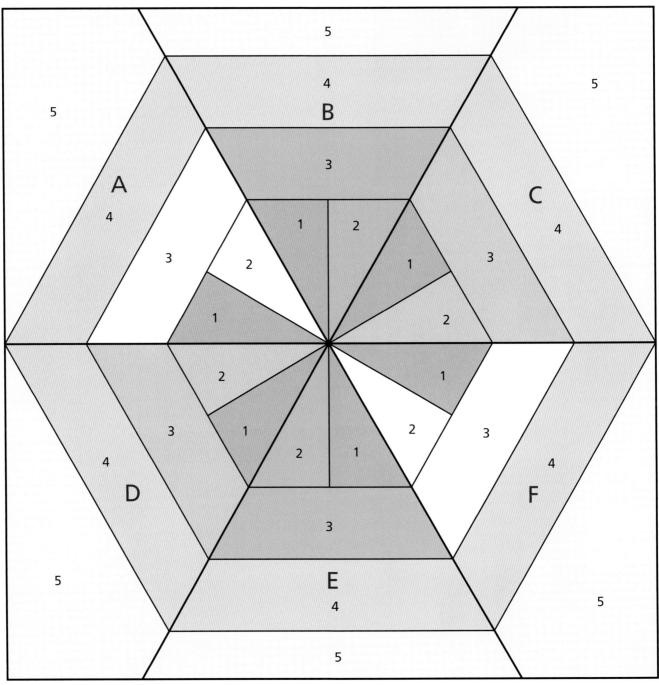

29

Starburst

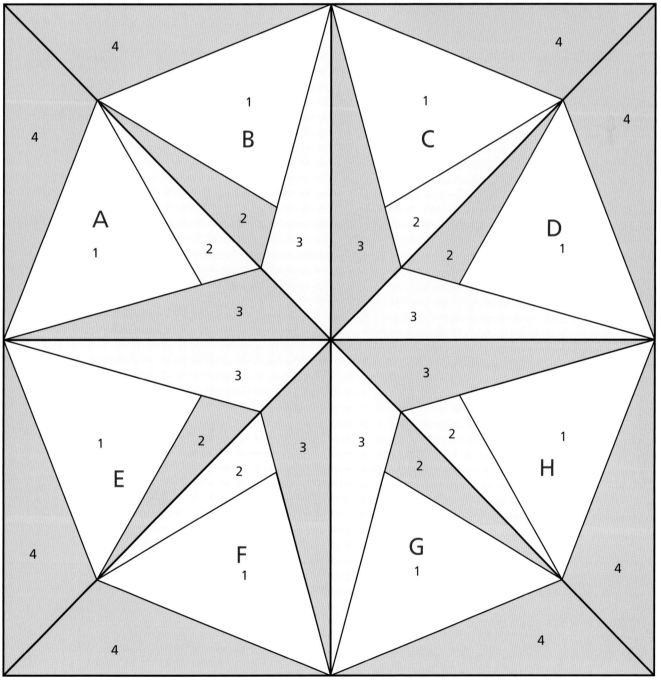

30

Whirlibird

G
4 2 1 3 5

5 4 5 4 4
3 3
A 1 B 3
E 3 5 2
1 5 3 2 1
2 2 2 5 F 1
C 2 2 5
1 3
D 3
2 3
4 4 5 4 1 1 4 5 5

H
5 3 1 2 4

31

Summer Log Cabin

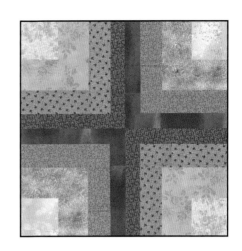

A
1
3
5
2
4
6
7

B
2
1
4
6
3
5
7

C
7
5
3
6
1
2
4

D
6
4
7
5
2
3
1

August

You've spent your vacation at the shore, and you'd like something to help remember all of the good times. Photos just end up in a box, and you're not in to making scrapbooks. Then why not a lovely quilt that can carry those memories forever? Start with a fabric that is reminiscent of the sea. Let the Seagull fly over the entire quilt, and the Sun Star shine brightly. Make certain to use a Sailboat to remind you of the wonderful days spent sailing. Add two Lighthouse blocks and a beautiful view of Hawaii. Tie the whole quilt together with a border made from Small Pinwheel blocks alternating with the sea fabric strips, and you've made a quilt that can't be forgotten.

1

Sun Star

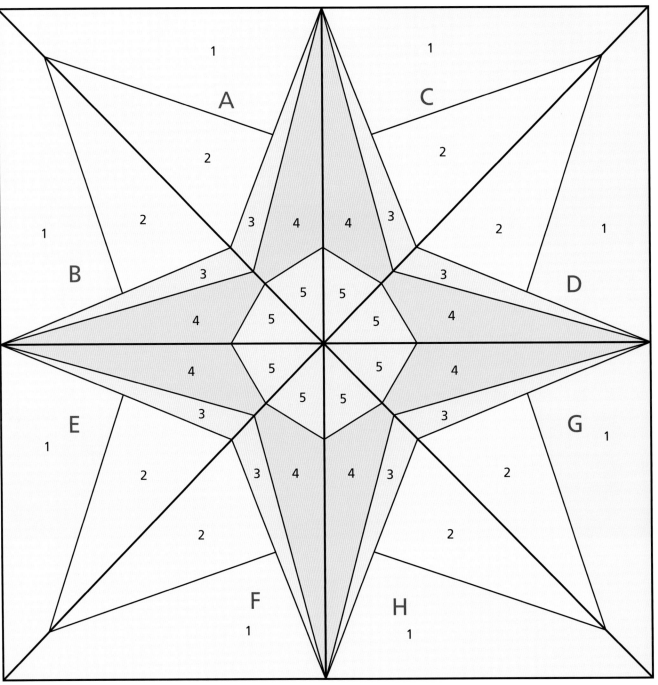

Weather Vane

4	2	1 **A**	3	5
4	2	1 **B**	3 / 5	6
4	2	1 **C**	3	5
6	4 / 2	1 **D**	3	5
4	2	1 **E**	3	5

3

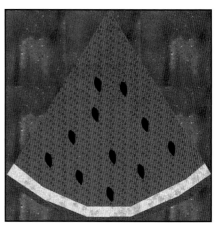

Watermelon Day

EMBELLISHMENT NOTE:
Use a black permanent fabric marker to add seeds.

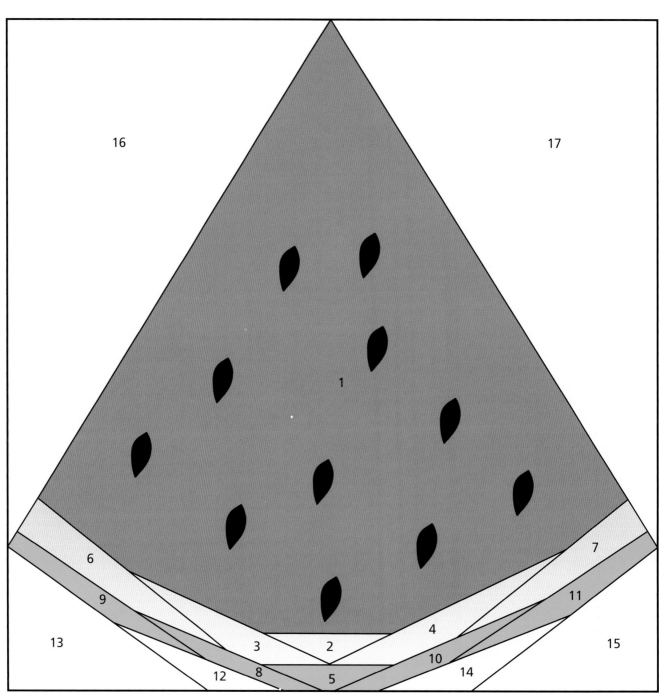

Sailboat

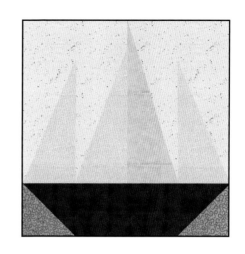

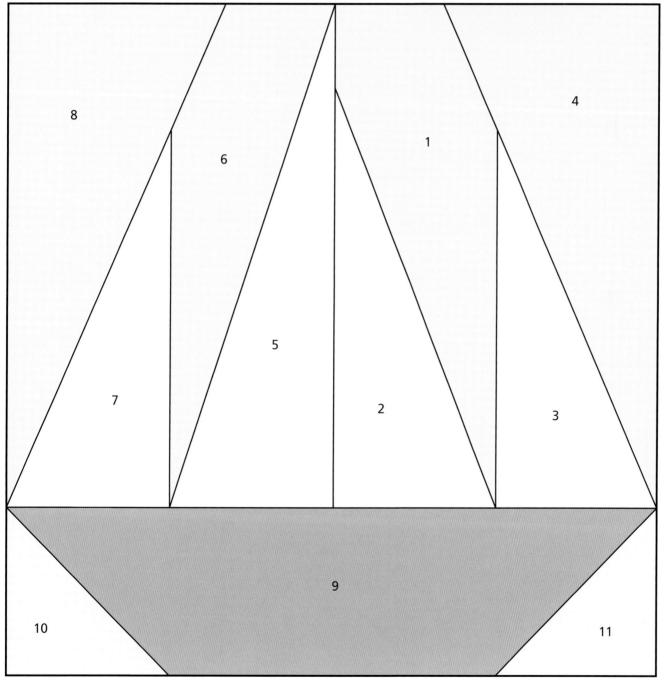

Lighthouse

A

7   6

5

8   4   9

2   1   3

B

2   1   3

5

C

6   4   7

2   1   3

8

6

Sea Gull

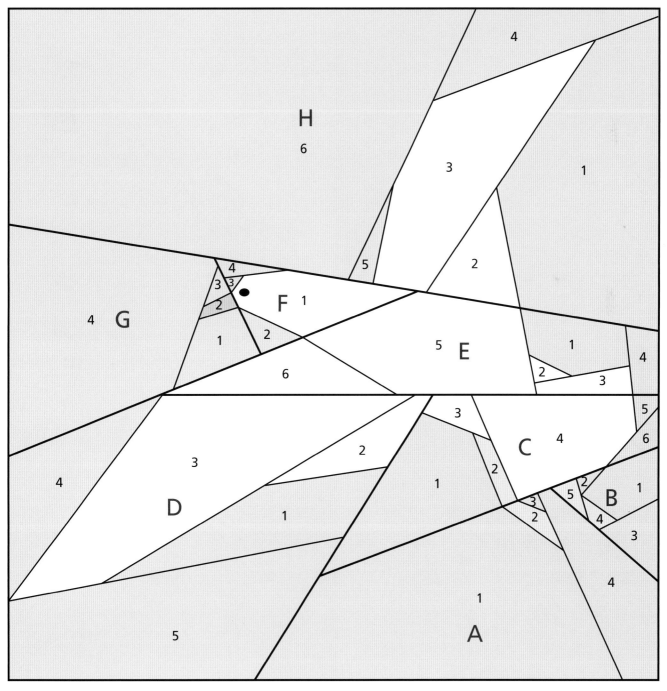

Pinwheel

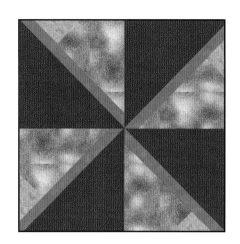

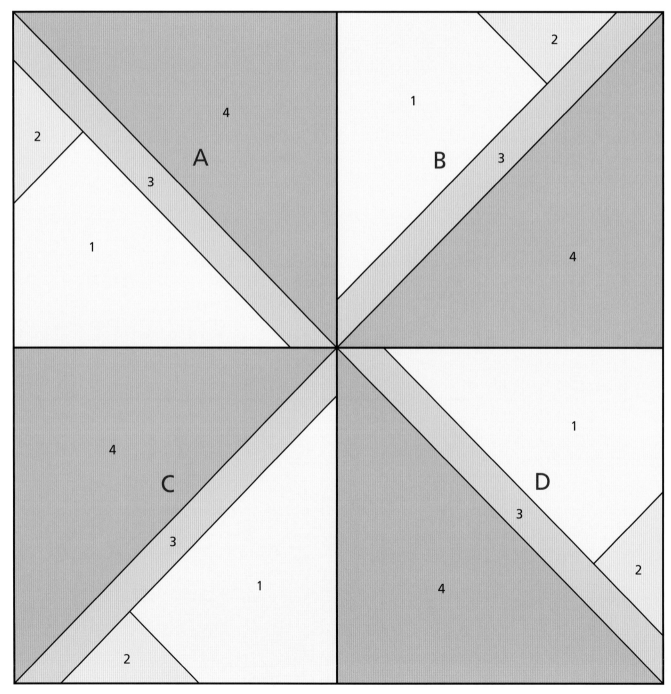

8

Lighthouse

C
8

A

6

7

8

9

10

D
8

4

1

2 3

1

2

7

6

5

4

3

1

2 5 2

3

1

3

4

7

6

5

4

9

5

3 1 4

2

B

6

9

10

7

10

Peridot—
August Birthstone

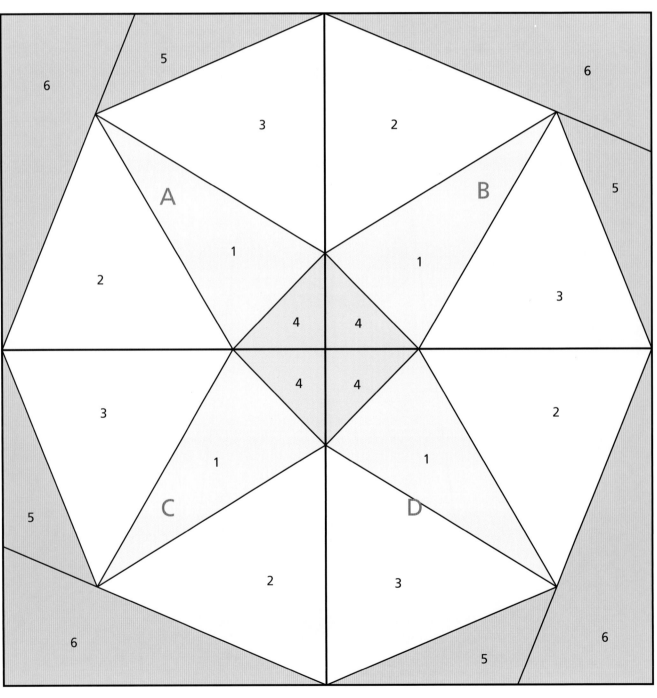

10

Chicago Becomes a City

6

4 1 L 5
2 3

3

2

M 1

6
5

N 1
2

3 4

1 2 O 3 4 5

3

I

2 1

2
1 3 J 4

2 1
3 K 4

4

H

3

2 1

6
D
4 1 5
2 3

2 1 3

5 E 4 6

5
F

2 1
3 4

2 1
G 3

4

A

2 1 3

5 4 2 1
B 3

1 C 2 3

2

P
1

11

Small Pinwheel

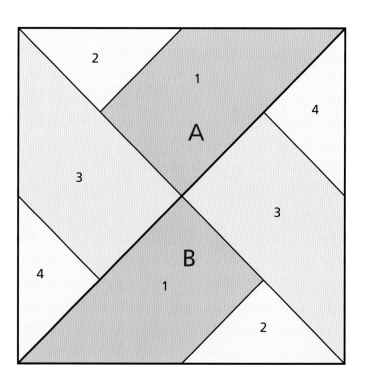

12

Stepping Stone

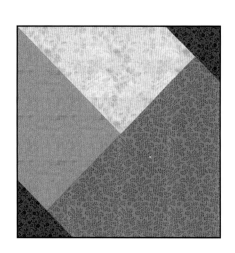

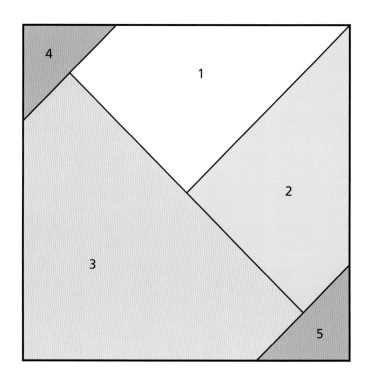

Log Cabin Pineapple

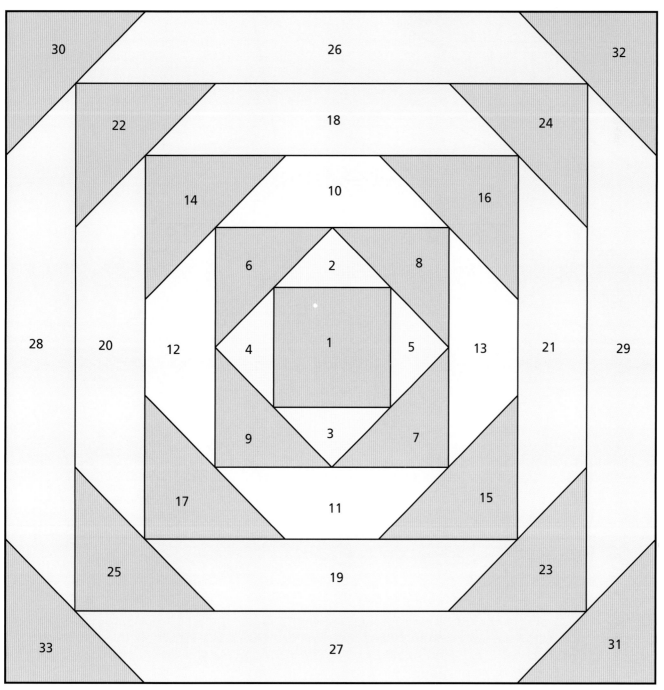

August

223

14

*Gladiolus —
August Flower*

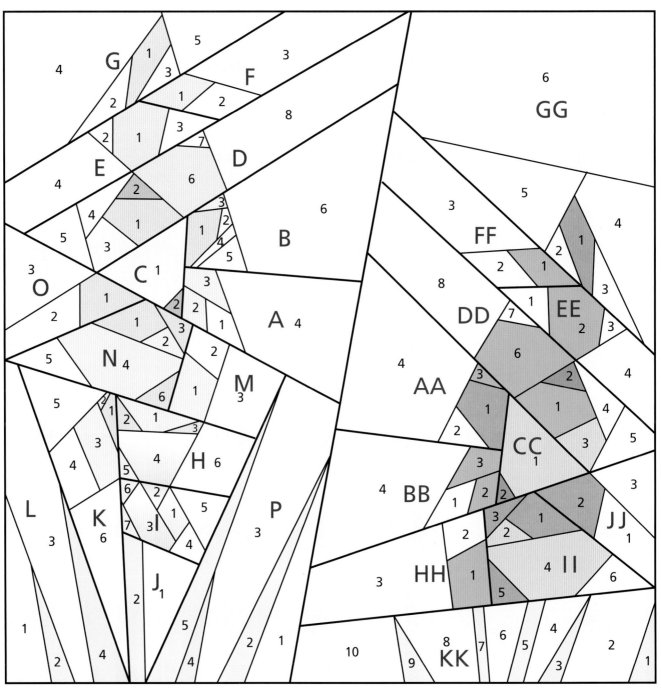

15

Pinwheel in a Star

16

Cosmic Star

17

Pinwheel Flower

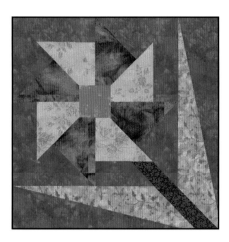

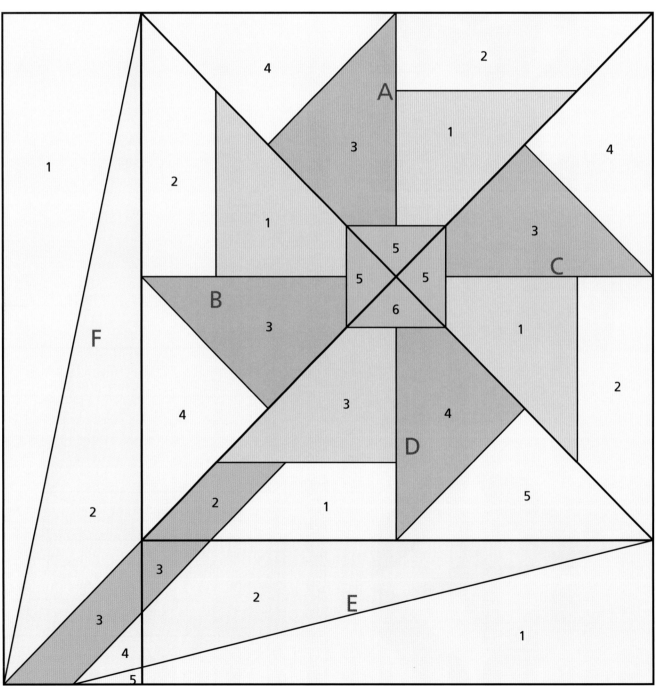

Aviation Day

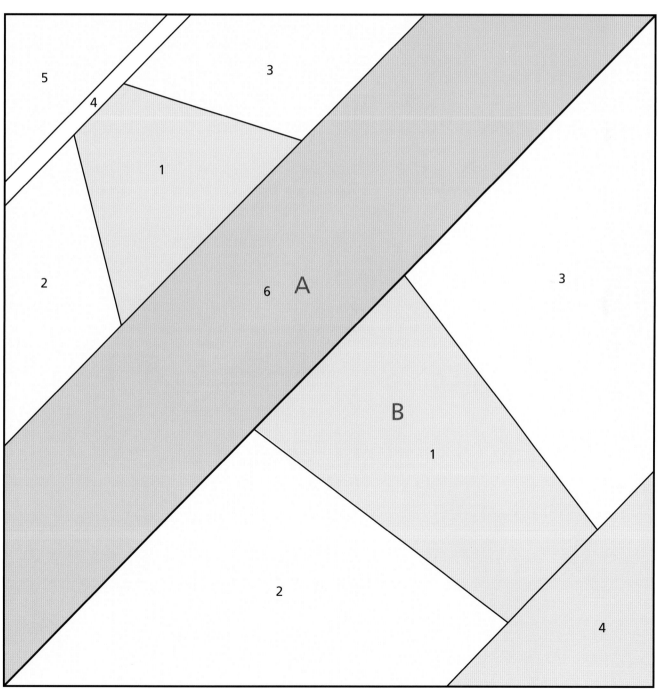

5

4

3

1

2

6 A

B

1

2

3

4

19

Rainbow Star

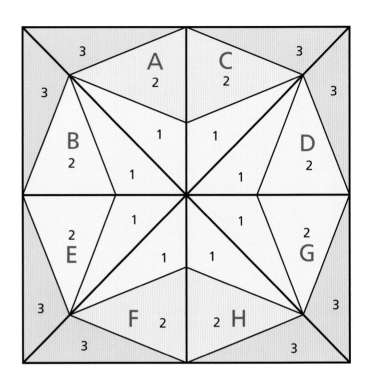

20

Rainbow Ripple

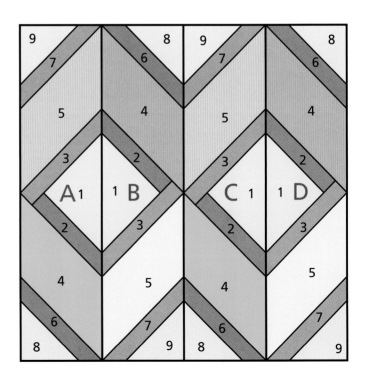

21

Hawaii Day

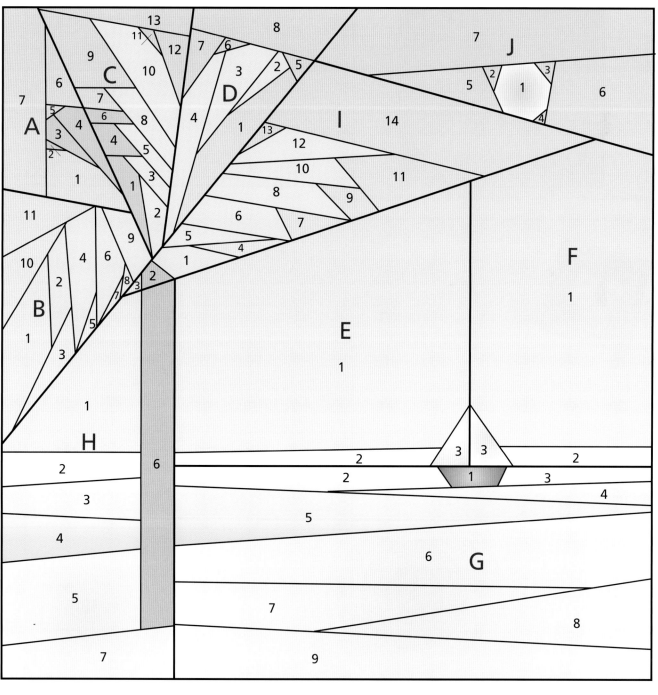

22

Ribbons

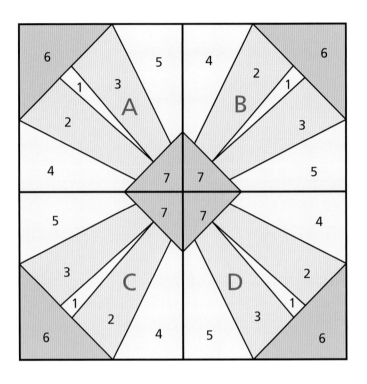

23

Summer Basket

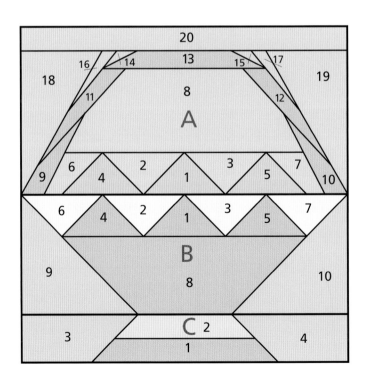

24

Hidden Star

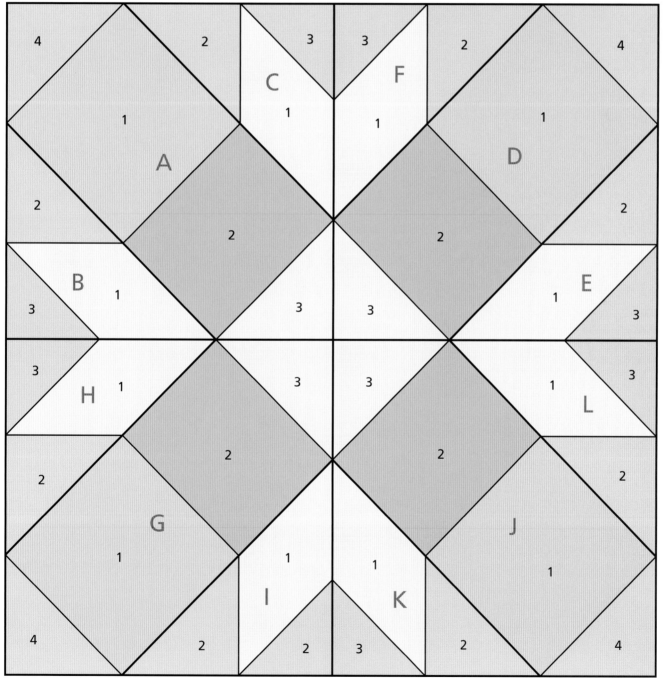

Palm Leaf

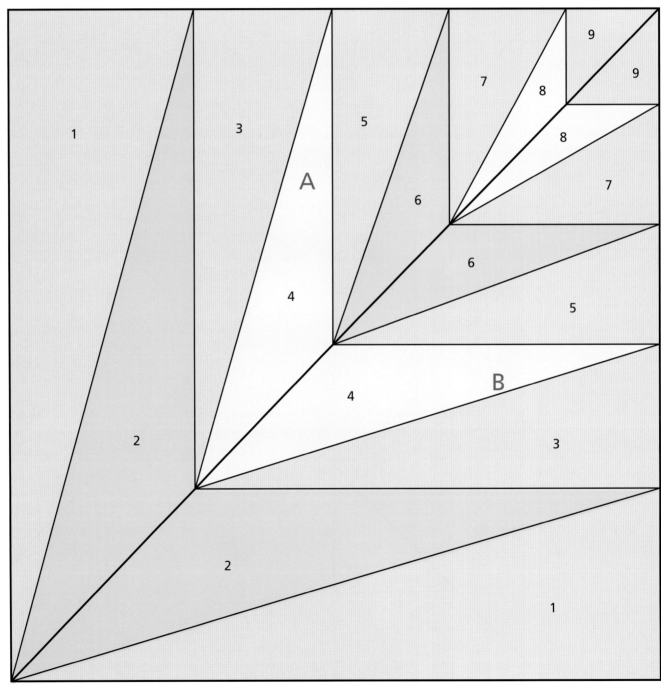

Summer House

A
5
3
1
4
4

10

B
4
6 | 2 | 1 | 3 | 7
5

F
7
7 6
8 9
1
4
3 2
5

C
4
6 | 2 | 1 | 3
7
5

7
8
9

D
3
2
3
2
1
5
4 4

E
1

G
2
1
3

August

233

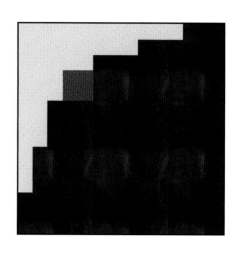

Uneven Log Cabin

11

7

3

4

1

2

8

6

12

10

5

9

13

28

Sunshine Stripes

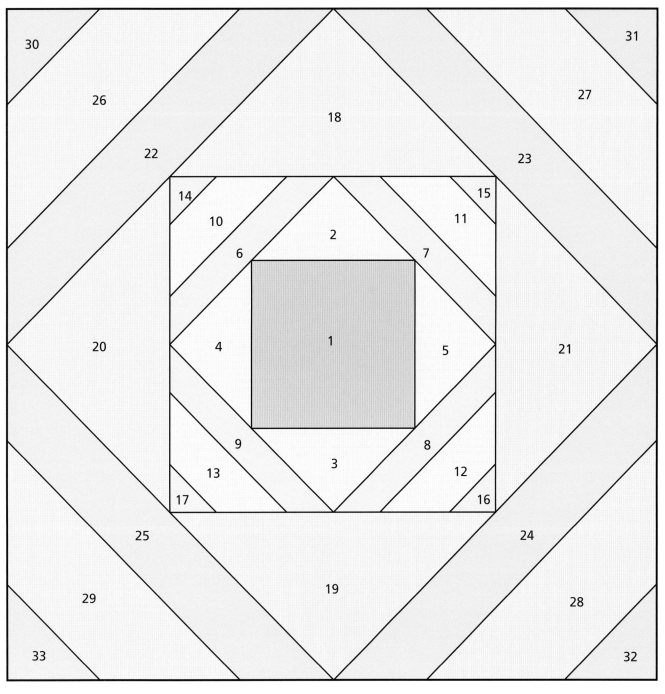

29

Bowties

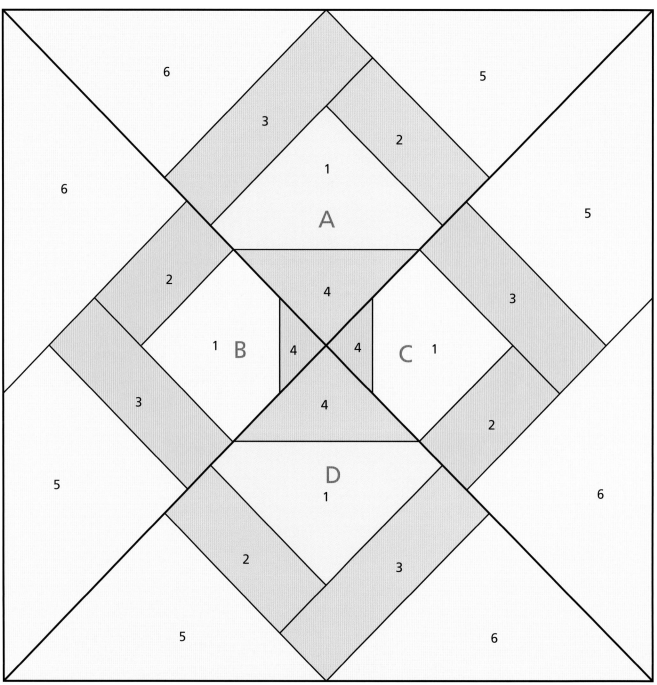

30

Crazy Squares

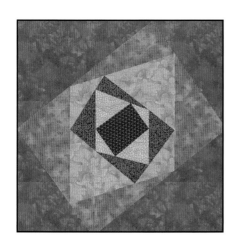

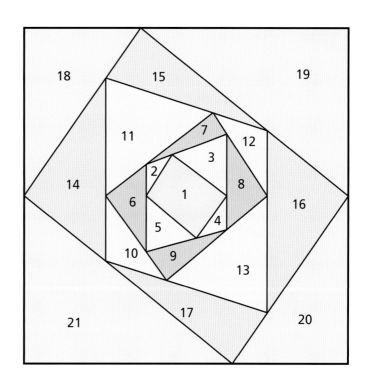

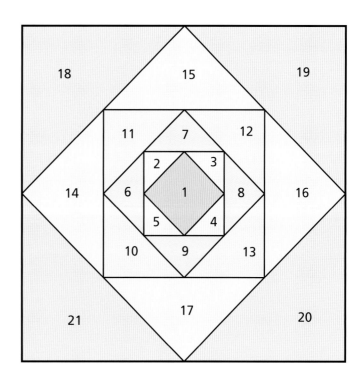

31

Colorful Squares

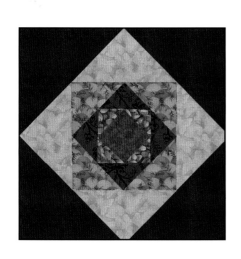

September

No matter how old we might be, the month of September turns us all into little children, heading back to school. Whether we went to school in a one-room schoolhouse or a huge city building, the sight of the little red schoolhouse reminds us of September. This quilt might be the perfect gift for a favorite teacher or a special scholar. It is made very simply, consisting of twelve Schoolhouse blocks, using a number of different red prints to give it interest. It's school time again.

Abstract Star

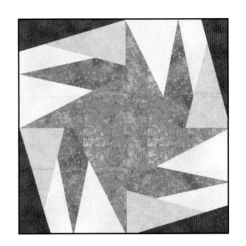

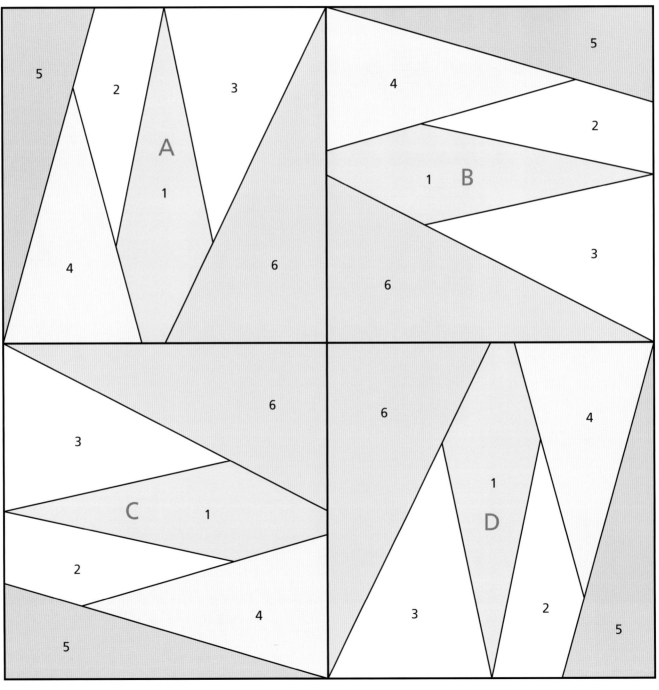

Pinwheel

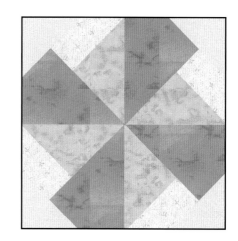

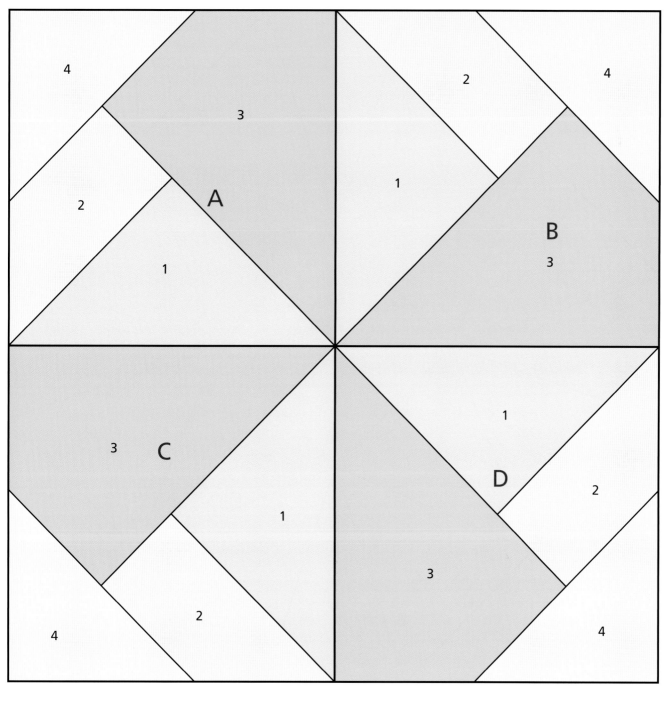

3

Cogwheel

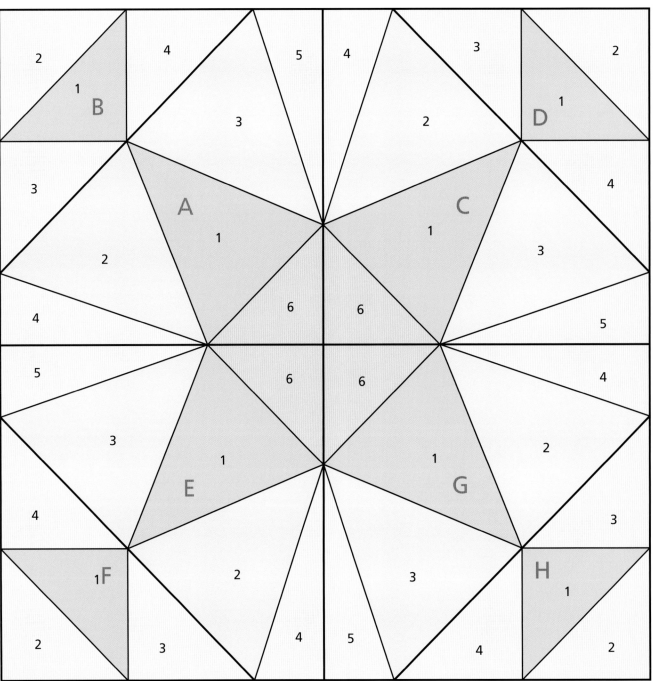

Schoolhouse

| 3 | 2 | D | 1 |

3

4

1   C

2

2

6   4

A   B

1   2   3   4   5   2   1   3

7

Labor Day
Picnic Basket

5	2	6
3	1	4
	A	

| 6 | 4 | 2 | 1 | 3 | 5 | 7 |

| 8 |
| B |

| 9 | | 10 |

6

Read a Book Day

6	7	9	4	6	

A: 3, 2, 1, 4

B: 3, 2, 1, 4, 5

C: 4, 3, 2, 1, 5, 6, 7

D: 3, 2, 1

E: 3, 2, 1, 4

5, 6, 8, 5, 5

Teddy Bear Day

EMBELLISHMENT NOTE:
Use white and black felt for eyes and a black permanent fabric marker for the mouth.

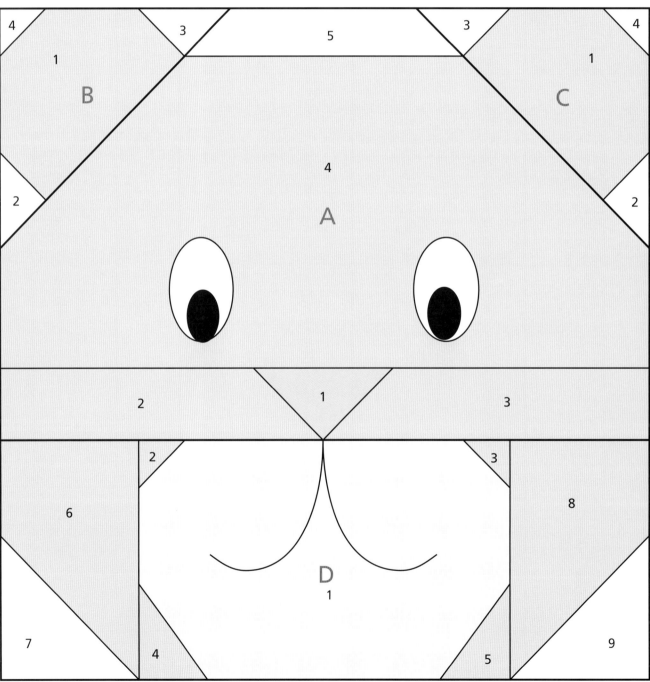

First Day of School

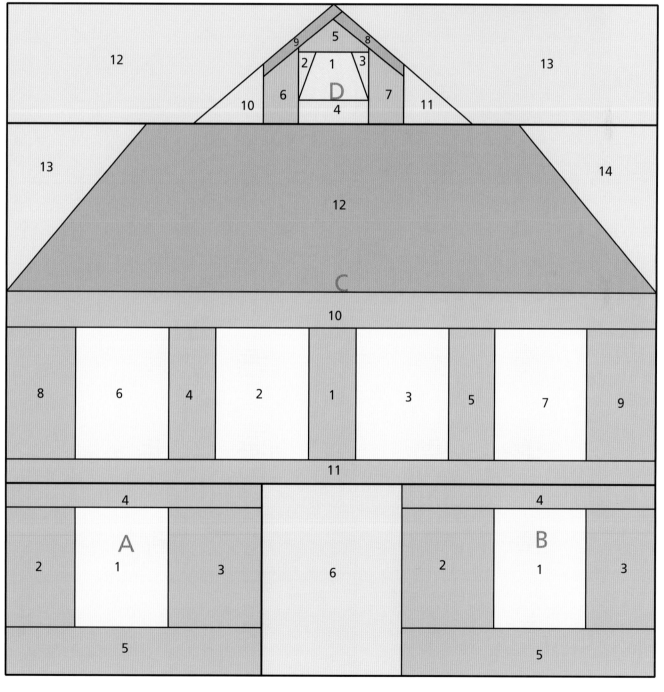

9

Star Log Cabin

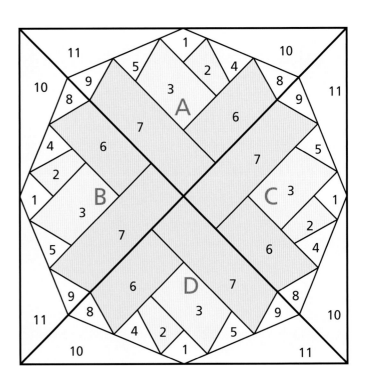

10

Diamond Stripes

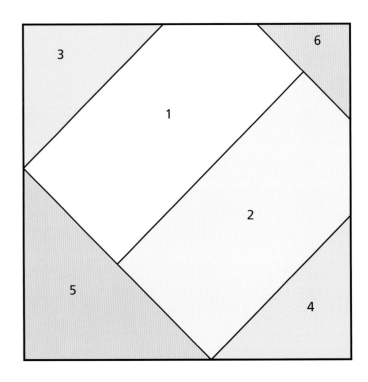

11

Remember 9/11

O 5

4

4

H 1

4

A

1　2　3

3
2 3 2
2 3 2

C 1

1

B 5

D 1 1

7　6　4

2

2　1 E　3

K 3

1

L 3

2 1 2

I 1

2

J

2

2

1 F

3

M 3

N 3

I 2

J 3

1

2

1

3

4 2

1

2 1

2 1

G 4

2

P 3 4 5

1

Q 1

5

5

12

Tool Time

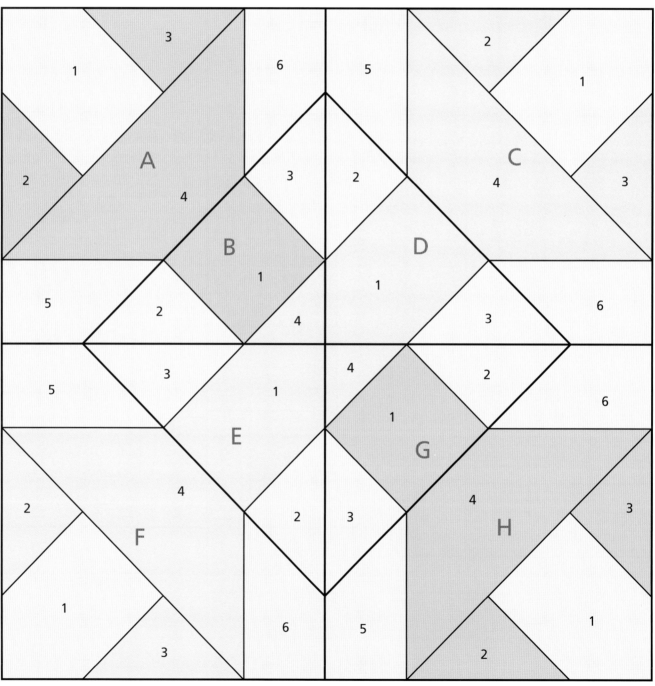

Aster — September Flower

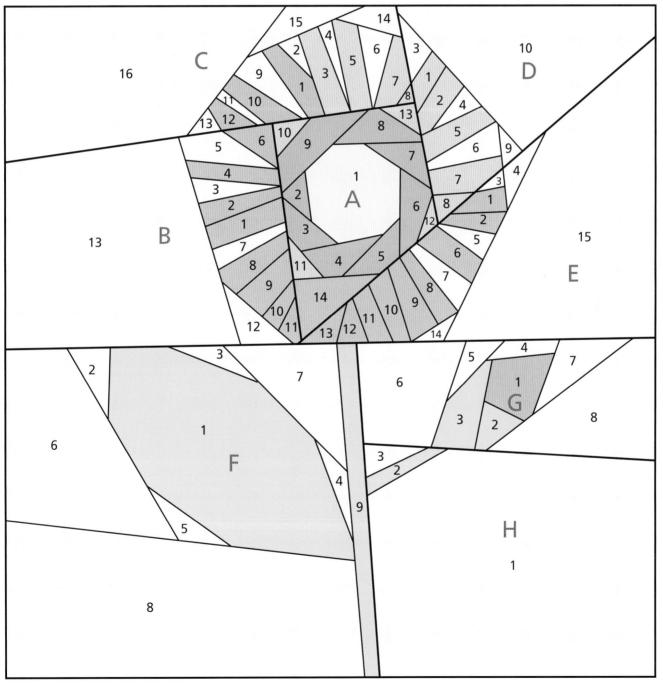

Sapphire –
September Birthstone

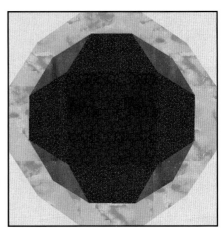

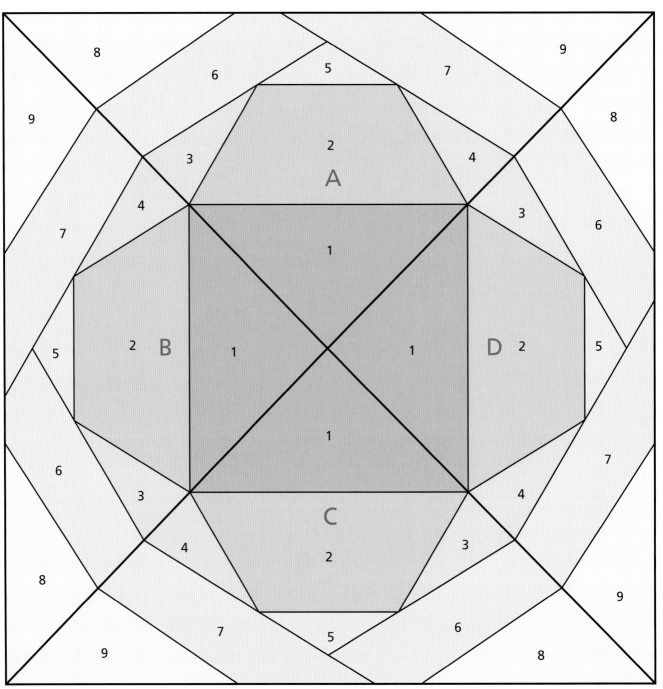

15

Pinwheel

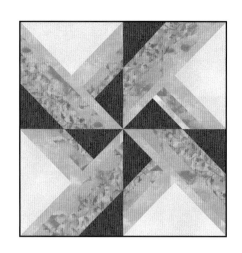

A
1
9
8
7
6
2
3
4
5

B
1
2
3
4
5
6
7
8
9

C
9
8
7
6
5
4
3
2
1

D
5
4
3
2
6
7
8
9
1

Mayflower

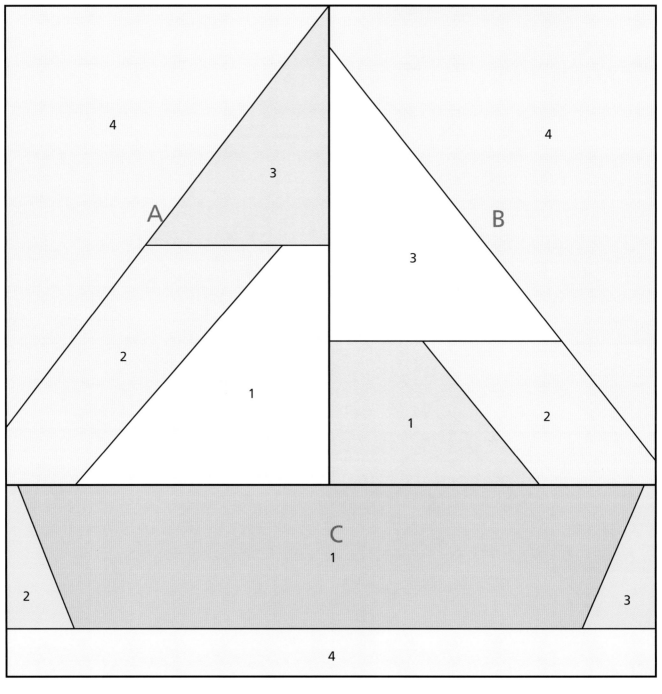

Star

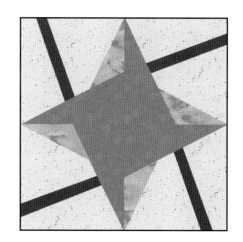

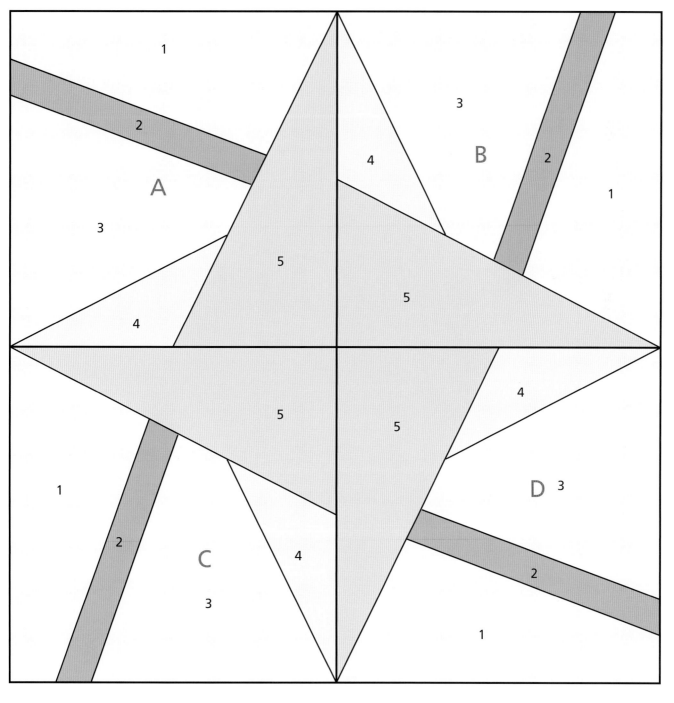

1

2

A

3

4

5

4

3

B

4

2

1

5

5

1

2

C

3

4

5

5

4

D 3

2

1

18

Owl

EMBELLISHMENT NOTE:
Use black and light yellow felt to add eyes.

19

Crazy Log Cabin

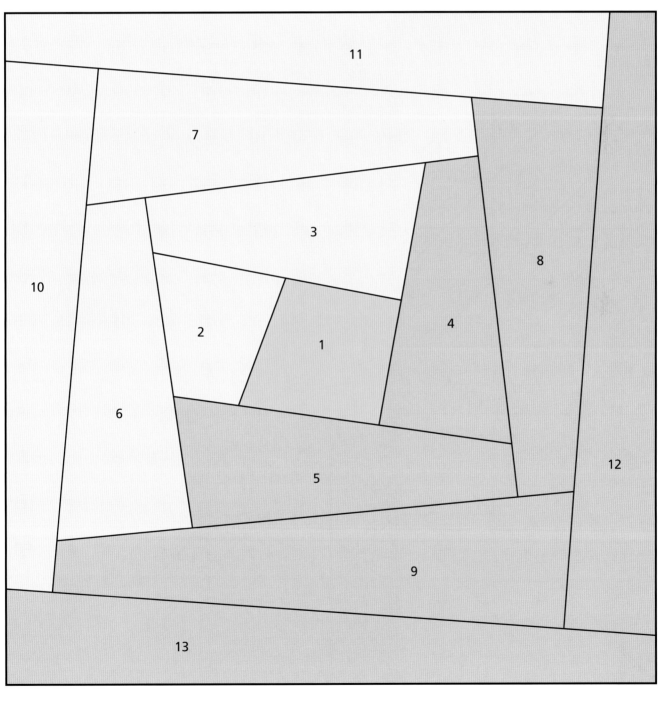

Carpenter's Wheel

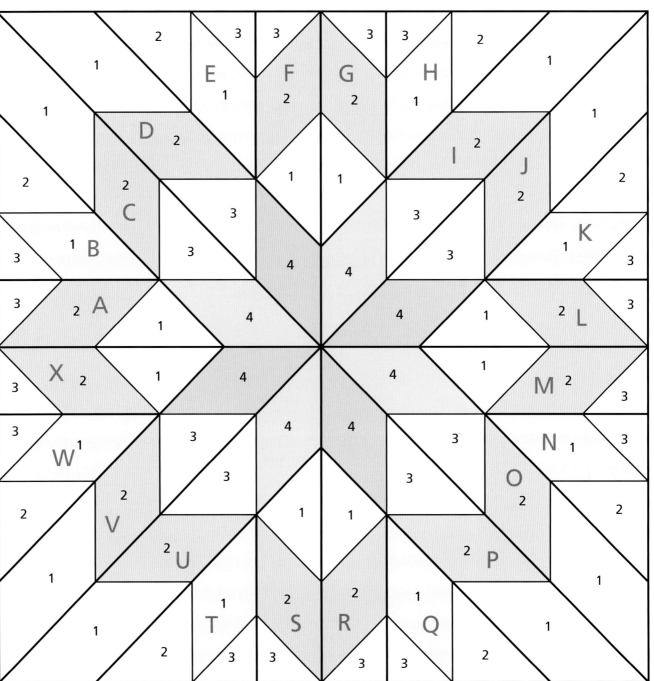

King's Diamond

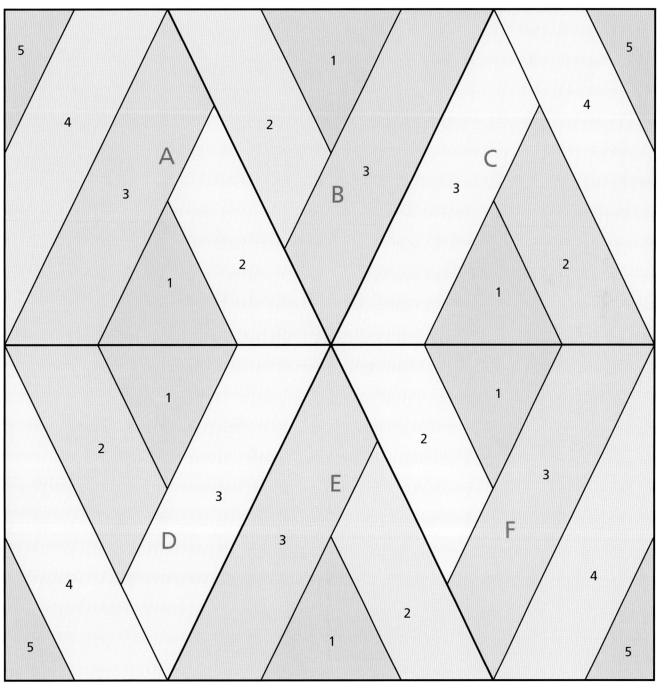

22

Autumn Flying Geese

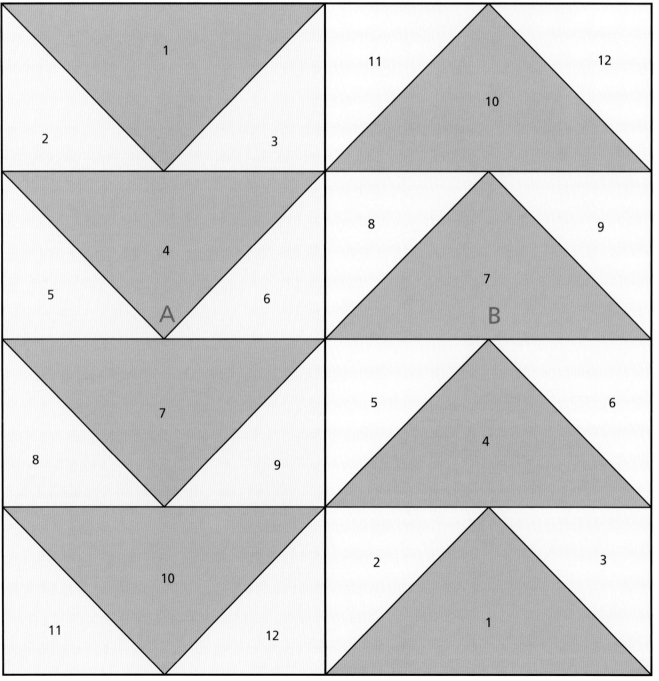

23

Native American Day

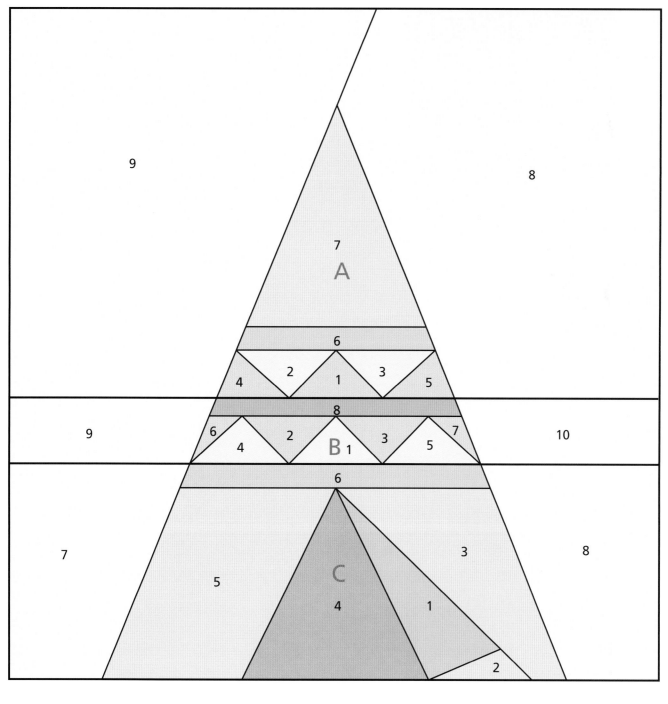

24

Diamond Shadow

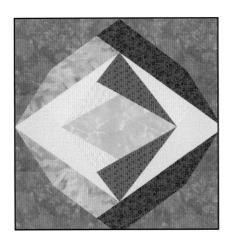

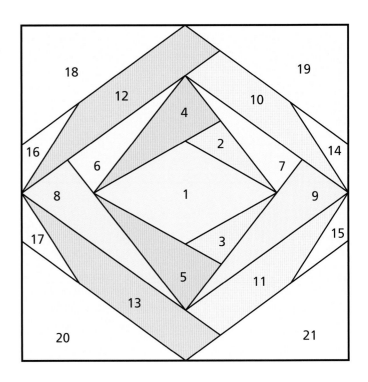

25

Spiraling Star

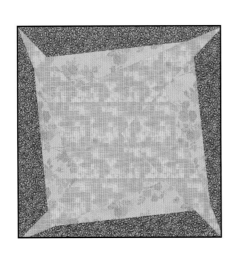

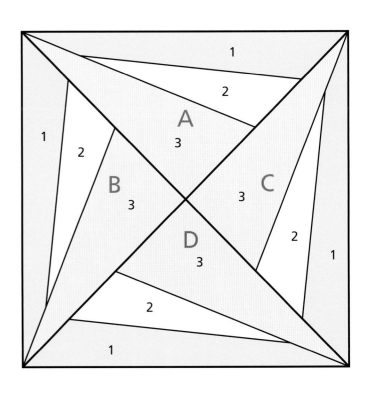

26

Solar Power

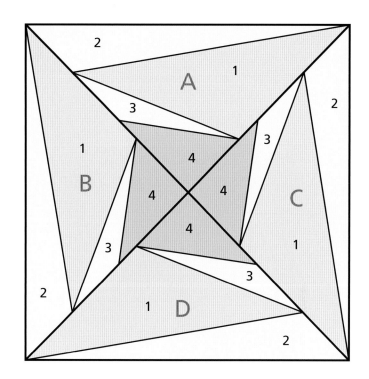

27

Star Cross

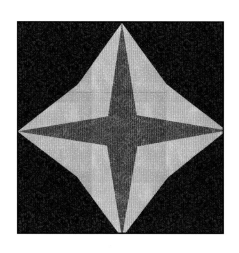

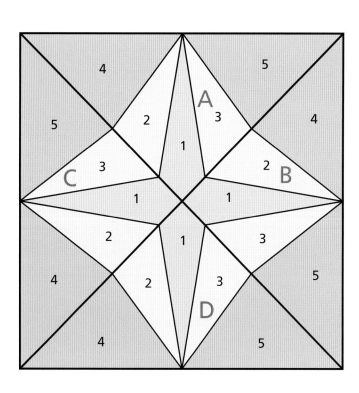

28

Skewed Log Cabin

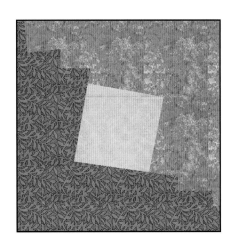

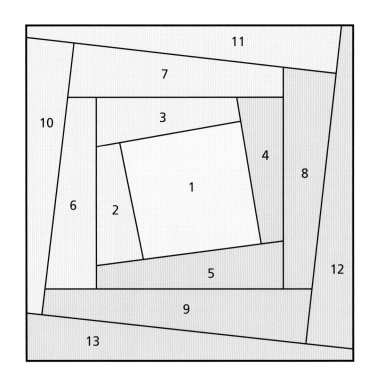

29

Fortune Cookie

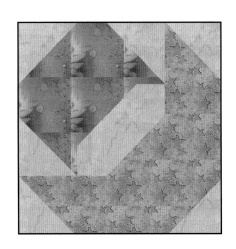

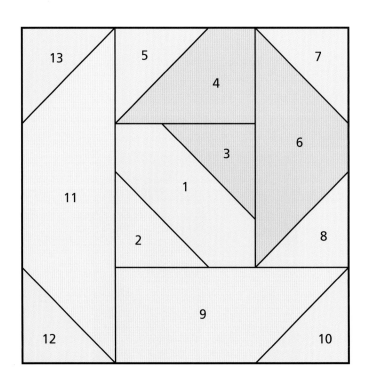

30

Birds in Flight

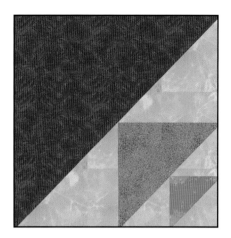

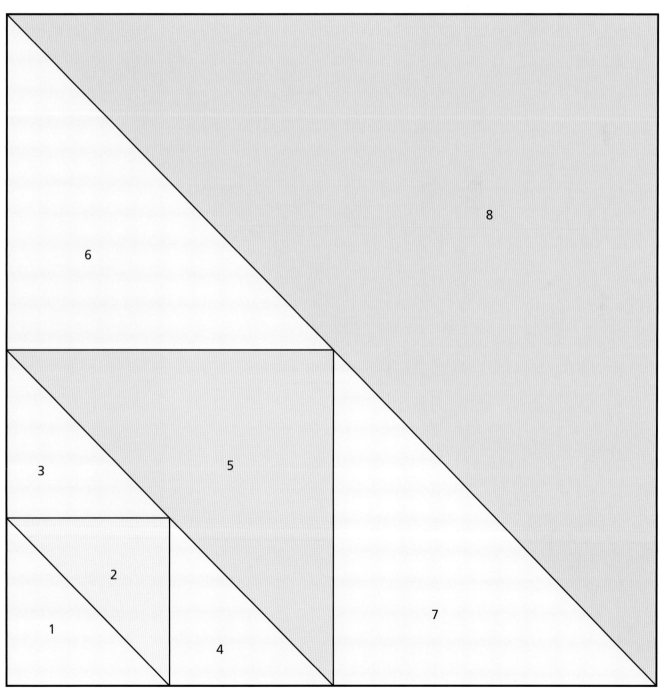

What could be more fun than Halloween! Hang this quilt where it can be seen by all the town's "trick or treaters," and they'll be certain that you are "open for business." Begin by collecting a Halloween print and lots of orange and black fabric. Then start out with the traditional Black Cat followed by a Halloween Pumpkin. The scary spider might be missing, but we have the Spider Legs. All we see of the famous lady in the Witch block is her hat and her broomstick, but we know she's here. What better bird to celebrate Halloween than the bird depicted in the Crow block, and finish the quilt with something a little sweet by making the Candy Corn block. We're ready for Halloween!

Cat

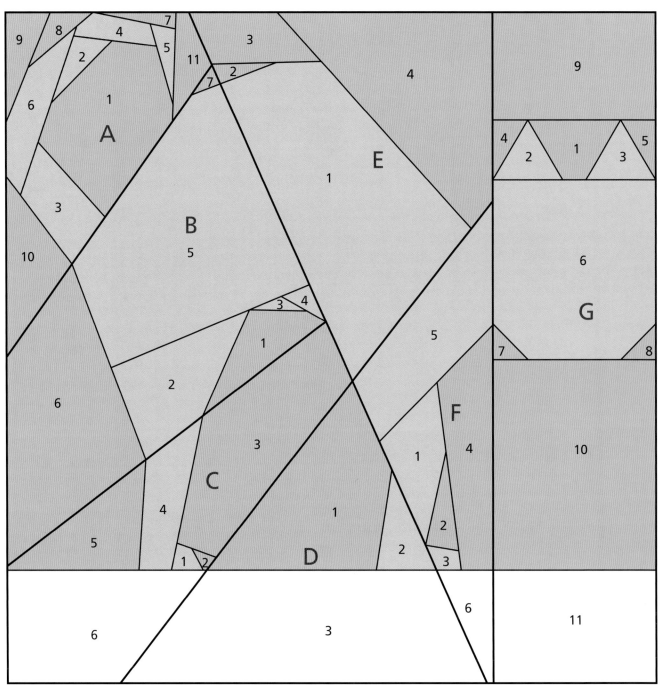

A

9 8 4 7
2 5
6 11
1 7 2
3
4
3
B
5
E
1
10
3
4
9
4 5
2 1 3
6 6
G
7 8
5
F
4 1 4
1 2
C 2
D 3
1 10
3
2 3
1 2
6
5
6 3 6
11

2

Cottage in the Woods

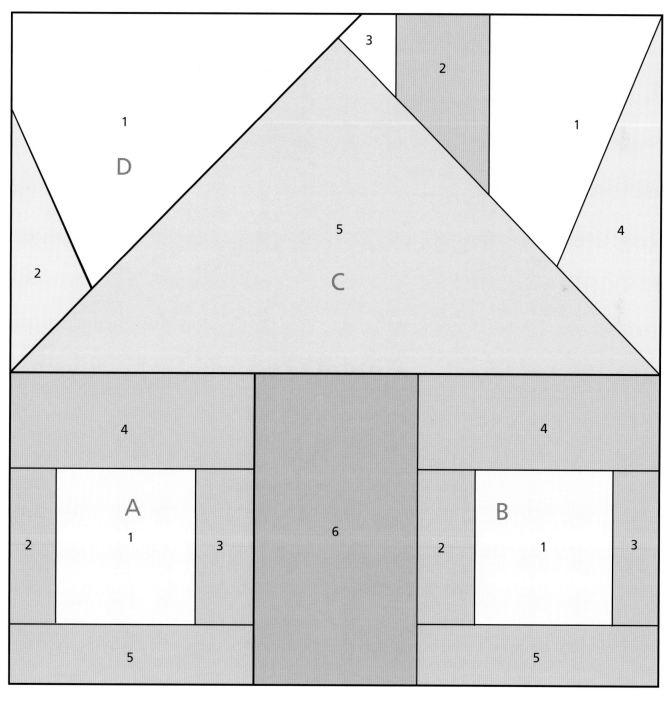

Witch

EMBELLISHMENT NOTE:
Use brown permanent fabric marker to add lines to broom.

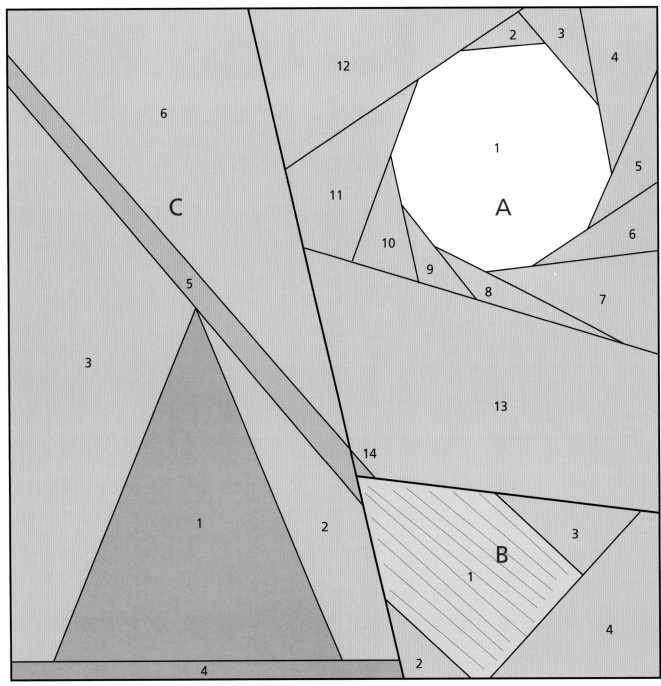

Star

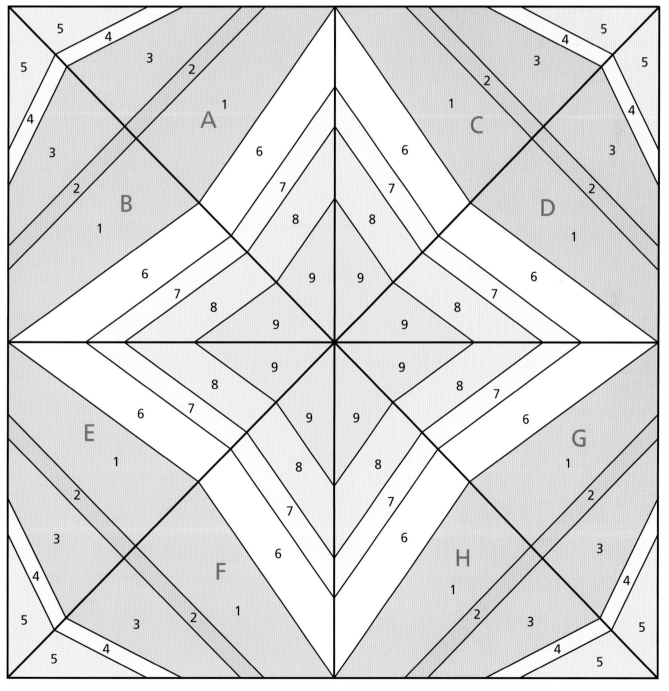

5

Candy Corn

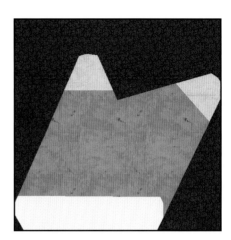

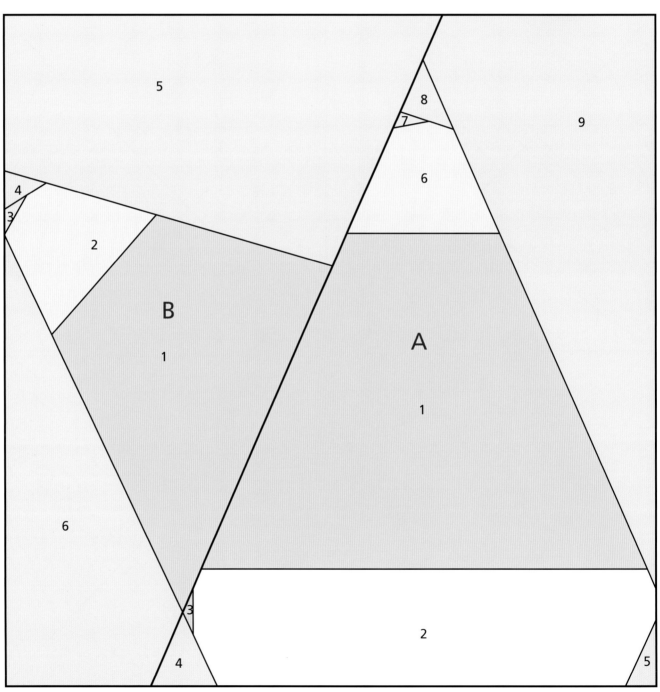

Crow

EMBELLISHMENT NOTE:
Use a large yellow seed bead for eye.

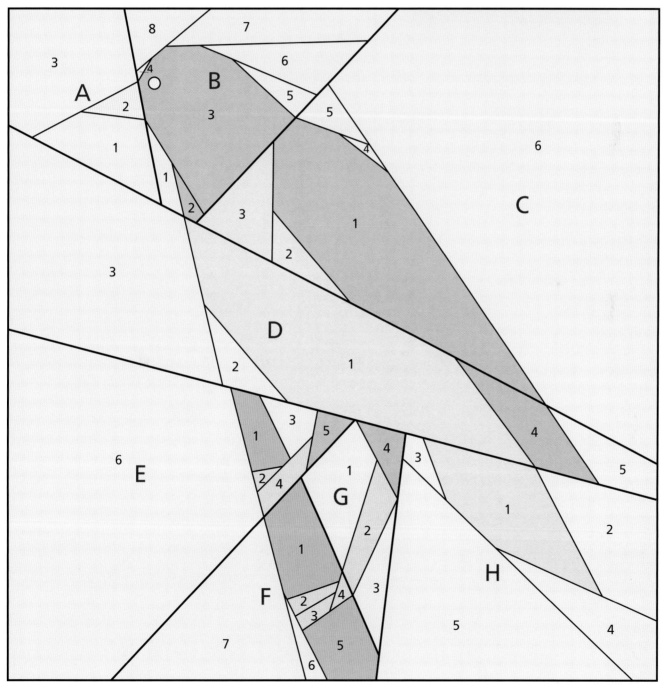

7

Spider Legs

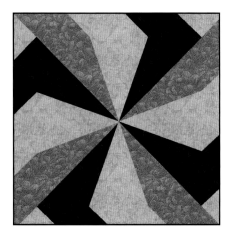

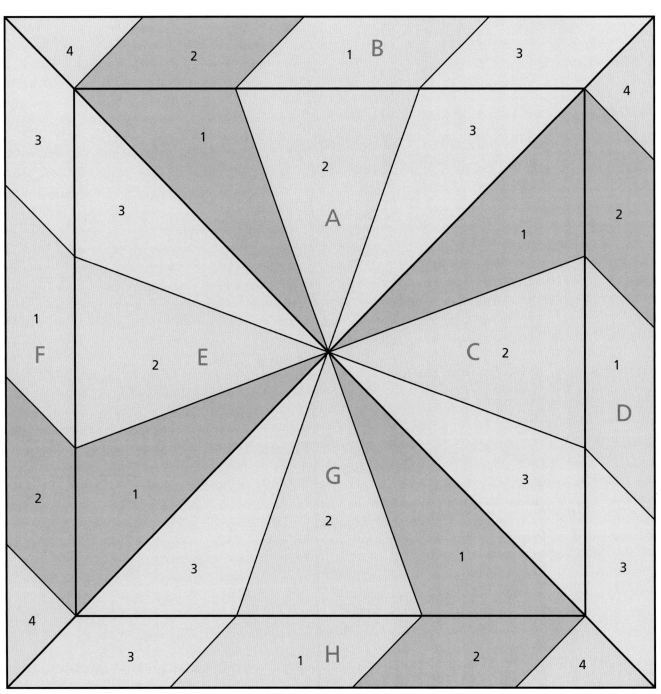

8

Opal – October Birthstone

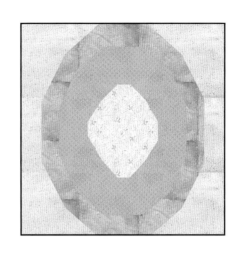

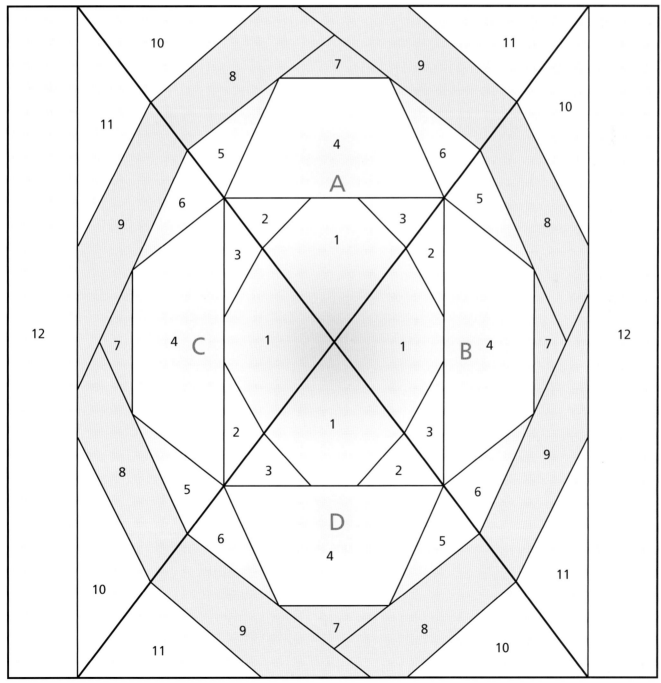

Pinwheel

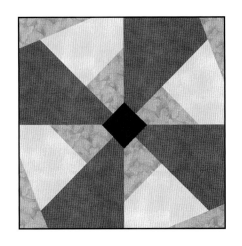

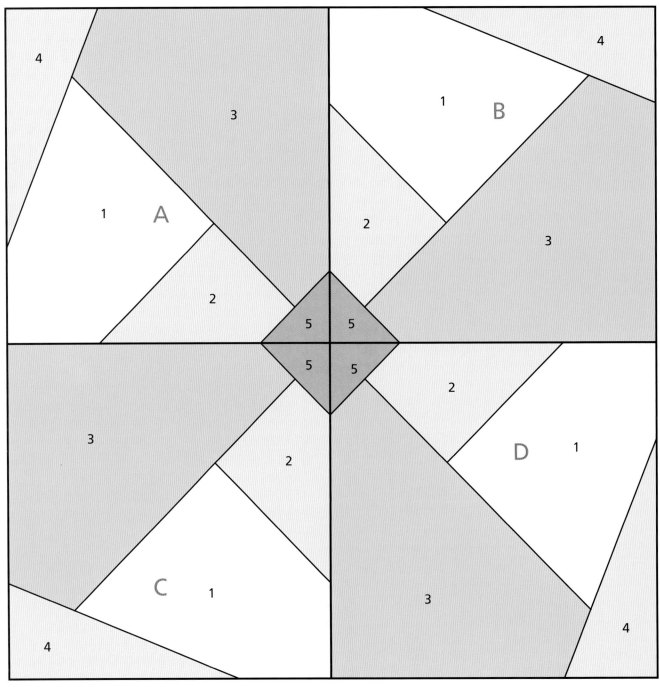

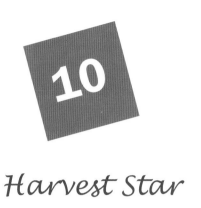

10

Harvest Star

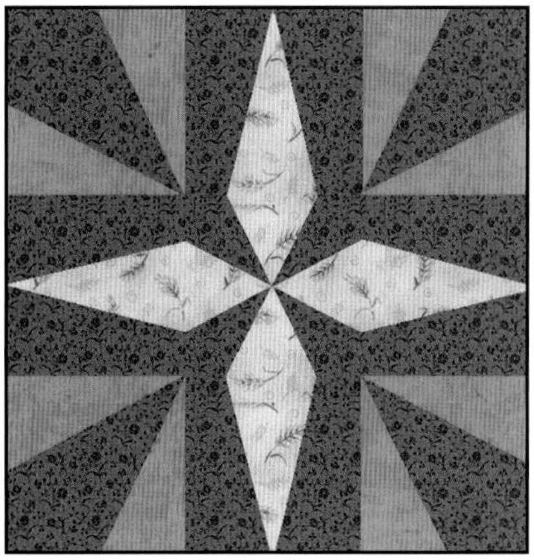

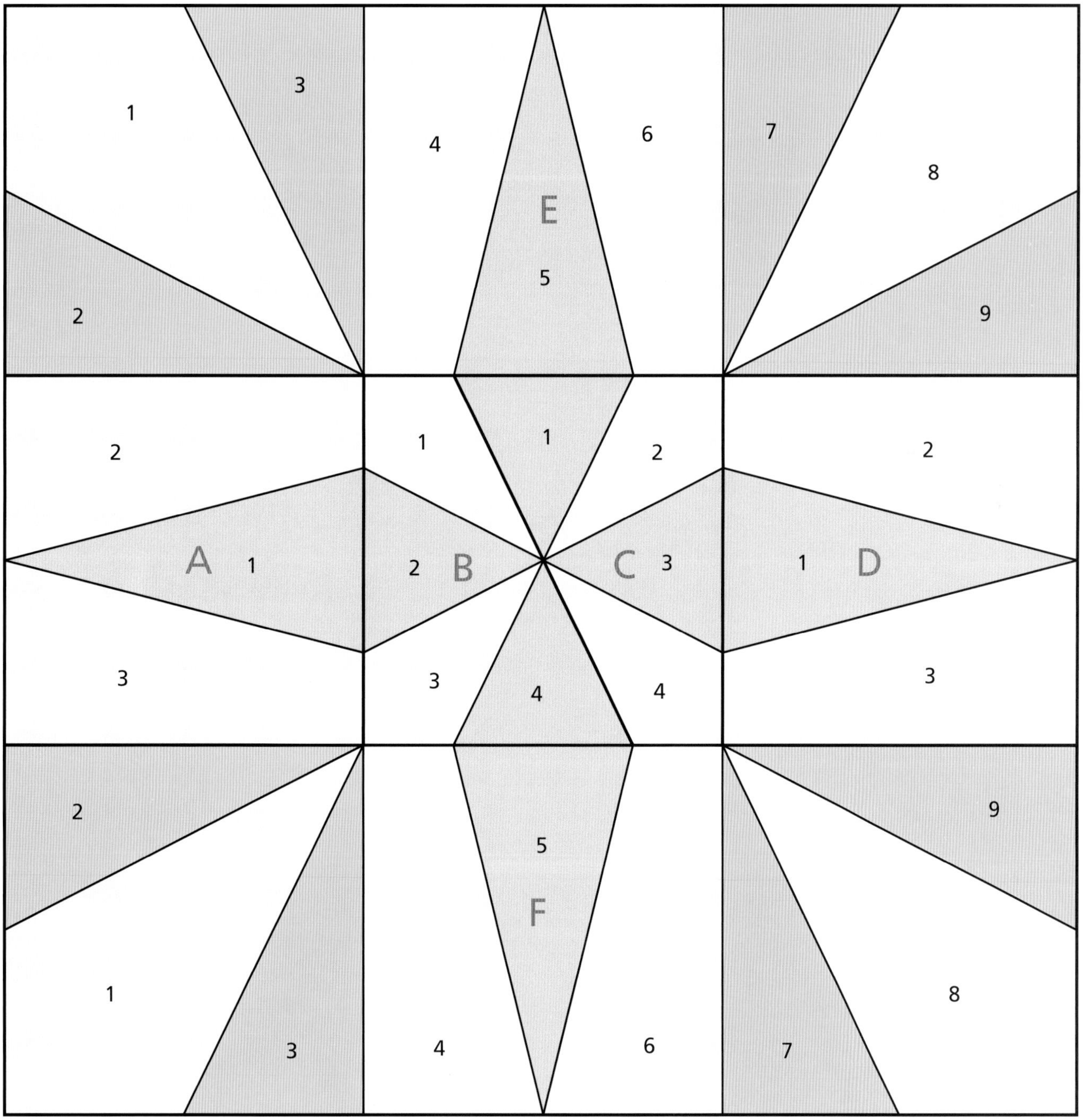

11

Cosmos —
October Flower

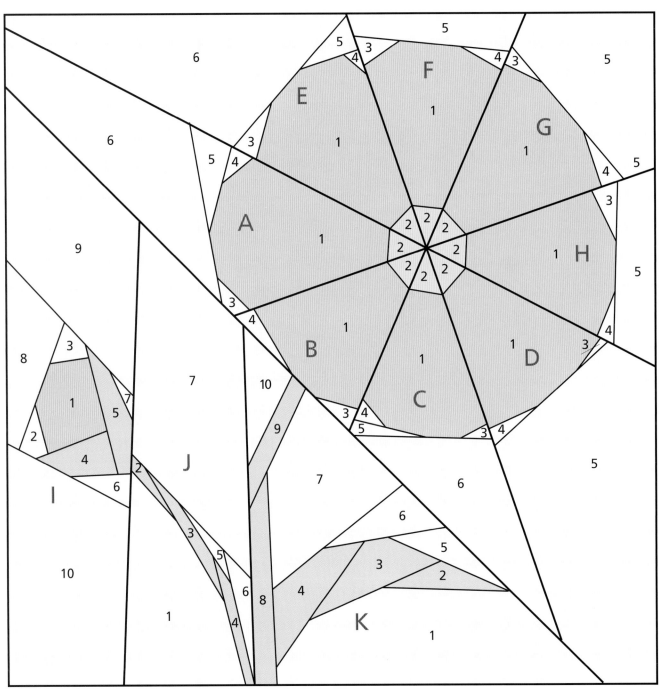

Columbus Day

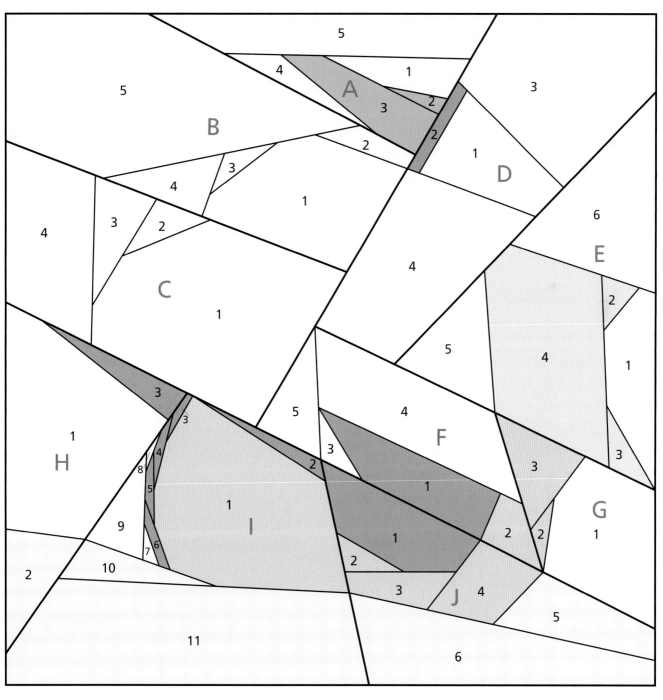

13

Pueblo Dragonfly

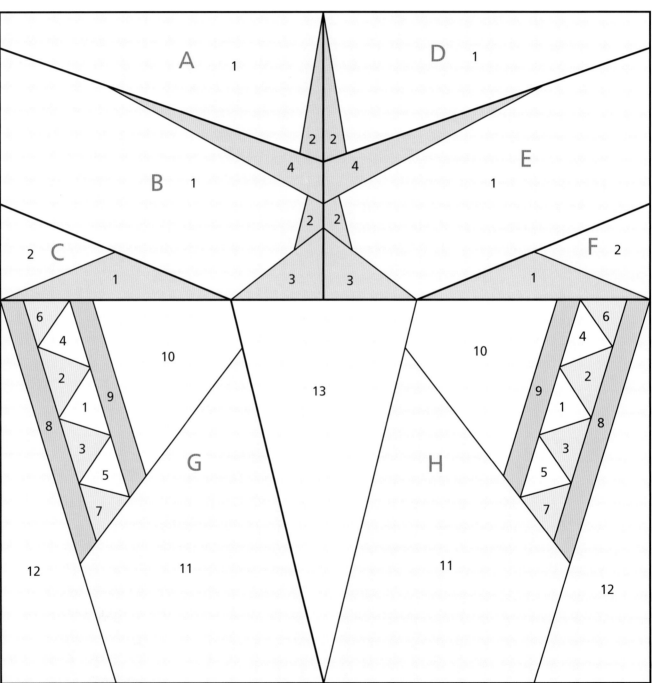

A 1

D 1

2 2

4 4

B 1

E 1

2 2

2 C

F 2

1

3 3

1

6

6

4

4

10

10

2

2

9

9

1

1

8

8

13

3

3

5

5

G

H

7

7

12

11

11

12

14

Mini-Star

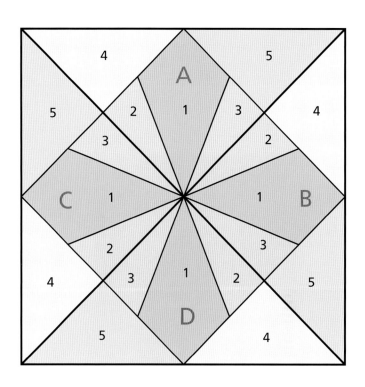

15

Mini-Starburst

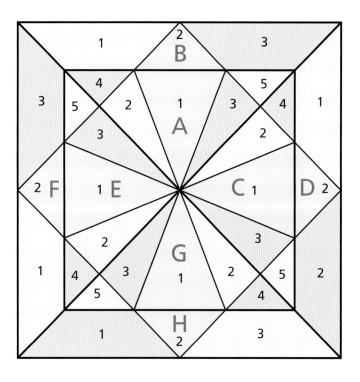

Pineapple Bit

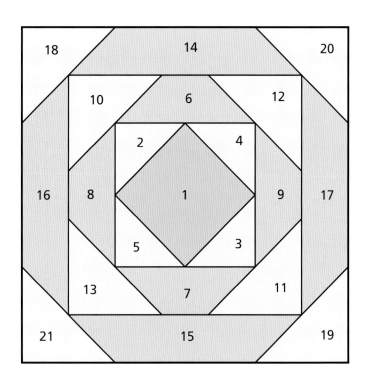

Pointed Corners

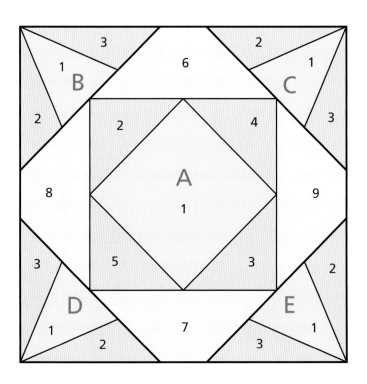

Siberian Husky —
Alaska Day

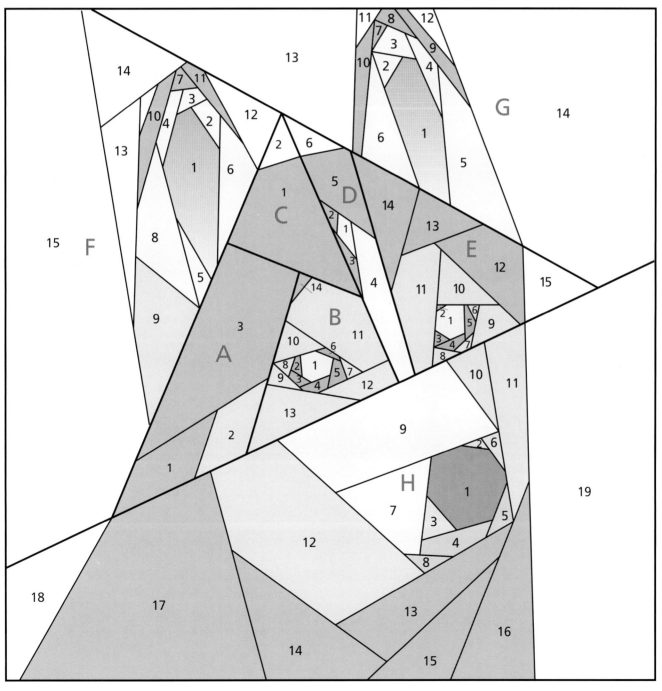

Propeller

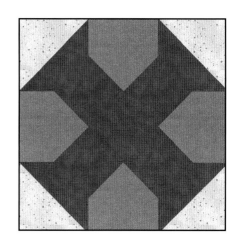

6

4

1

C

2

3

7

5

2

1

A

4

3

B

1

3

2

4

6

D

2

1

3

5

7

Harvest Basket

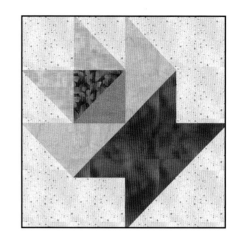

1

2

C

3

4

5

3

3

3

A

1

1

2

B

2

E

2

4

3

5

4

1

2

D

1

3

21

Twirling Ribbons

3

2

1

4

C

5

6

8

7

A

3

4

1

2

2

1

B

4

3

D

4

5

1

2

3

7

6

8

22

Shuffling Cards

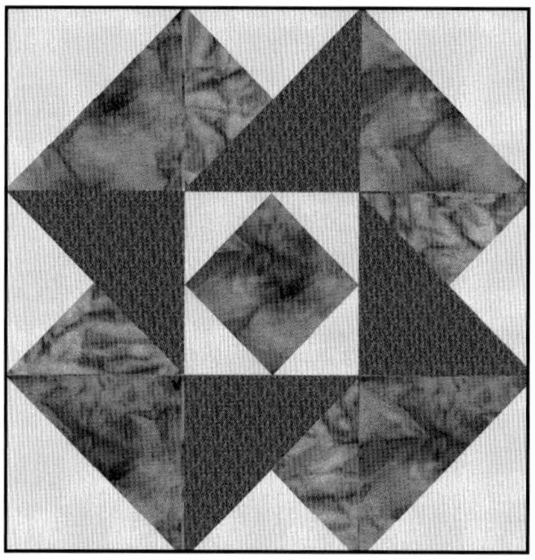

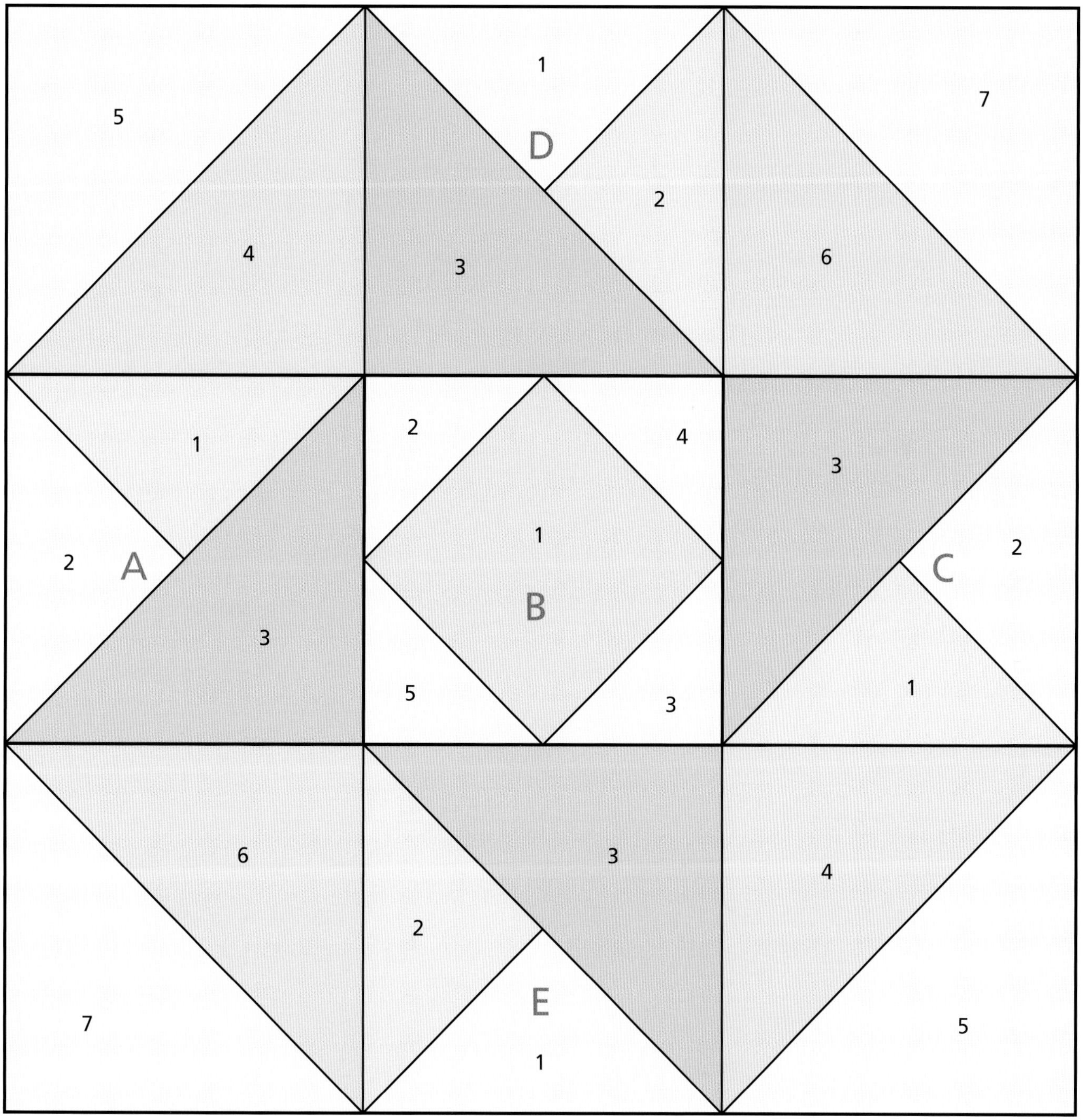

5

1

7

D

2

4

3

6

1

2

4

3

A

2

B

C

2

3

1

5

3

1

6

3

4

2

E

7

1

5

Card Tricks

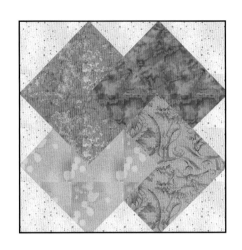

7

1

4

6

5

C

2

3

2

A

5

3

B

1

4

1

3

5

4

2

6

3

D

4

2

7

1

5

United Nations Day

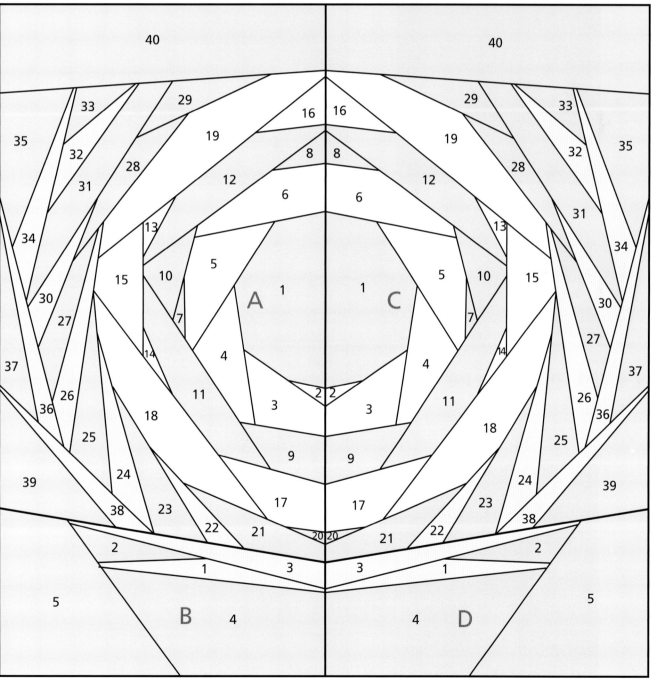

25

Fenced In

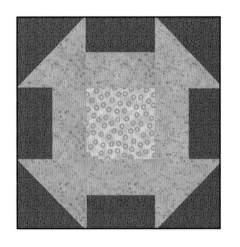

26

Log Cabin

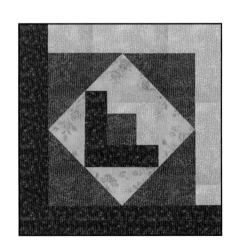

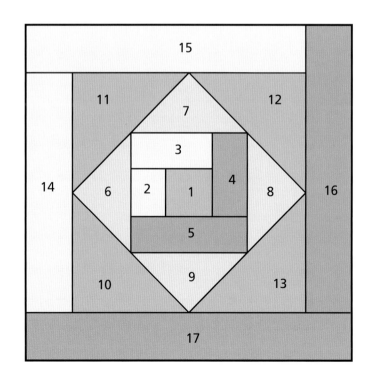

Star Snapshot

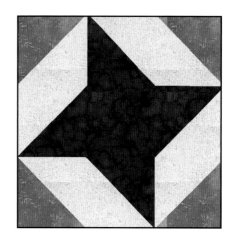

5

2

6

1

A

3

4

2

1

B

5

4

3

3

1

4

C

5

2

6

Gateway Arch

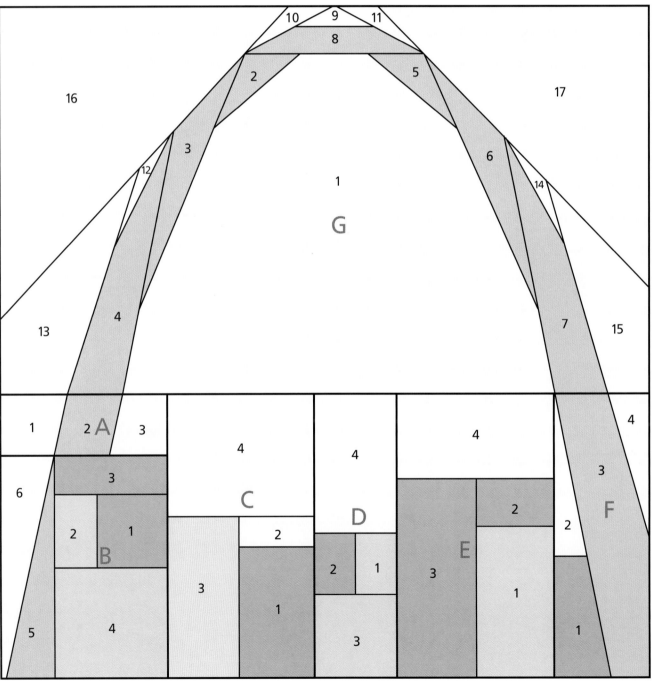

29

Spinning Pinwheel

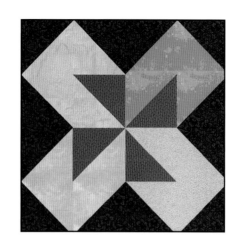

A

4

1

5

2

3

B

2

4

5

7

1

3

6

8

C

1

3

6

8

2

4

5

7

D

2

3

4

1

5

30

Spinner

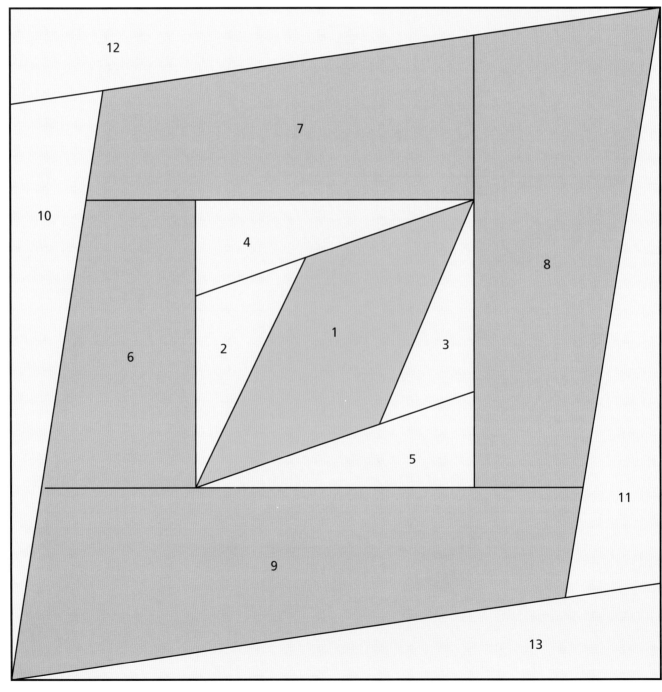

31

Halloween Pumpkin

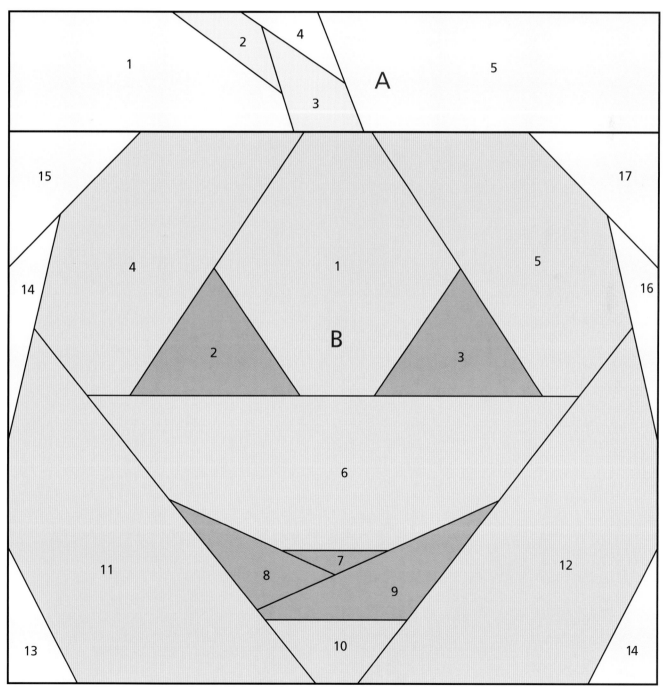

It's Autumn, and nature sends colorful leaves into the air providing the background for an artist's palette. Here that panoply of color is recreated in a quilt to celebrate the season. If you are fortunate enough to live in a part of the country that has a beautiful display of Autumn leaves, then you will certainly appreciate this quilt. If, however, your home is in an area that doesn't enjoy a colorful Autumn, this quilt will revive the season. The quilt uses the Leaf block and the Oak Leaf block surrounded by the colors of the season.

All Saints Day

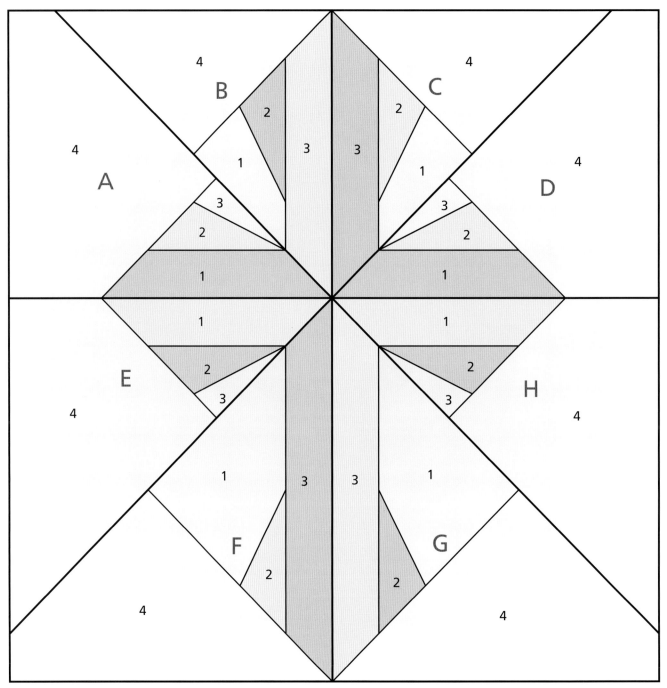

2

Election Day

6	1	7
4	A	5
2	3	

B: 2, 4, 5, 7, 1, 3, 6, 8

C: 1, 3, 6, 8, 2, 4, 5, 7

D: 4, 2, 3, 5, 6, 1, 7

3

Woven Ribbons

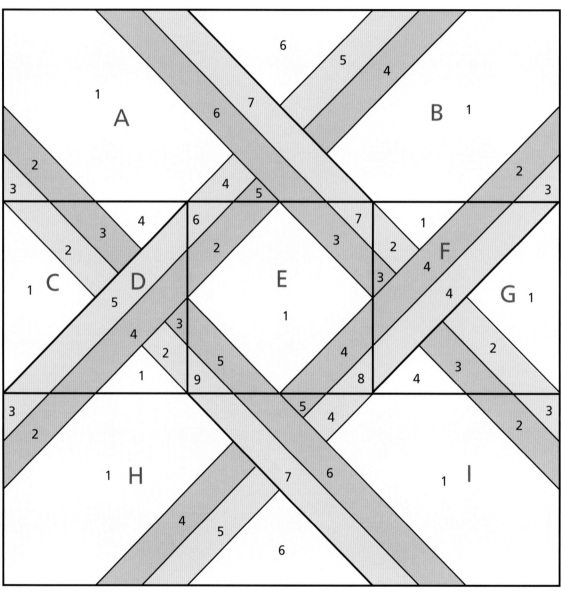

A 1
B 1
6
5
4
7
6
2
3

4
5
3

C 1
D
E 1
F
G 1
4
3
2
2
3
7
6
3
2
2
4
3
5
4
1
3
4
9
5
8
4

5
4
3
2

H 1
I 1
7
6
4
5
6
2
3

Oak Leaf

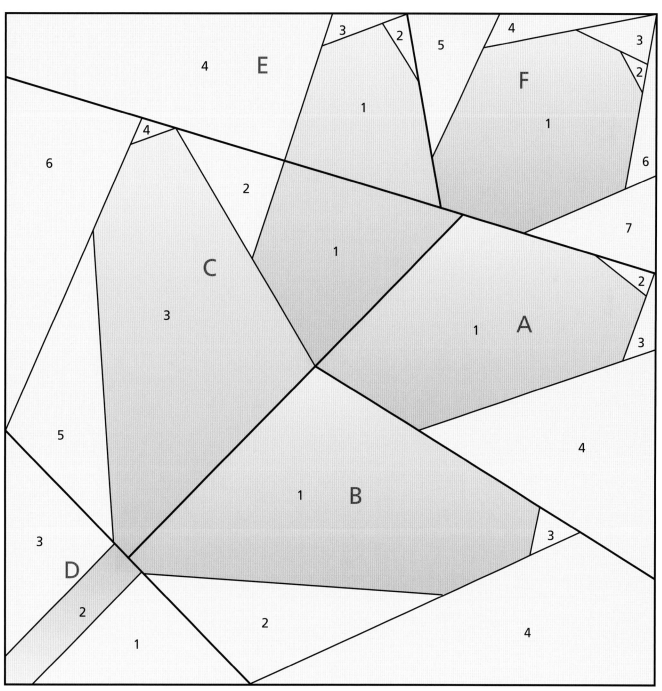

E 4

3 2 5 4 3

1 5 F 2

4 1

6 2 1 6

7

C 2

1 3 A 1

5 4

3

B 1

3

D 2

3 2

1 2 4

5

Topaz —
November Birthstone

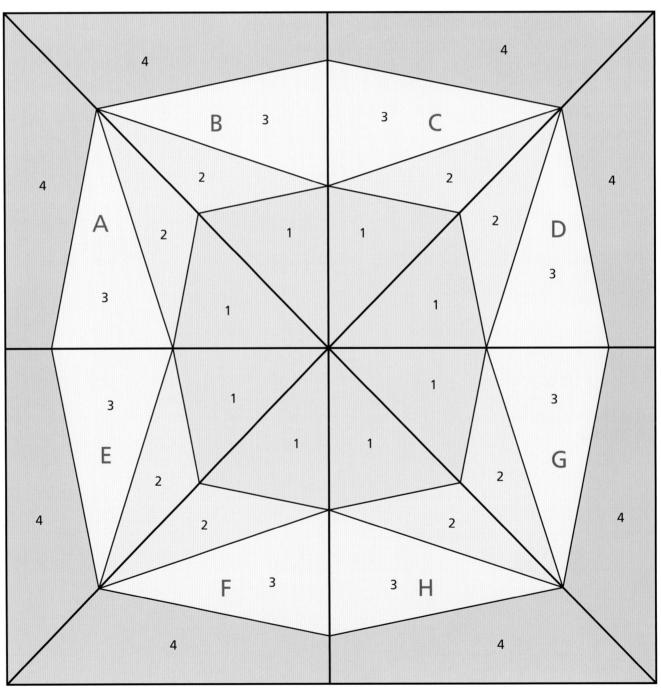

Pinwheel

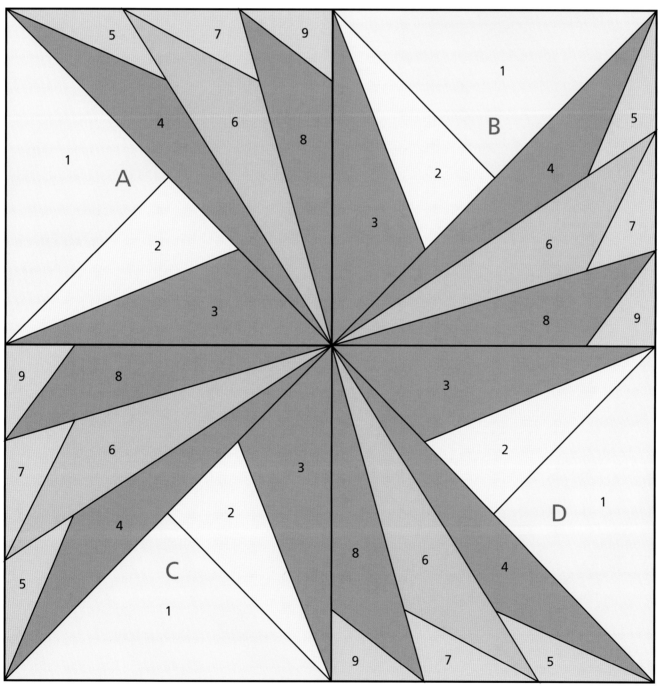

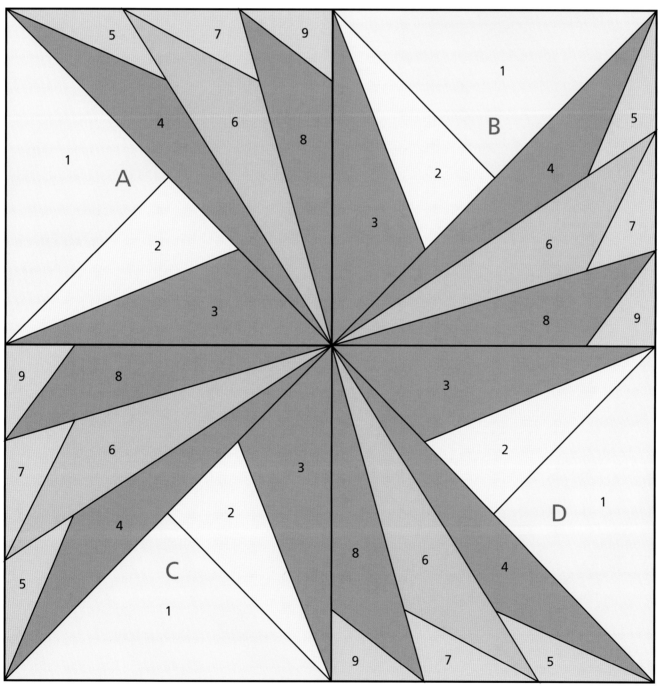

5 7 9

4 6 8

1

A

2

3

B

1

5

2

4

3

6

7

8 9

9 8

6

7

3

5

4

2

3

2

D

1

C

1

8 6 4

9 7 5

7

Star

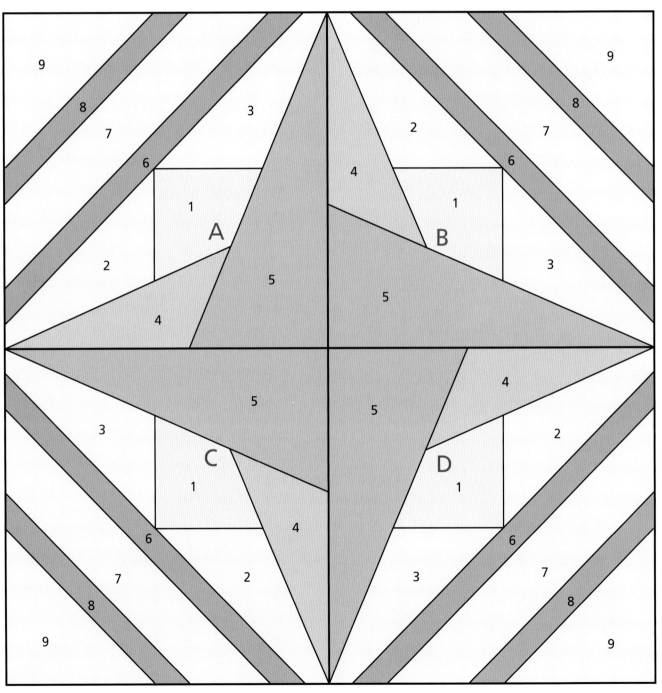

Mum —
November Flower

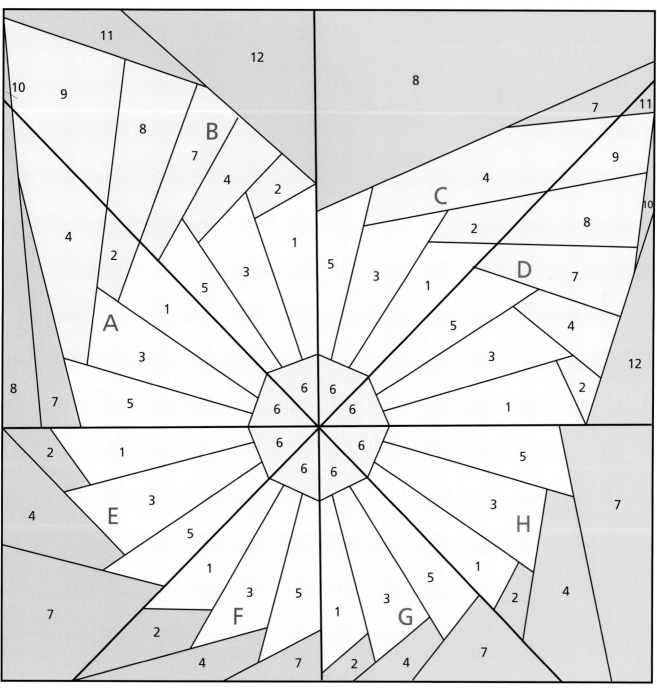

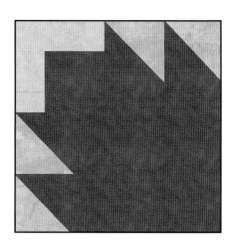

Log Cabin

11

7

2

3

1

5

9

4

6

8

10

Leaf

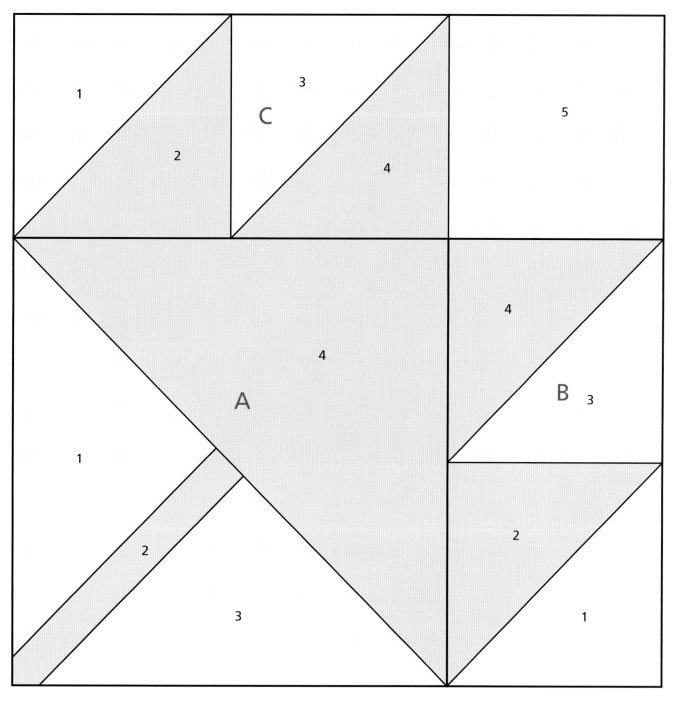

1

2

3

C

4

5

4

A

4

B 3

1

2

1

2

3

11

Veteran's Day

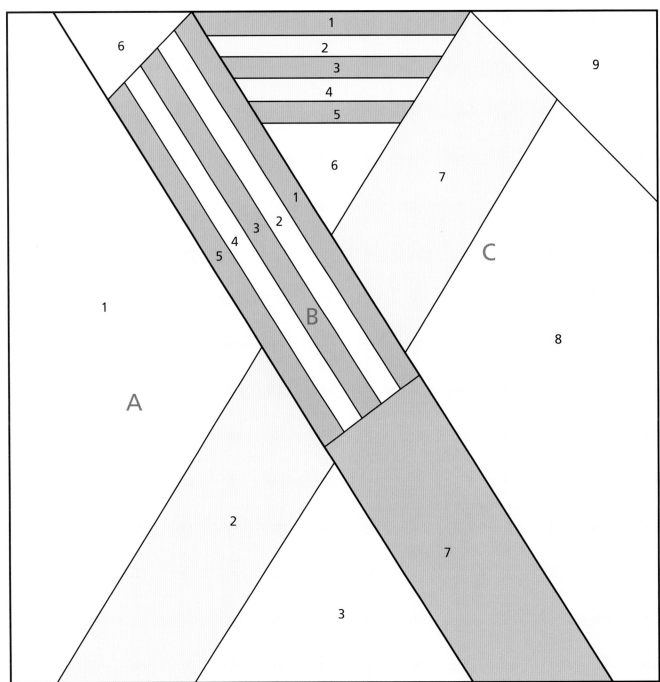

6

9

1

2

3

4

5

6

1

7

5 4 3 2

B

C

1

A

8

2

7

3

Thanksgiving Basket

1

D

2

3

4

5

6

2

1

A

1

1

B

C

2

3

3

4

4

2

2

3

E 1

6

4

5

13

Square Links

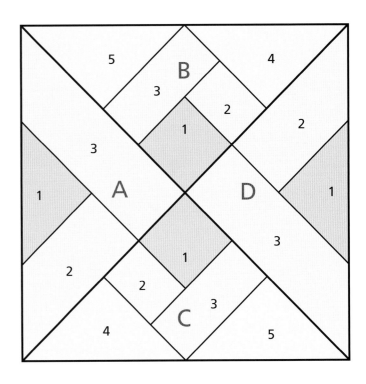

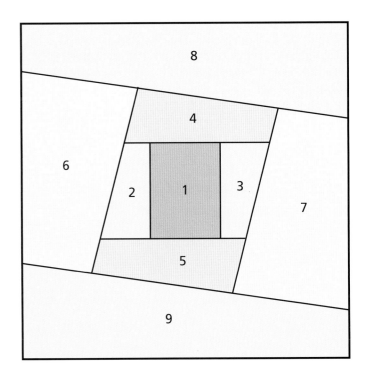

14

Tipsy Log Cabin

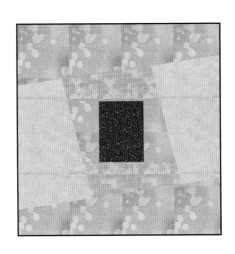

15

Bits and Pieces

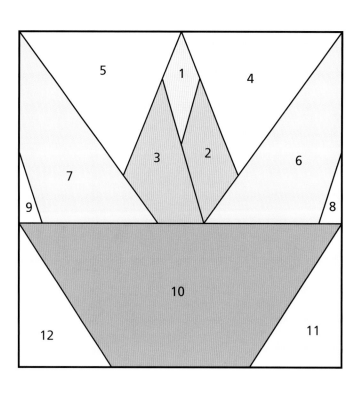

5		3	3		5
6					6
	1		1		
4	A		B		4
	2			2	
4	2			2	4
	C		D		
6	1		1		6
	3		3		
5					5

16

House Plant

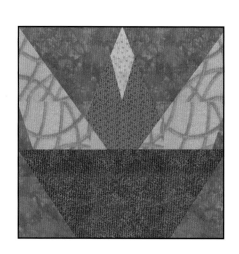

17

Nightingales

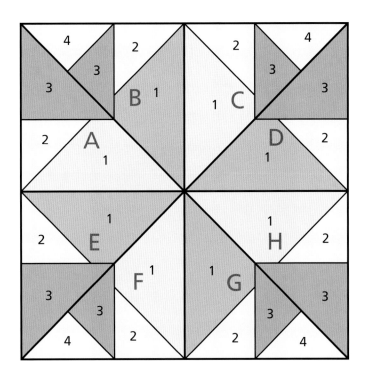

18

Gone Fishing

EMBELLISHMENT NOTE:
Use a black permanent fabric marker to add eye.

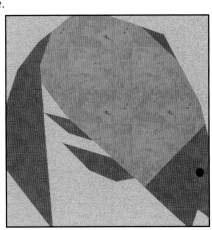

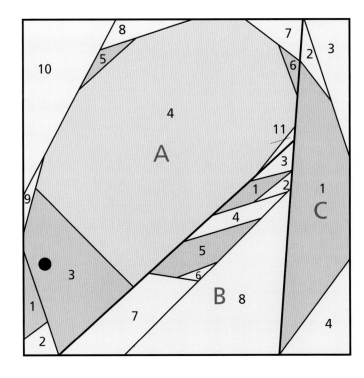

19

Thanksgiving Corn

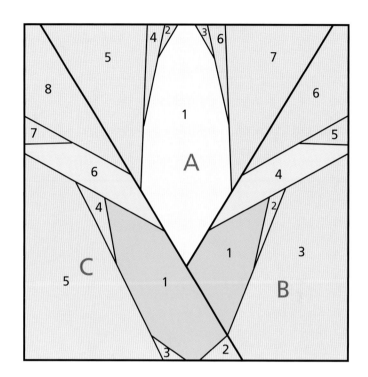

20

Autumn Colors

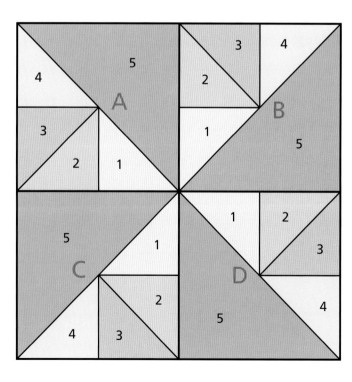

21

Autumn Tree

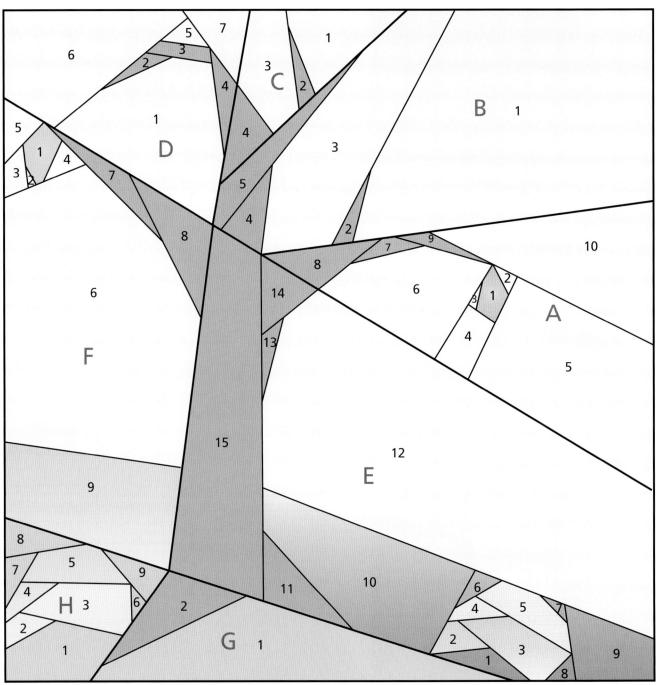

Autumn Leaves

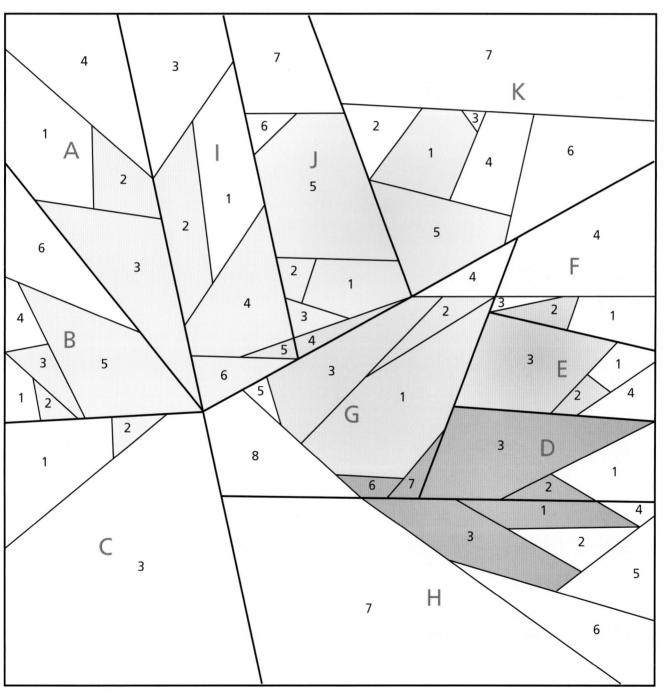

Grandmother's House

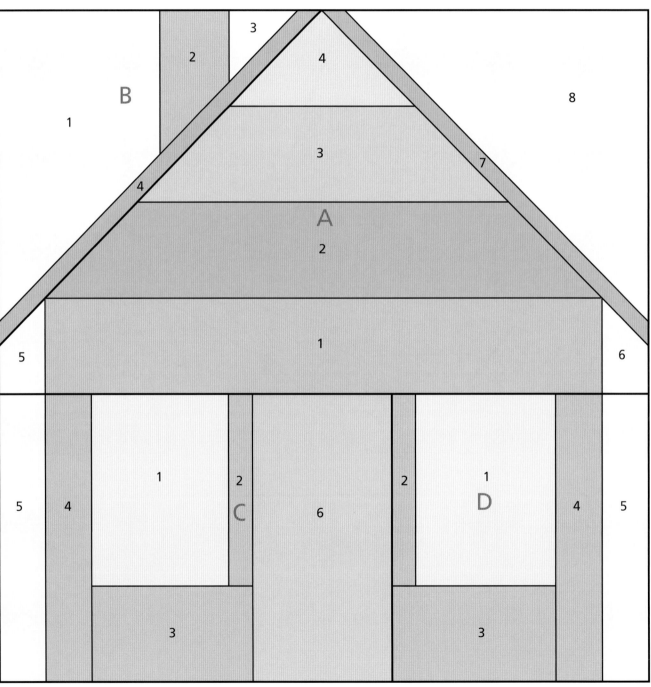

24

Pilgrim's Hat

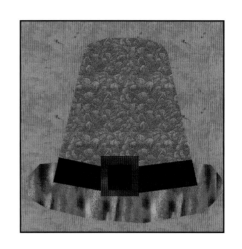

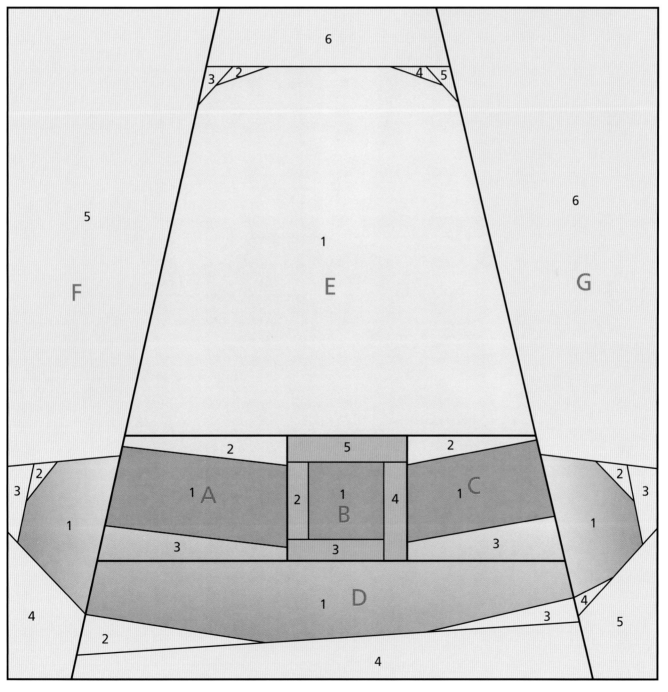

25

Thanksgiving Turkey

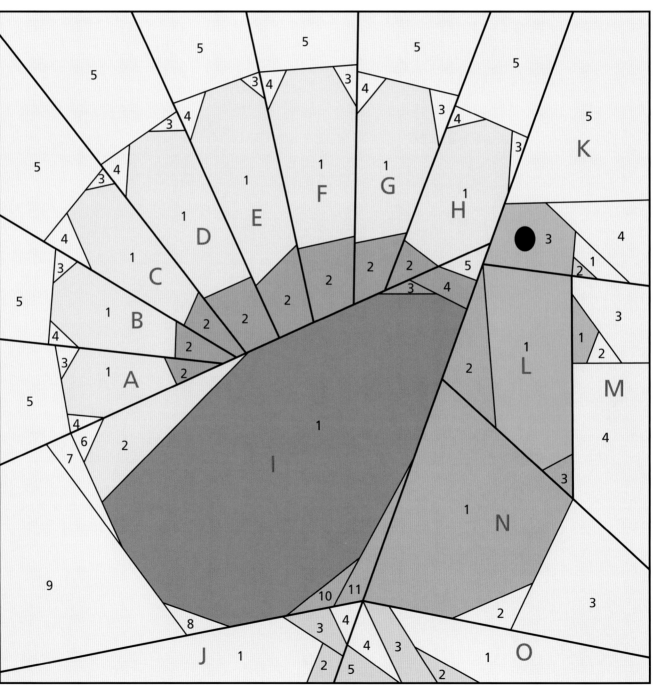

Radiating Star

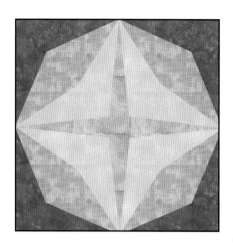

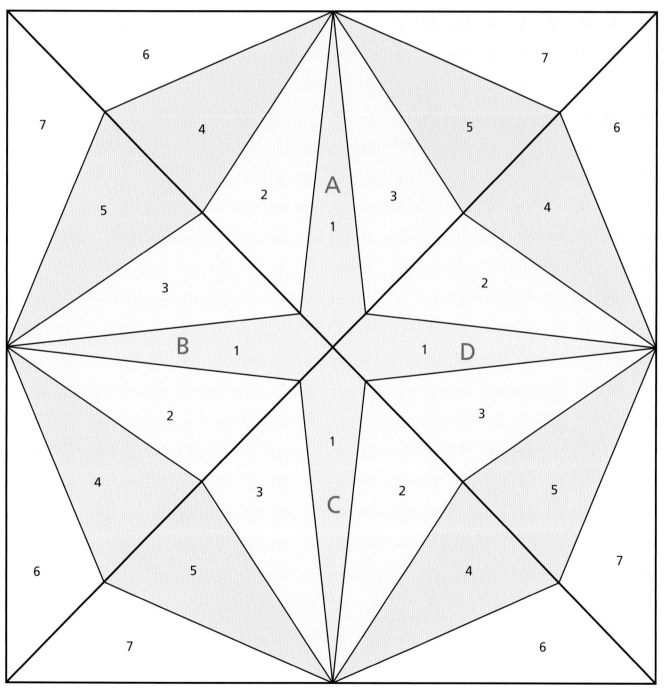

27

Shining star

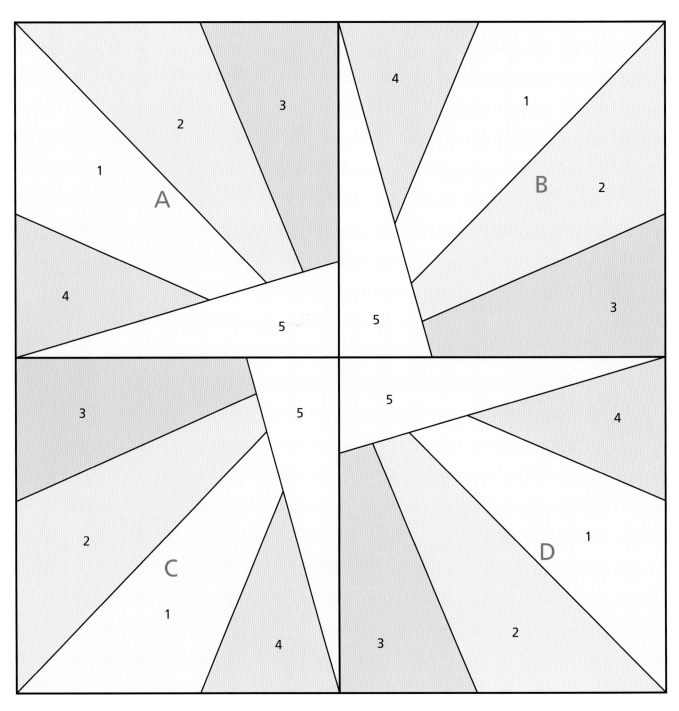

28

Southwest Design

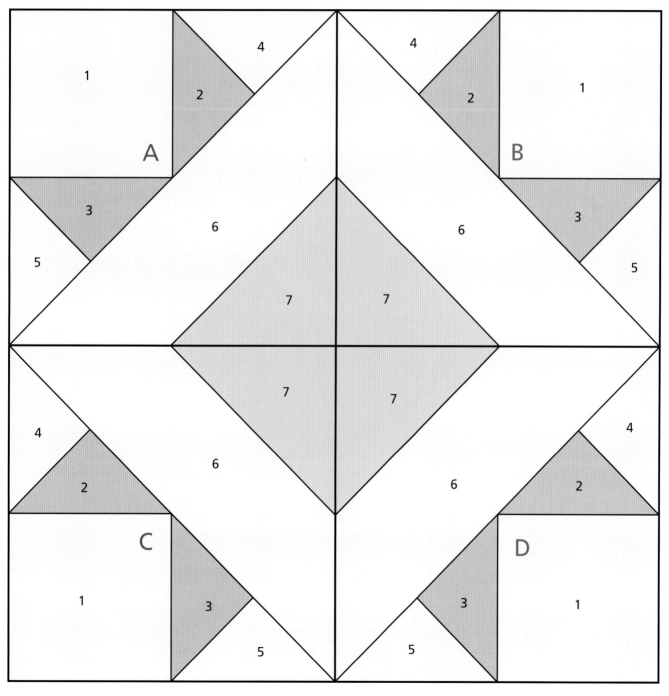

Flyfoot

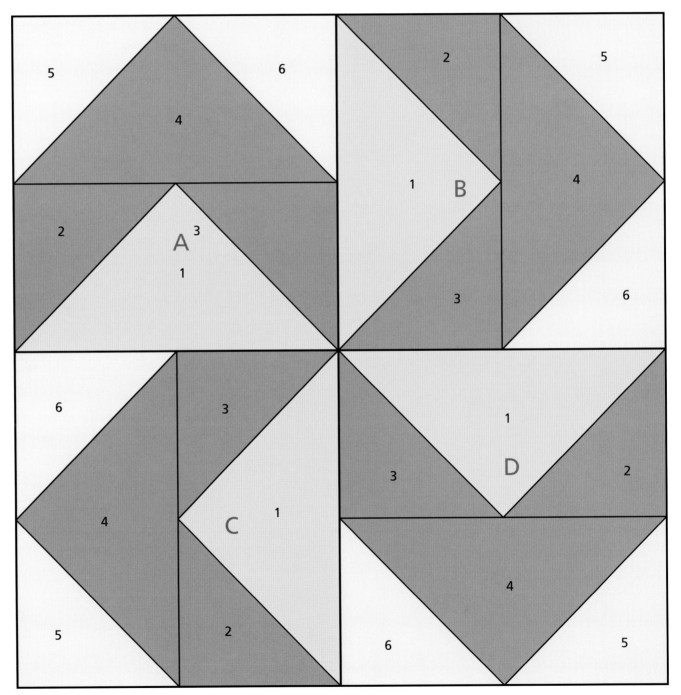

30

Scrapbag

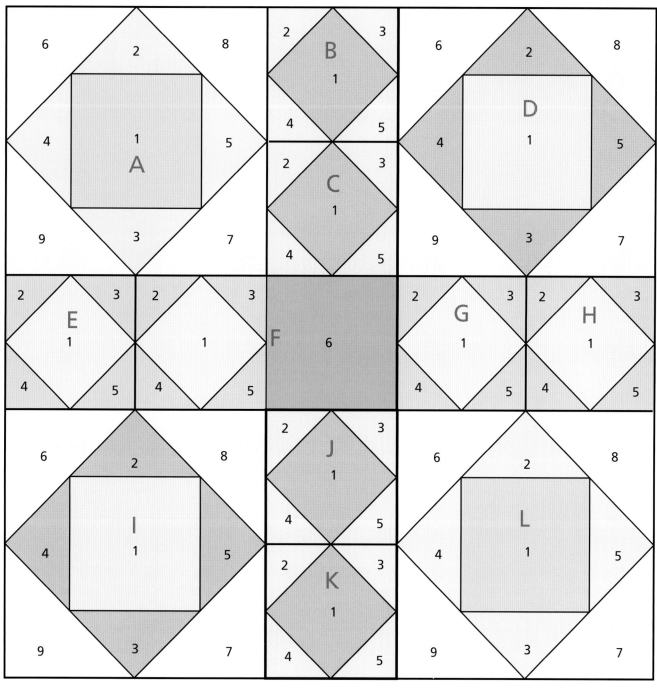

A Christmas tree to celebrate December is in order, and this one is simply made using squares and triangles of Christmas fabric. Use the small quilt blocks to make individual ornaments, and hang them on the tree. The Star block hangs at the top of the tree. The Angel block and a red and gold Ornament sit on the next branches. The Stocking block, the Santa block and the Candy Cane block all add another row of charming ornaments while a sparkling silver and gold Ornament and the Moose block complete the tree decorations. This is sure to become a family heirloom brought out each year – or give it as a gift when you are invited for a special holiday party.

Angel

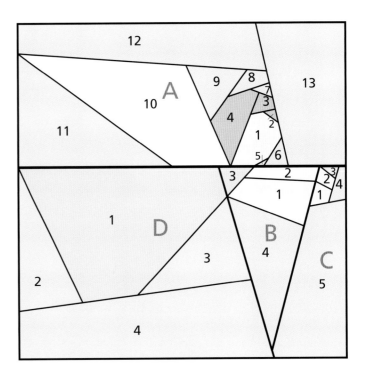

Candy Cane

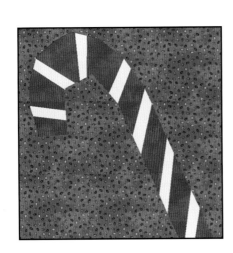

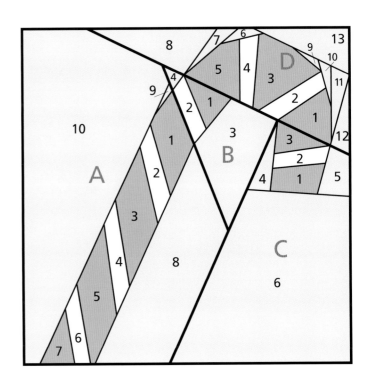

3

Santa

EMBELLISHMENT NOTE:
Use pink felt for nose and white felt for
pompom at tip of hat.

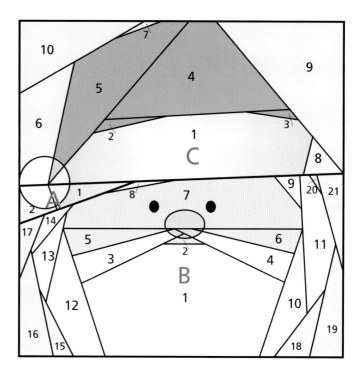

4

Stocking

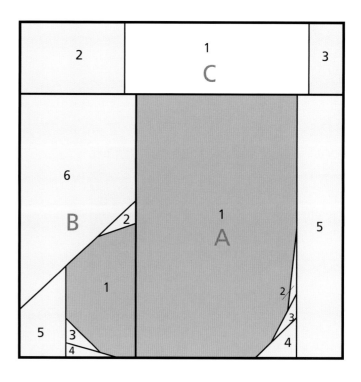

Ornament

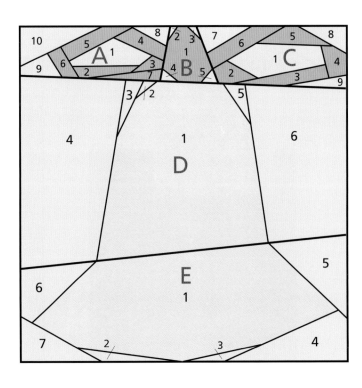

Silver Bell

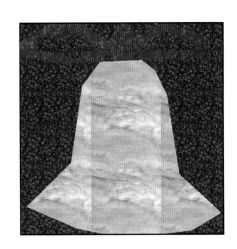

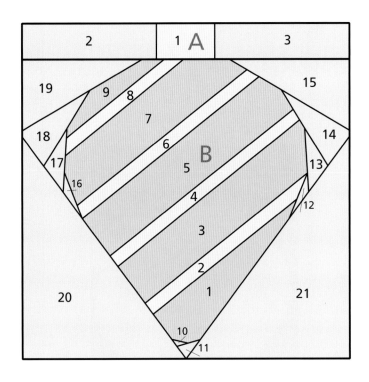

7

Pearl Harbor Remembrance

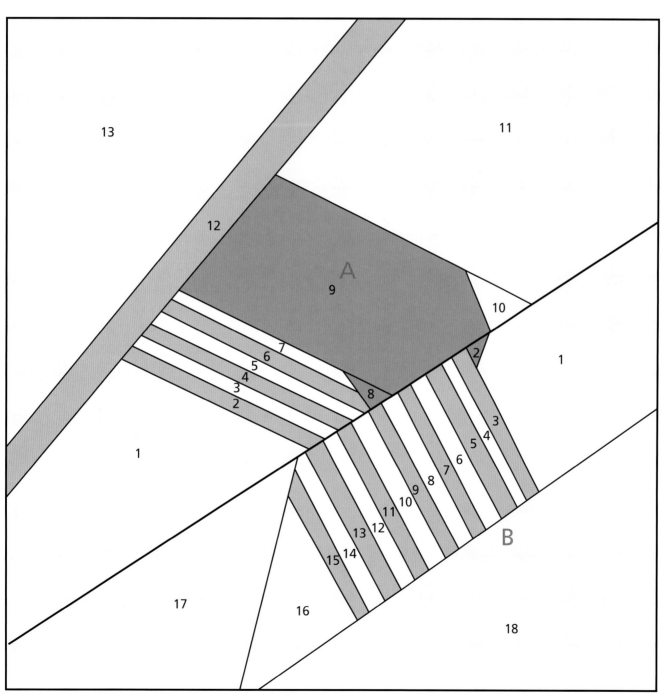

Star

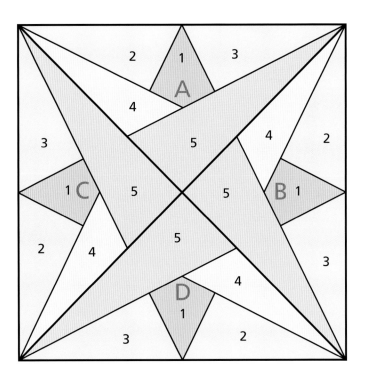

Moose

EMBELLISHMENT NOTE:
Use white and black felt for eyes and a black permanent fabric marker for the mouth.

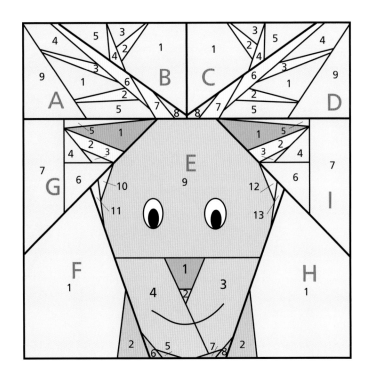

10

Christmas Star

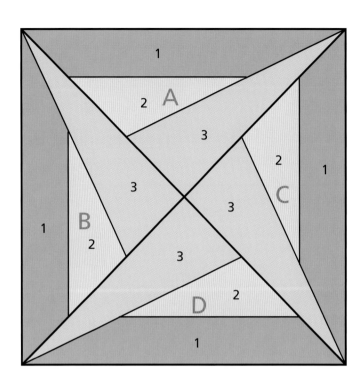

1

2 A

3

2

1

3

3 C

1

B

3

2

3

D 2

1

11

Chanukah Star

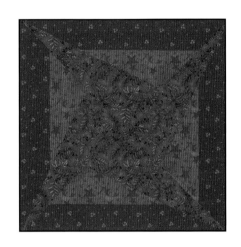

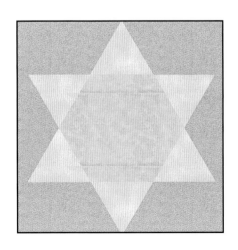

2   1   3

A

2   B   3

4   1   5

4   C

5

2   1   3

D

2   1   3

Star

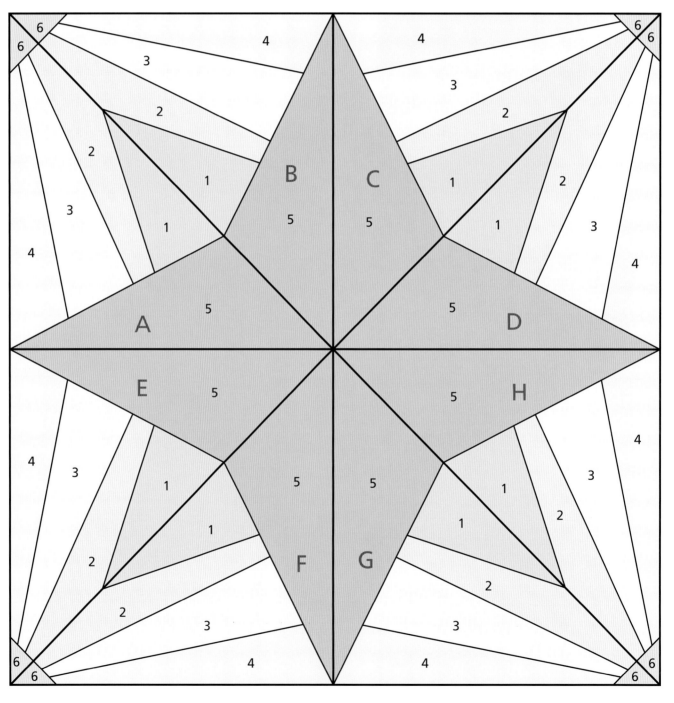

13

Partridge

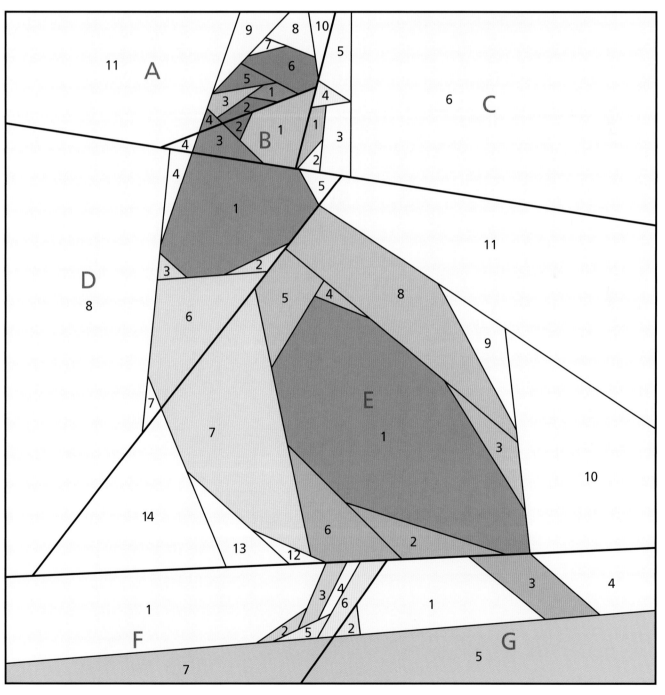

14

Log Cabin Tree

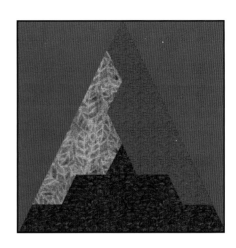

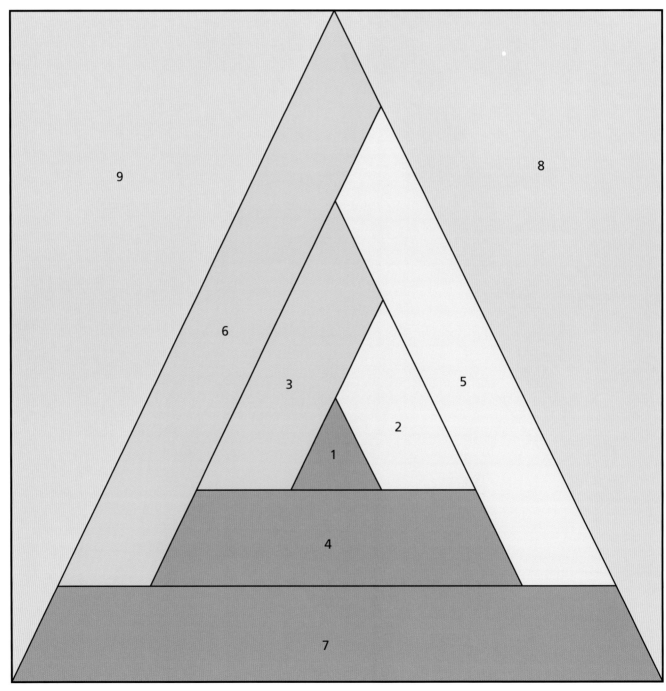

15

Narcissus —
December Flower

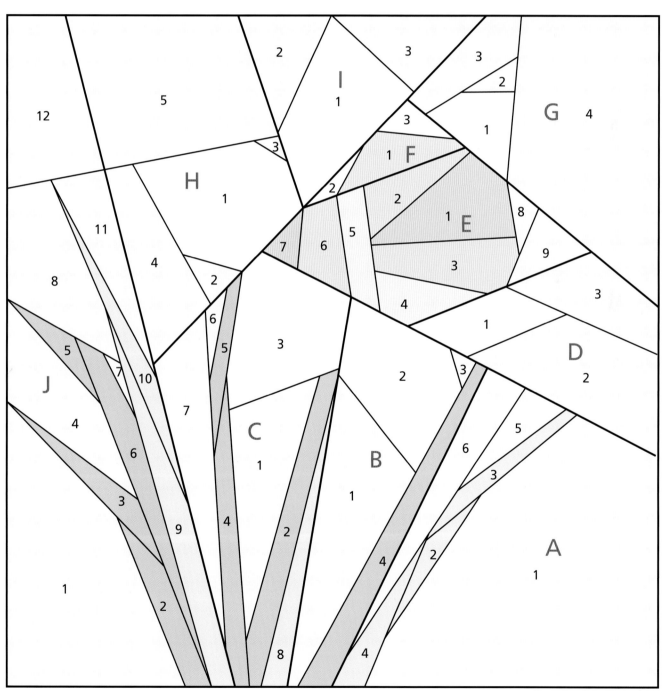

16

Chanukah Menorah

20

| 18 | 16 | 14 | 12 | 10 | 8 | 6 | 4 | 2 | 1 C | 3 | 5 | 7 | 9 | 11 | 13 | 15 | 17 | 19 |

21

A
10
9
8
7
6
5
4
3
1
2

11

B
10
9
8
7
6
5
4
3
1
2

Blue Zircon — December Birthstone

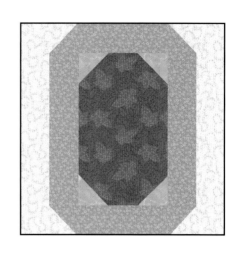

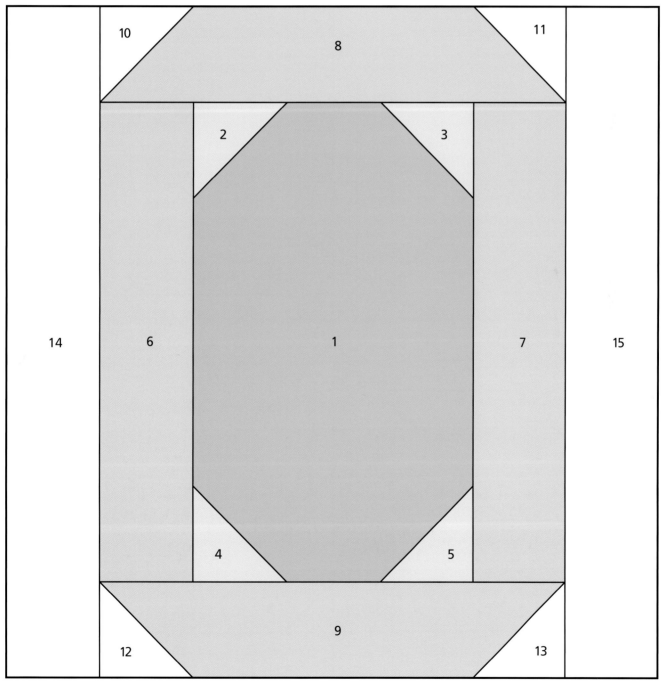

10 8 11

2 3

14 6 1 7 15

4 5

9

12 13

18

Pinwheel

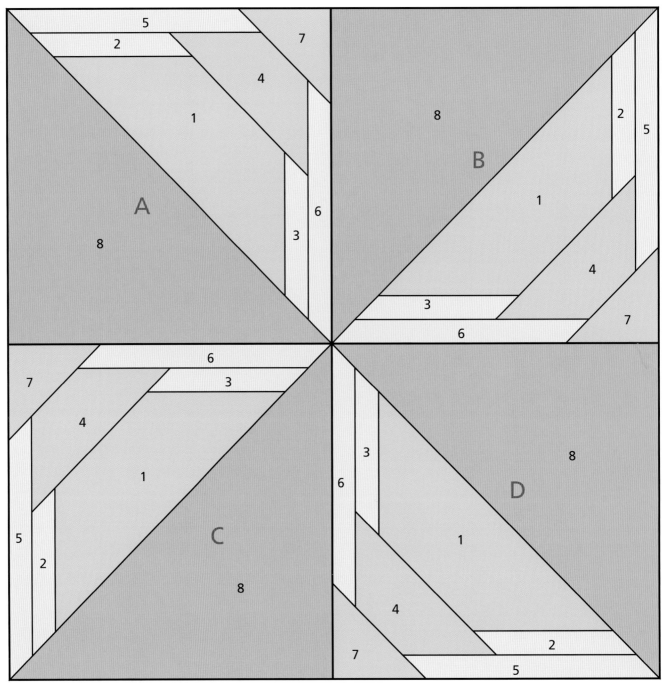

19

Snow Crystal

A

4
5
2
1
3

1
B
2
4
5

1
C
3
5
2
4

4
5
2
3
1
D

5
3
2
4
4
5

E
1
2
3
3
5
4

1
F
4
5
2
1
G
3
2
5
4
4

3
5
5

H
1

I
1
2
4
4
5
5
5
3
4
4
1
L

3
2
5
J
1
3
2
K
1
3
2
4

5
4
5
4
2
3
5

M
1
2
3
2
N
1
O
1
3
2
5
4
P
1

5
4
3

December

339

20

Poinsettia

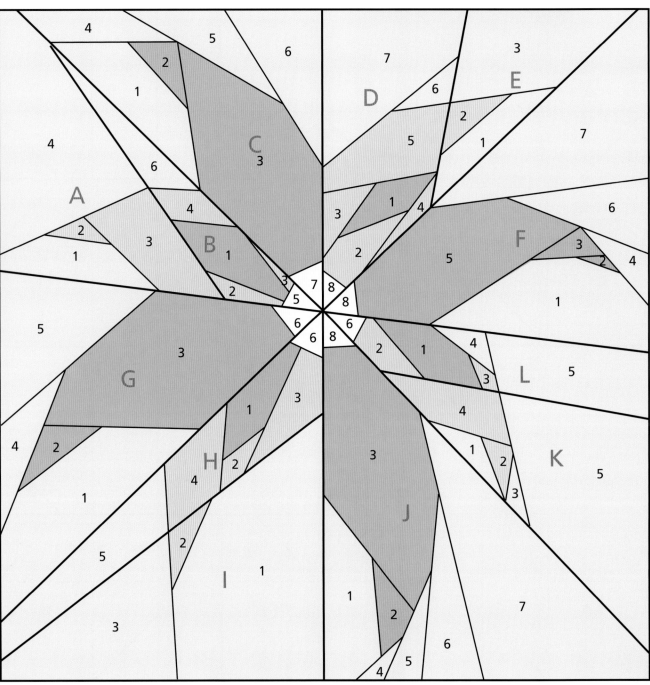

Mini
Christmas Tree

Diagram labels: A 1, 2, 3; B 1, 2, 3; C 1, 2, 3; D 1, 2, 3

22

Christmas
Present

Diagram labels: 7, 3, 8, 6, 2, 7; 2, A 1, 4, 5, B 1, 3; 6, 5, 4, 8; 8, 4, 5, 5, 6; 3, C 1, 5, 4, D 1, 2; 7, 2, 6, 8, 3, 7

23

Home for the Holidays

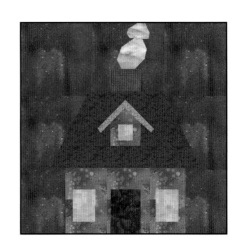

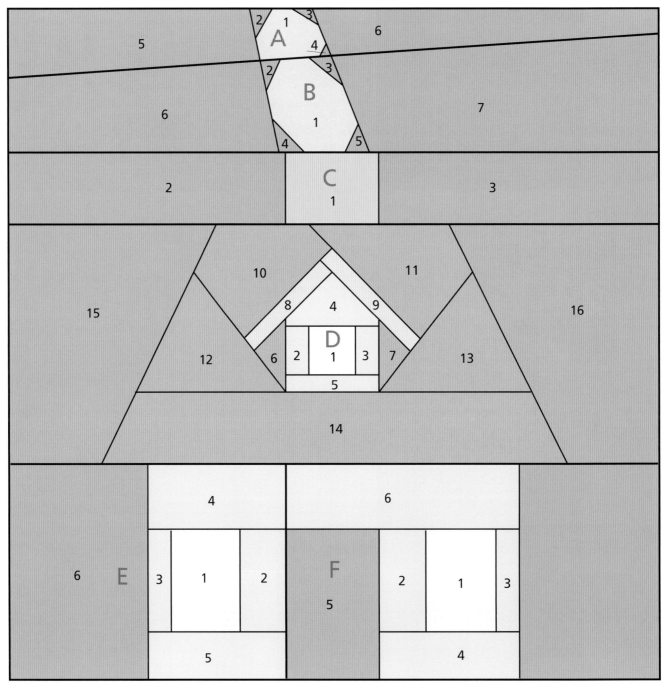

24

Alleluia

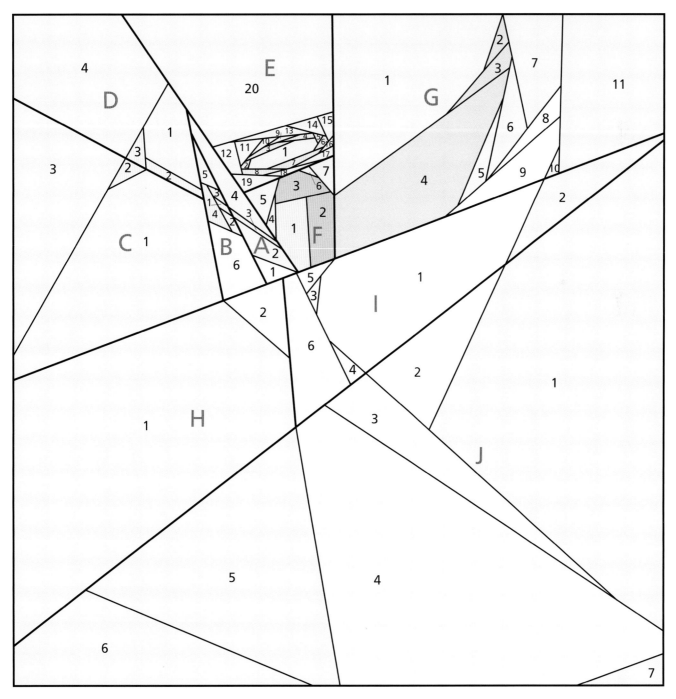

25

Noel

December

A
1

2

3

B
1
2
3
4
5

6

4

C
1
2
3

5

D
1
2
3
4
5

26

Children of Israel

A 1
2
2
B 1
3
3
4
4

4
4
3
3
E 1
2
F 1
2
2
3
3

4
3
3
D 1
2
2
C 1
4
4

4
3
3
G 1
2
H 1
2
2
4
4

27

Snowballs

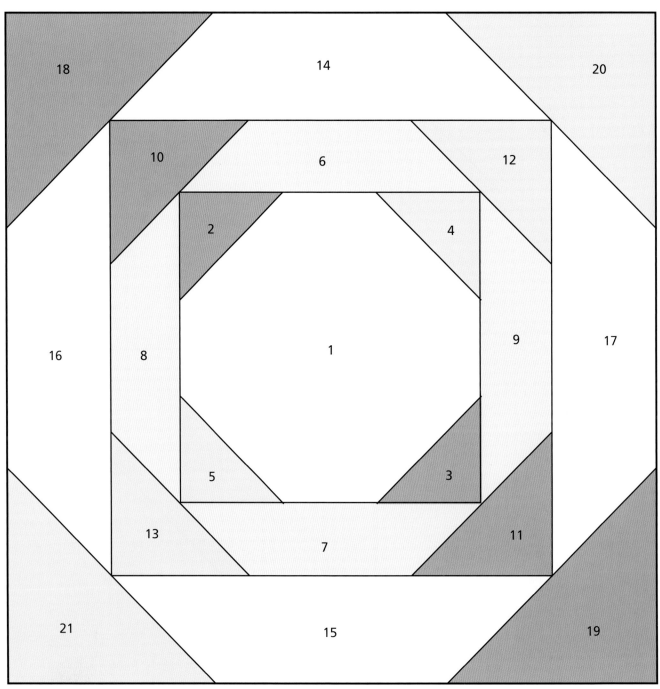

28

Center Log

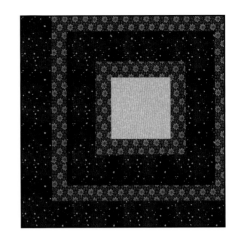

13
9
5
1	2	6	10	14
4
3
7
8
12
11
15

29

Christmas Cactus

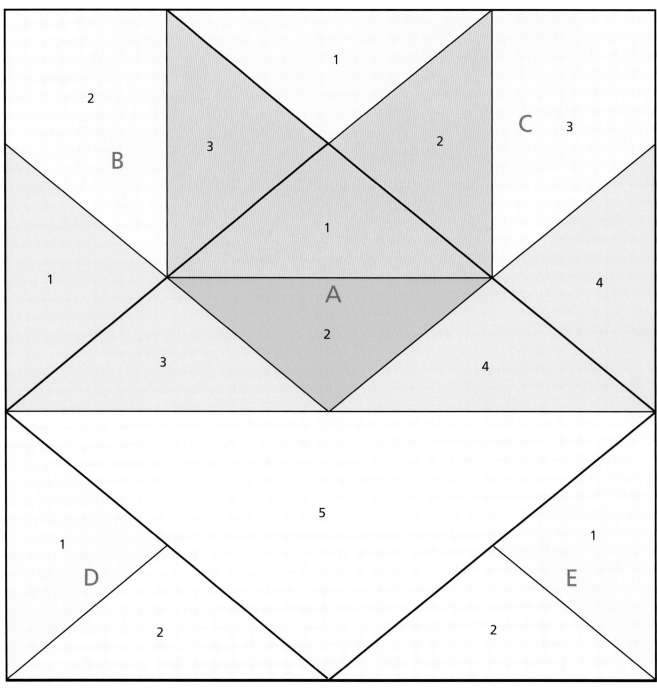

Within the diagram:

1

2

C 3

B

3 2

1

1

A

2

1 4

3 4

5

1 1

D E

2 2

The Pope's Star

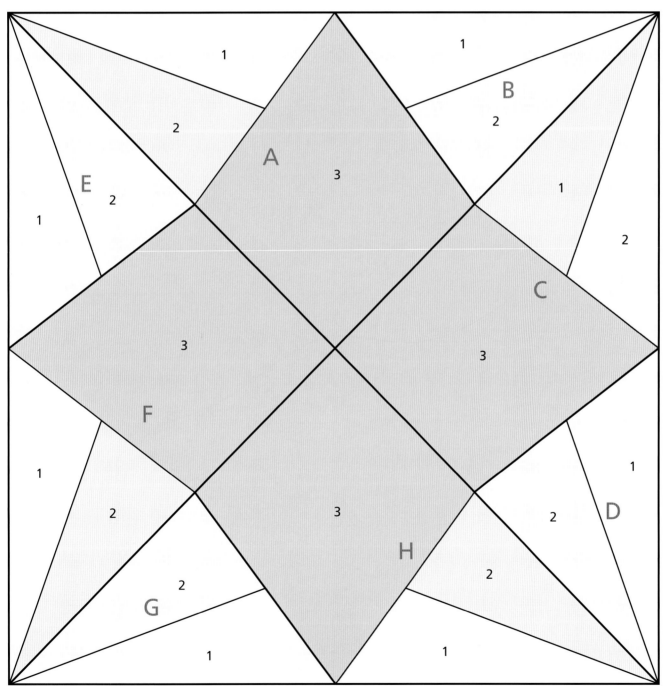

31

New Year's Toast

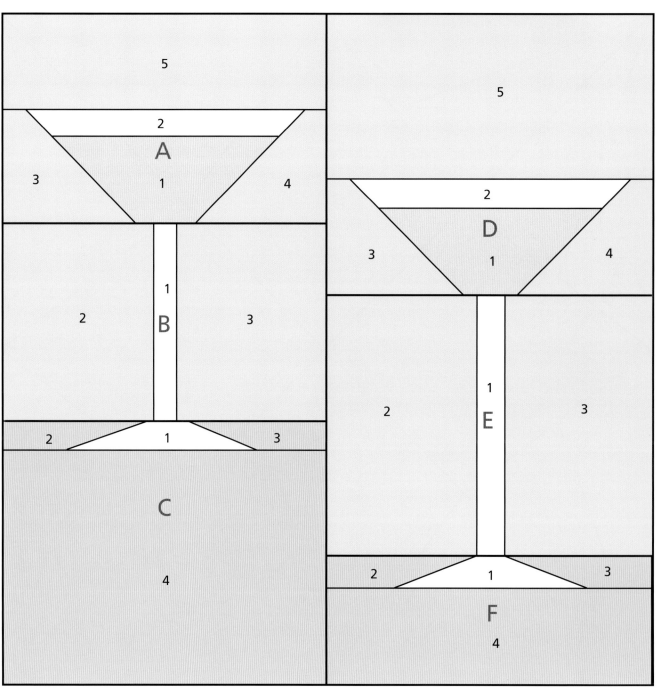

Index

Index